Dario Fo

Mistero Buffo, Accid[...]
Trumpets and Raspbe[...]
One Was Nude [...]

Dario Fo is Italy's leading contemporary performer/playwright, renowned throughout the world for his dazzling radical satires.

Mistero Buffo: 'Fo is the determined enemy of pomp, ceremony and the material aspects of religion but what shines out of this exhilarating show is his love of humanity and truth.' *Guardian*

Accidental Death of an Anarchist: 'Fo's play absorbs social indignation into mainstream Italian comedy.' *The Times*

Trumpets and Raspberries: 'We have political theatre and we have comic theatre, but the astonishing thing about Dario Fo is that he manages to combine the two. A deeply subversive farce.' *Guardian*

Also included are two short farces: *The Virtuous Burglar* and *One Was Nude and One Wore Tails*.

Dario Fo was born in 1926 in Lombardy. He began working in the theatre in 1951 as a comic and mime. Together with Franca Rame, he was highly successful as actor, director and writer of satirical comedies for the conventional theatre. In the Sixties they abandoned it; Fo began to write for a wider audience in factories and workers' clubs and produced work which was not only an important political intervention in Italy but has been internationally acclaimed. In 1970 Fo and Rame founded the theatrical collective, La Comune, in Milan. His work – and the work of Franca Rame – has been performed in England with great success: *Can't Pay? Won't Pay!* (Half Moon Theatre and Criterion Theatre, London, 1981); *Accidental Death of an Anarchist* (Half Moon Theatre and Wyndham's Theatre, London, 1980); *Female Parts* by Franca Rame (National Theatre, London, 1981); *Mistero Buffo* (Riverside Theatre, London, 1983); *Trumpets and Raspberries* (Palace Theatre, Watford; Phoenix Theatre, London, 1984); *Archangels Don't Play Pinball* (Bristol Old Vic, 1986); *Elizabeth* (Half Moon Theatre, London, 1986); *An Ordinary Day* (Borderline Theatre Company, Scotland, touring, 1988) and *The Pope and the Witch* (West Yorkshire Playhouse, Leeds, 1991; Comedy Theatre, London, 1992). *An Ordinary Day* has also been translated by Ed Emery as *A Day Like Any Other*. In 1997 Dario Fo was awarded the Nobel Prize for Literature.

DARIO FO

Plays: 1

Mistero Buffo
translated by Ed Emery

Accidental Death of an Anarchist
translated by Ed Emery

Trumpets and Raspberries
translated by R C McAvoy and A-M Giugni

The Virtuous Burglar
translated by Joe Farrell

One Was Nude and One Wore Tails
translated by Ed Emery

with an introduction by series editor
Stuart Hood

Methuen Drama

METHUEN CONTEMPORARY DRAMATISTS

This collection first published in Great Britain in 1992 by Methuen Drama
Reissued with a new cover design 1994;
Reissued in this series 1997 by Methuen Drama
Methuen Publishing Limited
215 Vauxhall Bridge Road, London SW1V 1EJ

13 15 17 19 20 18 16 14

Methuen Publishing Limited Reg. No. 3543167

Mistero Buffo first published in this translation in 1988
by Methuen London Ltd., copyright © 1988 Ed Emery
Accidental Death of an Anarchist first published in this translation in 1992
by Methuen Drama, copyright © 1992 Ed Emery
Trumpets and Raspberries first published in this translation in 1984
by Pluto Press, copyright © 1984 R C McAvoy and A-M Giugni
The Virtuous Burglar first published in this translation in 1992
by Methuen Drama, copyright © 1992 Joe Farrell
One Was Nude and One Wore Tails first published in this translation in 1992
by Methuen Drama, copyright © 1985 Ed Emery

This collection copyright © 1992 Methuen Drama
Introduction copyright © 1992 Stuart Hood

The authors and translators have asserted their moral rights

A CIP catalogue record for this book is available from the British Library

ISBN 0-413-15420-3

Printed and bound in Great Britain by Cox & Wyman Ltd, Reading, Berkshire

CAUTION

Contents

A Chronology

1926   Born in the province of Varese, North Italy. Attends art school in Milan and studies architecture at the Politecnico.

1952-54   Writes and performs monologues for radio which transfer to the theatre. Takes part in satirical revues and meets with censorship.

1957-59   Produces classical farces working with Franca Rame, his wife and close collaborator. They include *One Was Nude and One Wore Tails* and *The Virtuous Burglar*.

1959-67   Writes and produces a series of comedies for the bourgeois theatre, including *Archangels Don't Play Pinball*. He has difficulty because of his criticism of bourgeois society.

In 1962 Fo is asked to produce the popular TV programme *Canzonissima*, which is heavily censored because of its satirical content. Fo and Rame refuse to accept the cuts.

In 1966 he produces and works on *Ci Ragiono e Canto*, which draws on popular and folk songs.

1968-70   Together with Franca Rame sets up the Nuova Scena company, which breaks with the bourgeois theatre and works through the cultural institutions of the Italian Communist Party. It is to this period that *Mistero Buffo* belongs.

1970-74   Fo and Rame break with the Communist Party,

which they consider too reformist, and set up the theatrical collective La Comune. In the 1970-71 season they put on *Accidental Death of an Anarchist* and *Can't Pay? Won't Pay!*

1977   Franca Rame and Fo publish *All Home Bed and Church*, a volume of monologues for female voices.

1983   *The Open Couple* by Rame and Fo looks at the place of women in society.

1984   *Elizabeth, Almost by Chance a Woman*, set at the court of the ageing Elizabeth I.

1986   *An Ordinary Day* and a new edition of *The Open Couple* are published under the title *Female Parts*, by Rame and Fo.

1989   *The Pope and the Witch* looks at the problems of drugs and contraception. *Twenty-five Monologues for a Woman* (English title *A Woman Alone and Other Plays*) assembles texts by Rame and Dario Fo on the theme of woman's fate in society.

1990   *Zitti! Stiamo Precipitando*, looks at AIDS.

1991   Franca Rame's *Parliamo di Donne*, and Fo's *Johan Padan a la Descoverta de le Americhe*, a worm's eye view of the 'dicovery' of America

1997   Dario Fo is awarded the Nobel Prize for Literature.

Introduction

Dario Fo represents a tradition in Italian theatre that gave the world comic figures like Pulcinella and Arlecchino. The lineage of his writing and performance can be traced back to the Commedia dell'Arte of the Renaissance which established the cast of cunning servants, swaggering swordsmen, lecherous old men and star-crossed lovers with their masks and conventional costumes that held the stage for more than two hundred years and from which Punch and Judy derive. But further back still he draws on the older tradition of the *giullari*, the wandering performers of the Middle Ages with their tradition of disrespect for the authorities and the church, and on the slapstick of clowns like Zanni, which is the Venetian version of Giovanni and the name from which we get the word 'zany'. These Zannis – peasant clowns from the valley of the Po – developed a tradition of mime and the convention of *grammelot*: a mixture of dialect words and onomatopoeia, a language that was no language and yet one audiences could latch on to and understand and still do. These are kinds of theatre, Fo argues, that in turn have their roots centuries earlier in the Latin farces of Plautus and Terence, which drew on performances with masked actors that were popular and rude – indeed popular because rude and disrespectful. Fo's theatrical mission is therefore one with a trajectory that takes him away from the formal scholarly dramas of the Renaissance courts just as it does from the bourgeois plays of the nineteenth century and the 'well-made' plays of our own time. The art of comic acting, of working with masks, of mime and of *grammelot* he has taken and developed in order to create a modern popular theatre.

Born in 1926 in North Italy, he grew up in a society of lakeside fishermen, smugglers and storytellers; from them, he says, he learned 'the structure of dialect – above all learned the structure of a primordial, integral language'. That structure and that language were to be the basis of one of his theatrical monologues developed at first for radio and later for the theatre, which he reached by way of art school and stage design. In the Fifties – along with his extremely talented wife Franca Rame – he became the equivalent in Italian theatre of a successful West End actor; but the couple abandoned this career to search for a new audience that was not composed of middle-class playgoers. By the Sixties they had found that audience and were playing to huge crowds in new venues: circus tents, parking lots at factories or the cultural centres of the Italian Communist Party. They and their company became part of the radical political movements of the day. But their connection with the Communist Party was of short duration for the Communists were inflexible in terms of sexual and other politics and unable to understand or approve of that disrespect for established authorities, which large numbers of people – especially the young – felt in those days and to which Fo gave expression.

It is to this period that *Mistero Buffo* (1969) belongs. It is explicitly based on medieval and later texts and the traditions of the *giullari* but in terms of Fo's own development it reflects his subversive reading of Scriptures which is certainly anti-clerical but on another level reflects the view that the Christian tradition is capable of being interpreted in a radical, life-affirming way – the same view as inspired the radical priests working in the *favelas* of South America. Thus his version of *The Marriage at Cana*, as narrated by a drunken guest, is an affirmation of life and the need to enjoy it. What characterises these retellings of Bible stories is the fact that the narrator or chief character in the sketches is frequently a disadvantaged spectator of events – the man who is robbed at the raising of Lazarus or the blind man who, along with his lame mate with his trolley, sees Jesus pass on the way to Calvary and flees from the danger of being 'miracled' by a glance from him. For if they are made whole they will be robbed of their only livelihood. But Fo's anger, which is all the fiercer for being expressed in comic terms, is reserved for the Pope in all his magnificent vestments who spurns Jesus as a poor and worthless creature. It is not surprising therefore that Fo has had problems with the Church and with conventional believers – Franco Zeffirelli, the film director, took exception to the 'satirical reworking of the Gospels' for which the public, he argued, was not ready. Yet in the course of two and a half years, as Fo toured Italy, *Mistero Buffo* attracted a global audience which Fo puts at more than a million spectators – 25,000 on one evening alone in Milan and 14,000 in Turin.

Accidental Death of an Anarchist is a political play which is at once a farce and deeply serious. It dates from the Seventies, that murky period in modern Italian history which saw the discontents of young people – schoolchildren, students and workers – take aggressive form in dress and social behaviour. It was also a period of political hysteria in the media and the established political parties – a hysteria which encouraged certain forces on the Right, among the security services and the army, to pursue (with the connivance of the authorities) a 'strategy of tension'. The result was a series of bombings that killed a number of innocent people. One such explosion in a bank in Piazza Fontana, Milan, in December 1969 killed sixteen people and wounded eighty-eight. The authorities and the press laid the blame on 'anarchists', one of whom, Giuseppe Pinelli, 'fell' from a fourth-floor window in the police headquarters where he was being interrogated. Fo wrote his bitterly ironic play about this 'accidental death' as an act of political intervention when a Left-wing paper *Lotta continua* was on trial for accusing the police of murder. When, many years later, there was a proposal to remove the plaque commemorating Pinelli's death, his reaction typically was to go to Milan and restage the piece.

The play is a farce; the main character, who proceeds to investigate the incident and in doing so reveals the idiocy of the lies spun by officialdom, is on the face of it mad, but his madness is like Hamlet's – a weapon that uncovers truths no one dare formulate in the sensible, 'real' world. The power of the play derives from the tension which Fo deliberately sets up between the comedy arising from confusions of identity, always one of the principal elements of farce, and the tragic circumstances surrounding the death of an innocent man. It is one of his most important tenets that laughter opens people's minds and renders them receptive to ideas they might otherwise reject. The dangers of the course he and his wife, Franca Rame, embarked on during this highly volatile political situation are demonstrated by his arrest by the authorities for disrespect to the American president and – a much graver matter – her kidnapping by Fascists for her courageous support of movements on the Left that included women, workers and the parents and relatives of political prisoners. Franca Rame has explained their stance in these terms:

> In order to feel at one with our political commitments it was no longer enough to consider ourselves democratic, left-wing artists full of sympathy for the working-class and the exploited... the lesson came to us directly from the extraordinary struggles of the working people, from the young people's fight against authoritarianism and injustice in the schools and from their struggle for a new culture and relationship with the exploited classes... We had to place ourselves entirely at the service of the exploited and become their minstrels.

The movement of the Sixties and Seventies developed outside the framework of the established political parties and invented its own methods of struggle. Some of these were a kind of civil disobedience and *autoriduzione*, a tactic by which workers of their own accord limited their working hours and output; the tactic was extended to include the refusal to pay higher prices for pop concerts or cinemas. The slogan *Can't Pay? Won't Pay*, which has found an echo in the anti-poll-tax protests in Britain, was adopted by Fo as the title of one of his successful comedies from this period. But political protest took other forms such as the tactics adopted by the Red Brigades with their policy of armed struggle, kidnapping and political murder – what was described as 'the strategy of annihilation'. The most clamorous example was the capture and killing in 1978 of the Christian Democrat politician and ex-prime minister Aldo Moro. His fate was surrounded by mysteries which have never been resolved. One view is that having been held captive for almost two months – a period during which he appealed to his political allies and the authorities to come to terms with his captors – he was in the end abandoned by his own Christian Democrat colleagues in order to demonstrate that they were not 'soft on terrorism'.

The hysteria and hypocrisy of the times led Fo to write *Trumpets and Raspberries*, a two-act play which is included in this volume as another example of his use of comic invention to make a political intervention. It concerns, again, a confusion of identities: a Fiat shop steward sees what appears to be a terrorist attack on Agnelli, the boss of Fiat; he covers the badly-burned industrialist with his jacket before fleeing from the scene; the disfigured Agnelli is taken to hospital where he is mistakenly identified as the shop steward. He is interrogated by the police, who are convinced that he is a Left-wing terrorist, but they break off their investigations when it becomes clear that their 'terrorist' has such knowledge of dubious goings-on in high places that any further police action would be dangerous.

In the original performance in January 1981, Fo played both the workman and the industrialist, the latter being so swathed in bandages and connected to pulleys that he is little more than a human puppet (a situation that recurs in Fo's work). The mainspring of the comic action derives, in the tradition of classical farce, from confusions and misrecognitions; the cutting-edge, in the original Italian production, was provided by sharp comments on prominent politicians of the day, their hypocrisy and 'the stench of corpses' (to use Fo's words) which accompanied it. The political temperature was raised several degrees when at the end of one performance three women, all relatives of political prisoners, came on stage and read the text of a complaint about conditions in the maximum security gaols where the prisoners were and on whose behalf Franca Rame had sent an appeal to Amnesty International. The ensuing press campaign was astonishing and unrestrained. The row over what was inaccurately described in some papers as a demonstration in favour of the Red Brigades spread to Parliament and the Senate where there were calls for the censorship of parts of the play. Today we read and see it at a different political conjuncture but it stands up as splendid comic writing and a comment on power and its abuse that is still valid.

Fo's work came to be strongly marked by the thinking of the women's movement and by the impetus he received from collaboration with Franca Rame. He was thus inspired to write a number of plays like *The Open Couple*, along with monologues for his wife dealing with the position of women in our society. What was remarkable about them was the degree to which the texts evolved in a dialogue with audiences – to the point where it is very difficult to discover what the final text is. The view of the text as something open to alteration, without closure, is in a tradition familiar in the popular theatre and to the travelling troupes like the family into which Franca Rame was born; it goes back to the Commedia dell'Arte in which the plot was merely an outline around which the actors improvised and in which they inserted their *lazzi*, their comic routines, and reactions to the audiences of the day.

Fo's skill as a performer lies precisely in his ability to improvise, to spin out a comic moment to its limits in a manner that draws on these traditions. His skill as a writer lies in his prolific ability to write texts for farces, of which two examples have been included here. *The Virtuous Burglar* is based on a classic confusion of identities, on the improbable assembling in one place, one flat, one room, of couples who had rather not be discovered there. Fo has an apparently inexhaustible repertoire of variants on these age-old situations which to this day never fail to work with audiences. Such a piece too is *One Was Nude and One Wore Tails* which exploits the same mechanisms while driving home the old saying about clothes making the man. These are texts which on the page are deceptively simple; they depend for their success on a highly developed style of acting to which speed and agility give an almost balletic quality.

Since the heady days of the Sixties and Seventies Dario Fo has faced the problem that confronts many people on the Left – how to express their feelings about the great social changes in European society, the shifting of the political parameters, the confusions about goals, about ends and means. In one of his latest works *The Pope and the Witch* he takes as his target social attitudes to the drugs problem -- in another he deals with the prejudices inherent in certain perceptions of AIDS, always using to discuss these most controversial topics the skills he has learned from the past, whether as performer, writer or director.

Fo has done some work since then, acting in and directing the work of Angelo Beolco (1502–42) known as Il Ruzzante, the Playful Man. He wrote in Paduan dialect comedies for which he invented the peasant character from whom he takes his name. His work with its use of dialect and *lazzi* – comic business – is obviously close to the heart of the author of *Mistero Buffo*. But it looks as if in a period of self-assessment Fo is returning more and more to direction. It is a measure of his reputation as a director that he was invited – the first foreigner to be so honoured – to direct a production of Molière's *Malade Imaginaire* at the Comédie Française.

Fo is a controversial figure. Not everybody accepts his interpretation of the medieval texts on which much of his work is founded and some dispute his version of the history of the Italian theatre. There are those who find that he has in the past devalued the role of the director in favour of the performer. A recent volume on the Italian theatre by an important Italian publisher contains no reference to his work. There are those who reject his attempt to create a popular culture drawing on old traditions as a counter to consumerism and the mass media – an attempt that belonged to a historical and cultural conjuncture that is now past.

What there is no denying is the range and variety of his work. This volume aims to provide a sample drawn from an immense output that goes back more than thirty years.

Stuart Hood, 1991

Mistero Buffo
Comic Mysteries

Translated by ED EMERY

Translator's Note

Fo originally played these pieces in dialect (an aspect of his theatrical enterprise that often goes unnoticed when his works appear in translation). As Stuart Hood shows in the Appendix to this book, the pieces can also be translated in dialect form.

My brief, however, was to produce a translation in standard English, suitable for reading as a playtext, but also suitable for performance. This translation was in fact used by the 1982 Theatre Company in their memorable ensemble performance of *Mistero Buffo* at Riverside Studios in 1983.

In translating the words *giullare* and *villano*, I have used two words introduced into English by the Normans and current in the times of Chaucer: *jongleur* and *villeyn*. I have tended to use 'the people' to render *il popolo* (a term which has a political connotation). I have rendered *Mistero Buffo* as *The Comic Mysteries*.

The text as published in this edition is drawn from the 1977 Bertani version; some of Fo's introductory material about Italian cultural history is not included here.

ED EMERY

ACTOR: The term 'mystery' was already in use by the second and third centuries AD. It means a play, a religious representation, a performance.

We still hear the term used nowadays, during the mass, when the priest says: 'In the first glorious mystery... in the second mystery... etc.' The word 'mystery' means 'a religious performance'; comic mystery, on the other hand, means a grotesque performance.

The comic mysteries were invented by the people.

As far back as the second and third centuries after Christ, people used to entertain themselves (and this was not merely a form of entertainment) by playing, performing dramas in a form which was both grotesque and laden with irony. The reason for this was that, for the people, the theatre, and especially grotesque theatre, has always been a primary means of expression, of communication, and also a vehicle for the development and spreading of ideas. The theatre was the spoken and dramatised newspaper of the people of that time.

The *jongleur* used to turn up in the streets of the town, and reveal to the people their own condition — that of being beaten as well as being taken for a ride. Because the law prescribed beatings as well as hangings. There were plenty of other examples of vicious laws like this. Anyway, the *jongleur* was a figure who, in the Middle Ages, was part of the people. As Muratori[1] says, the *jongleur* was born from the people, and from the people he took their anger in order to be able to give it back to them, mediated via the grotesque, through 'reason', in order that the people should gain greater awareness of their own condition. And it is for this reason that in the Middle

1. Muratori: 18th century Italian scholar.

Ages, *jongleurs* were killed with such abandon; they flayed them alive, they cut out their tongues, not to mention other niceties of the time.

Photo 1: A *Buffonata*.

But now let us return to the 'Comic Mysteries'. Here (photo 1) we have a picture showing a scene of buffoonery, a procession preceding one of the ironic-grotesque performances. We see the people also taking part, dressed up in fancy dress. It is clear that the figures portrayed here are ordinary people, dressed up in *mammuttones*. What does *mammuttones* mean? They were an extremely ancient design of mask, half goat and half devil. In Sardinia today it is still possible to see peasants wearing these extraordinary masks during particular festivals. As you can see from the slide, they are almost all portrayed as devils. Here we have a *jongleur* portraying the Joker, the Fool (a popular allegorical figure), and here we have another Devil... and another...

Here (photo 2), further along, we see devils, witches, and a picturesque passing friar. Another particular that you should note is that everyone has instruments for making noises. The business of making a din, a racket, was an essential part of those festivals. (*He points to one of the figures*) This person is carrying a *ciucciué* – one of the names they give it in Naples. This is a pair of special leather bellows. When you squeeze them, they give out a tremendous farting noise. (*He points to another figure on the slide*) This fellow with his leg half cocked doesn't need a fart-machine. As you can see, he makes his own

Photo 2: A *Buffonata*.

noises... He's a naturalist... So, here you have all these people making a racket. These folk would put on their masks, and gather in the street, whereupon they would set up a kind of make-believe trial of the noblemen, the rich, the powerful, and bosses in general. In other words, merchants, emperors, grasping moneylenders, bankers... all of which anyway amount to more or less the same thing. Bishops and cardinals were also included.

I really can't imagine why, in the Middle Ages, they put bishops and cardinals together with the rich and powerful.... This was a particularly striking element of these performances, but we have not yet tracked down the reasons! Obviously, the bishops and the rich people in question were make-believes... For some curious reason, real rich people preferred not to come down and join in people's fun on these occasions. The make-believe noblemen were dressed to fit the part. A kind of trial took place, amid scenes of some violence, and on the basis of specific charges. 'You did such and such... You have exploited... You have robbed... You have killed... etc.' The crowning moment of this performance was a big bonfire, into which all these rich people and noblemen were hurled, with imaginary pots of boiling oil poured over them, and they were subjected to make-believe executions and skinning alive.

Obviously, real rich people used to stay at home on days like this, because, who knows, they might have been walking down the street and... gotcha! 'Oh, excuse me, I thought you were only a make-believe rich person.' So, in order to avoid being taken for make-believe rich people, they stayed locked up in their houses. In fact, there is an interesting if slightly mischievous theory of a major French historian, by name of Bloch,[1] who came from Alsace and who was killed by the Nazis for being a Communist. Bloch maintained that slatted shutters for windows were invented precisely in that period, in order to enable the rich to watch these demonstrations in the streets of the city without being seen from below.

On the final day of the festival, all these people, the *jongleurs* and the buffoons, would process into church. In the Middle Ages, the church still had its original character as an *ecclesia* – in other words, a meeting place. So, the people entered this meeting place. This would be at the end of eight to eleven days of buffoonery, which took place in December and maintained a continuity with the traditions of the Roman Fescennine[2] festivals, the Roman carnival. So, the people entered the church, and there, in the transept, stood the bishop. The bishop would remove all his trappings, and hand them over to the chief *jongleur*. The chief *jongleur* then went up into the pulpit, and began to preach, imitating the bishop's

1. M. Bloch: French scholar and authority on Middle Ages.
2. From Fescennia, a town in Etruria, famous in classical times for scurrilous dialogues in verse (OED).

own style of preaching. He would imitate not only the bishop's mannerisms and his style, but also the content of his sermons. In other words, he stripped bare the whole mystification and hypocrisy; he revealed the operations of power for what they were.

The *jongleurs* were very good at imitating the style of priestly hypocrisy and paternalism. In fact it is said that San Zeno of Verona was so well taken off by one of the *jongleurs*, so well imitated, that for six months afterwards, every time he tried to go up into his pulpit to preach his sermon, he never once succeeded in getting to the end; after the first three or four sentences, he would begin stuttering, and would have to leave. You would have the following scene. He would begin: 'My beloved faithful, I am here, as a humble shepherd...' And everyone would begin sniggering. 'The Sheep...' 'Baaaah!!' The poor devil would find himself covered in confusion and forced to flee the scene.

Now, in the next picture (photo 3) we see two figures. They are two *milites*.[1] This is a picture of a mosaic to be found in a church in Milan. It's a part of the floor mosaic in the church of Sant'Ambrogio, and even I, when I was an architecture student and had to go and work on this mosaic, never noticed this amazing bit. These figures represent two *jongleurs*, two *jongleurs* dressed as *milites*, as you can see from the theatrical nature of their gestures.

The *milites* found themselves in the popular firing line fairly frequently, because they were particularly hated by the people. Basically, the *milites* consisted of those professional agents of law and order whom today we know as the *police*. With a bit of imagination, you can remove their medieval dress and re-dress them in modern clothes, and you will see how well their faces fit the part.

On your left is a building; this building is not part of the theatrical stage portrayed; it is part of another scene. As you can see, this building outside the arch is made up of several storeys; it has four, five, six floors. Now, we have made inquiries and carried out profound historical researches, and

1. *Milites*: Literally 'soldiers'.

we have discovered that in the Middle Ages, police stations were all built on one floor only. This was in order to guard

Photo 3: *Milites*, from a twelfth-century mosaic in the church of Sant'Ambrogio Milan.

against dipsonomy, a disease which has been known to strike, in particular, policemen and officers of the law. It is a curious disease, whereby during interrogation sessions, they sometimes make mistakes in giving directions. Confusion sets in and they begin to mistake their left for their right. They say: 'You're free to go now... There's the door', and they point to the window! This has happened several times... but only in the Middle Ages, of course.[1]

While we're on the subject of making jokes out of things that are extremely serious and dramatic, yesterday I got a letter from a comrade, a lawyer, saying that allusions like this, to certain events that have happened recently in our country,

Photo 4: 'Fourteenth-century travelling players', Cambrai library.

which are presented here in order to make people laugh, had *upset* him. Well, that is precisely what we intended. In other words, we wanted to make people understand that this was the element which both permits and permitted (in the *jongleur* tradition) the popular actor, the folk player, to scratch people's consciousness, to leave them with a taste of something burned and bitter. The reference to pyres is purely by-the-by.

If I limited myself just to acting out oppression, in the tragic mode, employing rhetoric or melancholy or drama, I would

1. This is a reference to the death of the anarchist Pinelli who "fell" from a window while being interrogated by the Milan police – the story that inspired *Accidental Death of an Anarchist*.

only move my audience to indignation. Inevitably, the message would be lost like water off a duck's back.

I wanted to make this point because I often hear people asking why we should 'laugh' at things that are so serious.

This is something which, precisely, the people have taught us. Speaking of the people, we should remember what Mao Tse-tung says about satire. He says that satire is the most powerful weapon that the people have ever had in order to make clear to themselves, within their own culture, all the misdeeds and corruption of their rulers.

Let's proceed with the slides. In this picture (photo 4) you see another religious performance, which this time is both dramatic and grotesque. This is a performance in Flanders,

Photo 5: Comic-grotesque performance in Antwerp city
      square (1465).

around the year 1360 (the date is inscribed on the print). As you can see, here we have a woman with a lamb in her arms. I am pointing this out now because it will become relevant during a piece that follows later, the 'Slaughter of the Innocents'.

Here too (photo 5) we have a fairly important picture. Here we are in Antwerp in 1465, which was the year prior to the Edict of Toledo.

The Edict of Toledo forbade the people to take part in comic mysteries. The picture speaks for itself, in the sense of explaining why this censorship was necessary. If you look, here you see an actor representing Jesus Christ. Here you have two ruffians. Over there, you have a town crier, who would have been one of the actors, and the people, in front of the stage, react and respond to the crier.

What is the crier saying? He is shouting: 'Who do you want to be crucified? Jesus Christ or Barabbas?' And down below, the people reply by shouting: 'Jean Gloughert!' – who was the Mayor of the city. As you can imagine, little ironies like this, expressed so pointedly and directly, were not calculated to please the Mayor and his friends... Obviously, they began to think: 'Wouldn't it be better if we banned these performances?' Here, in the next slide (photo 6), we have another performance, which is perhaps a little more violent.

Here we are in Paris, in the Place du Louvre, around the same period. If you look, you can see Jesus Christ, an actor playing the part of Christ, together with other actors. Here we have Pontius Pilate, with his little bowl all ready so that he can wash his hands, and here we have two bishops. Note that they are two Catholic bishops. Strictly speaking, they should have been dressed at least in Hebrew dress, don't you think? They should really have been dressed completely differently: pudding basin haircuts, curling sidelocks, clothes of another era, which the people would have recognised as such.

Instead, the people went ahead and stuck two bishops there, dressed in the clothes of our very own Catholic bishops! In other words, they were saying: 'Alright, all this happened in Palestine, agreed, and at that period there weren't yet any Christians, and obviously those priests up there would have

Photo 6: A Passion Play. Place du Louvre, Paris (fifteenth century).

been Hebrews, and so they would have been of another religion, another reality! Yes, admitted. But at the same time, they
were still two bishops, those who insisted on Jesus Christ
being sent to the cross. And the fact is that, throughout the
ages, bishops have always taken the rulers' side when it comes
down to it, and end up sending poor sods like us to the cross!'

Naturally, sentiments like these were not pleasing to the
Pope, let alone to the bishops and cardinals. So they decided
to hold a conference in Toledo. They said: 'That's enough! We
can no longer permit a situation where the people use this kind
of theatre – where they start with religion and then turn everything into burlesque and irony.'

And so they banned the representation not only of the Gospels, but also of the Bible as a whole.

Speaking of the ways in which bible stories turned to effect, here (photo 7) we have a picture of a *jongleur*. He is enacting

Photo 7: 'King David's drinking session', from a medieval manuscript.

David's famous drinking session. In the Bible, it relates that David went on a drinking session that lasted for seven days. Remarkable! During this time, he picked on just about everybody in sight. He began by insulting his father, his mother, and the Holy Father, but in particular he picked on his own subjects, in other words, the people. He said, more or less: 'You people, vulgar, wretched, and also a bit stupid, why do you believe all these stories?'

The *jongleur* enacted all this in the grotesque, and shouted to his audience: 'But do you really believe that the Holy Father came down to earth and said: "Right, that'll do with all these arguments about division of wealth and land. I'm going to sort it out, I'll sort everything out. Right, you, you with the beard, come here, I like you. Take this crown: you can be king. You... come here. And your wife? You're nice, you can be queen. Oh, what an ugly face you've got... here, you can be Emperor. What about that fellow over there... He looks pretty crafty... Come on, come on, you can be bishop. As for you, you're going to be a merchant. And you, come on, come on... you see that, all that territory, all that land that stretches to the river over there... that's all yours... I like you... But be sure that you hold on to it! Don't ever let anyone else get their hands on it, and make sure that you work it well. And you too... Here's some land for you... That fellow's a relative of yours, you say...? That's good! That way you can keep everything in the family! Now, let's see... you can have all that bit over by the sea. Fishing rights, on the other hand, go to you... And you, down there, miserable shrivelled wretches that you are, you, and you, and you, and you, and also your wives, you're going to *work* for him... and for him... and for him... and also for him... And if you complain, I shall hurl you into Hell, otherwise my name is not God! And it is, by God!"'

Well, performances like this did not at all please the wealthier elements of the community. So, it was decided, or rather the bishops decided, that any *jongleur* who was found uttering such unpleasantnesses before the people was to be burned alive.

However, there was a famous German *jongleur*, one Hans Holden (photo 8), who was extremely good at playing this piece about David's drinking session. He took the liberty of performing the piece after the Edict had been issued. They burned him at the stake. The poor soul believed that the

Photo 8: 'The arrest of Hans Holden'.

bishops were only joking with their threat: 'You don't really think that they're going to put me on a bonfire, do you?' But he was wrong. Bishops are serious people, and they never joke! As I say, they burned him alive. End of story.

During the Middle Ages, there was also a popular technique for drawing people's attention to these particular plays and their performance. Remnants of it are still found today, in Puglia, during the feast of St Nicholas of Bari, a famous bishop, a saint and a black man, who came from the East. Nowadays this festival has been reduced to a fairly normal procession, of people carrying placards which, in the Middle Ages, would have served to indicate the scenes, the performances that were to be enacted that same evening. Bringing up the rear were the *battuti*, the flagellants, who went through the streets flogging themselves like mad. It wasn't for nothing that this was a religious performance!

In addition, when the procession had finished winding its way through the streets and squares of the city, these flagellants would gather around the stage where the performance was to take place, and would chant, shout, lament and even breathe chorally, together, in order to underline the dramatic and grotesque moments of the performance. My reason for bringing this up is because, in the course of the various pieces that I shall perform, you will hear passages of choral chanting. Their chant was more or less along the following lines:

THE FLAGELLANTS' LAUDE

(*Modelled on examples from Pordenone, Brescia and Mantua*)

Ahiiii. Beat yourselves. Beat yourselves. Ahiiiiah!
    Friends, get in line.
    Beat yourselves hard and with good heart.
    Complain not of the pain. Beat yourselves.
    Fear not that you are naked,
    Fear not the whip's lash and the scars it makes,
    The torn and broken flesh.

Ahiiii. Beat yourselves. Beat yourselves. Ahiiiiah!
    If you hope for salvation,
    Beat yourselves with the lash,

With the lash, hear it crack.
Do not flinch. Beat yourselves!
For the Lord Almighty was beaten, in truth!

Ahiiii. Beat yourselves. Beat yourselves. Ahiiiah!
If you seek to do penance
And reduce the dread sentence
That is shortly to come,
And which nobody can escape – Beat yourselves!
This sentence hangs over us all,
So let us beat ourselves. Feel the pain.

Ahiiii. Beat yourselves. Beat yourselves. Ahiiiiah!
In order to save us from sin
Jesus Christ was beaten.
On the cross he was nailed
And in his face they spat. Beat yourselves!
And gall was given him to drink!
And St Peter was not there.

Ahiiii. Beat yourselves. Beat yourselves. Ahiiiiah!
And you rulers, you usurers,
You will suffer misfortune,
For you have spat in the face of Christ,
Enriching yourselves with ill-gotten gains. Beat yourselves!
You who have squeezed, as a person would crush grapes,
The money out of those who sweat and toil.

Ahiiii. Beat yourselves. Beat yourselves! Ahiiiiah!

THE SLAUGHTER OF THE INNOCENTS

Introduction

A few years ago, an extraordinary exhibition was held in the Abbey of Chiaravalle in Milan. It was an exhibition of theatrical machines. These were magnificent statues, whose limbs were articulated so that they moved just like puppets or dolls. The movement was controlled by a series of levers and hooks which were operated by a puppeteer concealed in the rear of the statue (only the front of the statue was figuratively portrayed). One of the exhibits was a magnificent Madonna and Child, dating from the twelfth century, where both the figures were mobile. Their arms, torso, elbow joints and even their eyes moved, by a mechanism which functioned on the *déséquilibre* principle invented by Flemish puppeteers. For example, there was a balance mechanism in the forearm, whereby the hand was articulated, and any movement, however slight, would cause the hand to rotate at the wrist, before then coming to a stop. The slightest impulse would make the hands, or some other part of the body, move with an extraordinary grace. And this really did give the impression of an object come to life.

The same principle underlies the construction of another famous statue, the Christ of Aquileia. The mechanism cannot be seen, because clothing covers the statue's whole body; but when the garment is removed, you can see that the whole body is articulated, from the head on downwards.

Now, why was it that the people, when they put their plays on, decided to use these machines in order to represent the godhead. Were they perhaps worried about being blasphemous, scared of encroaching on the sacredness of the divine person? No! Not at all. It was done because the actor, the player, wanted his audience to focus their attention not on the divine presence, but on the man. If an actor had been seen to come on stage wearing a costume depicting Jesus Christ, he would have drawn everyone's attention to himself. On the other hand, the statue could be present as something purely indicative and symbolic, and the player had space to develop and emphasise the dramatic content of the *human* condition: desperation, hunger and pain.

I have gone into the question of theatrical machines because the piece which I am now going to perform does in fact require the use of a machine portraying the Madonna with the Child in her arms. In this piece another woman also figures, a crazy woman, who holds a lamb in her arms – and this is why I mentioned previously that Flemish picture, in which you see a woman with a lamb in her arms. This woman's baby had been killed during the Slaughter of the Innocents, and she found a lamb in a sheep-pen; she took it in her arms and went around telling everybody that this was her own baby. The allegory behind this is clear: the lamb is the *agnus dei*, the Lamb of God, the Son of God, and so this woman is also the Madonna.

This double-play of the Woman/Madonna figure is extremely ancient. In fact, it comes from the Greeks. The Woman is in a position to say things which a real Madonna, an actress playing the Madonna (or rather, an actor, as was the custom in those days) would never have been able to say. This woman goes so far as to curse God, with an incredible violence. With her lamb in her arms, she begins to shout: '...Why didn't you keep your son with you, if you knew that he was going to cause us so much suffering, so much pain! Your turn will come, to understand the suffering of mankind, you who tried to enact this exchange to your advantage... For one little cup of blood you have caused a river of blood to flow... A thousand babies killed for your one single child. Why didn't you keep your child with you, if you knew he was going to cost us so much suffering, so much pain! You will come to see pain too, the pain, the desperation of mankind, on the day when you too will see your son die – on the Cross. On that day, you will understand the tremendous suffering you have imposed on mankind, for a sin and by an error! No father on earth, however ill-meaning, would ever have thought to impose this on his own son. No matter how evil that father was!'

This is certainly an outrageous blasphemy! It is like saying: 'Eternal father, you are the scum of all scum! No father on earth could ever be as evil as you.' And why should the people feel such a deep-seated hatred towards the Eternal Father? We have already seen why. Because the Eternal Father represents the impositions which rulers have forced upon the people; it is he who introduced divisions among the people, who gave land, power and privilege to certain groups of people, and handed out suffering, desperation, subjection, humiliation and mortification to the rest. This is why God is hated, because he represents the rulers; it is he who hands out thrones and privileges. On the other hand, Jesus Christ is loved, because it is he who came to earth seeking to give people back their Spring. Above all else he represents dignity, and in these folk traditions the question of dignity is raised over and over again, with an incredible persistence. Dignity...

Now let us move on to the piece representing the *Slaughter of the Innocents*.

Before I start, I would like to draw your attention to one thing, the dialect (or rather the language) of the piece. It is a 13/15th century Lombard dialect, but reworked by an actor who, in the course of a week, might find himself moving from one village to another, from one town to the next. One day he might be in Brescia, the next in Verona, and then in Bergamo, etc etc. So, he would find himself having to play the piece in dialects that were quite different from each other. There were hundreds of dialects in those days, with considerable differences between them, even between neighbouring cities. Thus, the *jongleur* would need to know hundreds of dialects. So what did he do? He invented one of his own, a language formed from many dialects, and containing the possibility of substituting key words. Should he find himself in a moment of difficulty, not knowing which precise word to choose in order to convey his meaning, you would find him giving three, maybe four, even five synonyms.

There is a striking example of this: a *jongleur* from Bologna tells the tale of a girl who came to kiss a man whom she loved. But suddenly she was afraid. She wanted to make love with him, but when it came to the delicate moment, she suddenly pushed him away, and said: *Non me toccar a mi, che mi a son zovina, son fiola, tosa son e garsonetta.* In other words, she said: 'I am a girl, I am a girl, I am a girl, I am a girl.' All the words he used mean simply 'girl'. And his audience could simply pick out the word that they understood best.

In the piece that follows, in the original text, you will find many of these reiterations. But they are also used with another purpose in mind: in order to increase the poetic content of the moment, and, particularly, to expand its dramatic content. This is something quite unique to the art of the *jongleur*, to the theatre of the people – the ability to choose and select words and sounds that are best fitted to the moment. This is why you hear, for example, *croz*, *cros*, *crosge*, etc, all of which mean *croce* or 'cross', and each of which is taken from different dialects in order to give the best feeling to what is being enacted on the stage. The piece is performed by only one player, and afterwards I shall explain why. This is not to do with exhibitionism; it has an important underlying rationale. There will also be a moving statue onstage, as I explained, as well as the chorus of flagellants which opens the piece. At a certain point, as you will see, a soldier is killed on stage, and the flagellants' chorus sings a funeral dirge.

THE SLAUGHTER OF THE INNOCENTS

CHORUS OF FLAGELLANTS:
  Ahiii! Beat yourselves. Beat yourselves! Ahiiiiah!
    With pain and lamentation
    For the slaughter of the innocents,
    A thousand innocent children.
    They killed them like lambs.
    From their fear-stricken mothers
    King Herod plucked them.
  Ahiiii! Beat yourselves. Beat yourselves! Ahiiiiah!

WOMAN: Pig, murderer, don't touch my baby.

SOLDIER: Let it go, let go of that baby, or I'll cut your hands off... I'll kick you in the belly... Let go...

WOMAN: Nooo! Kill me instead... (*The* SOLDIER *snatches her baby and kills it*) Ahiiii, ahiiii, you've killed him! Dead!

SOLDIER: Hey, here comes another one. Stop where you are, Woman, or I shall run both of you through, you and your baby!

WOMAN: Run us both through, I would rather you did...

SOLDIER: Don't be crazy... You're still young, you have time enough to have a dozen more children... Give me that one... Don't make a fuss!

WOMAN: No! Get your dirty hands off him.

SOLDIER: Ouch! Bite me, would you? So, take that! And drop that bundle.

WOMAN: Have pity, I pray you... Don't kill him. I'll give you all that I have.

The SOLDIER *seizes her bundle and finds that it's a lamb.*

SOLDIER: What's this, eh? An animal, a lamb?

WOMAN: Oh yes! It's not a baby... It's a lamb... I don't have any children... I can't have children... Oh, Soldier, I pray you, don't kill my lamb... Because it's not yet Easter, and you would commit a great sin if you kill him!

SOLDIER: Look, woman, are you trying to play a joke on me... Or are you crazy, perhaps?

WOMAN: Me, crazy? No, I am not crazy!

Another SOLDIER *joins in.*

SOLDIER II: Come on, leave her lamb alone... The poor woman is out of her mind with grief because we've killed her son. What's the matter with you? Come on, there's still a lot more to be killed.

SOLDIER I: Wait, I think I'm going to be sick...

SOLDIER II: What do you expect! You eat like a pig –

onions, salted mutton, stuff like that, and afterwards...
Come over here, there's a tavern on the corner. I'll buy you
a nice stiff drink.

SOLDIER I: No. It's not because of what I've eaten... It's
because of this butchery, this slaughter of the children that
we've been doing. That's what's turned my stomach.

SOLDIER II: If you knew you were such a delicate soul, you
shouldn't have joined up as a soldier in the first place.

SOLDIER I: I joined up in order to kill enemies, to kill men...

SOLDIER II: And presumably to send a few women tumbling
in the hay as well, eh?

SOLDIER I: Yes, maybe... But only if they were enemy
women!

SOLDIER II: And butcher their cattle...

SOLDIER I: Only enemy cattle.

SOLDIER II: And burn their houses... And kill their old
people, their chickens, their children... Enemy children,
of course!

SOLDIER I: Yes, babies too. But only in war! There is no
shame and dishonour in war; the trumpets sound, the
drums roll, and there are hymns of war, *and* the captains'
fine speeches at the end!

SOLDIER II: Oh, you'll get captains' fine speeches at the end
of this slaughter too...

SOLDIER I: But here we're killing innocents.

SOLDIER II: What do you mean! Aren't people innocent in
wars too? What have those people ever done to you? Have
they ever done anything to you, those poor souls whom
you kill and maim, to the sound of your trumpets?

A machine representing the MADONNA AND CHILD
passes across the back of the stage.

SOLDIER II: Well, blind my eyes if that's not the Virgin Mary
with her Child, the one we're looking for. Let's grab her
before she can get away... Get a move on... This time we'll

get that big reward that's been posted.

SOLDIER I: I don't want the dirty, stinking reward.

SOLDIER II: Alright, then, I'll have it all for myself.

SOLDIER I: No, you're not taking it either!

He bars his way.

SOLDIER II: But have you gone mad? Let me pass. We've got orders to kill the Virgin's child!

SOLDIER I: I shit on those orders. Don't move from there, or I'll cut you down!

SOLDIER II: Wretch, don't you understand that if this child lives, he will become King of Galilee in place of Herod? That was what the prophecy said!

SOLDIER I: I shit on Herod and on the prophecy!

SOLDIER II: Alright, so you need to take a shit… Go and do it in a field somewhere, since you've got no stomach for this. Let me pass, because I don't want to lose that reward!

SOLDIER I: No! I've had enough of seeing babies killed!

SOLDIER II: Alright then, so much the worse for you!

He runs him through with his sword.

SOLDIER I: Ahiiii… You've killed me… Wretch… You've run me through!

SOLDIER II: I'm sorry… You were being really stupid… I didn't want to…

SOLDIER I: My blood's pissing out all over… Oh mamma, mamma… Where are you, mother…? It's getting dark… I'm cold, mother… Mamma.

He dies.

SOLDIER II: I never killed him. That one was a corpse from the moment that he began to have pity. As the proverb says: 'A soldier who feels pity is already as good as dead.' And now he's made me lose my chance of capturing the Virgin and her Child.

The FLAGELLANTS *sing a funeral dirge. Exit the*
SOLDIER, *dragging away his companion's body. Enter the*
MADONNA, *or rather the model of the Madonna. Behind
her, enter the* MAD WOMAN.

WOMAN: Don't run away, Madonna... Don't be scared, I'm
not a soldier... I'm a woman... a mother, too. I've got a
baby too. Hide yourself here and rest, because the soldiers
have gone away... Sit down, you poor woman... You look
as if you've been running... Let's see your baby. Oh how
pretty he is. What a bonny colour! How old is he? Pretty,
pretty... Look how happy he is, he's smiling... Pretty,
pretty... He must be just the same age as mine...
   What's his name? Jesus? Oh, that's a lovely name:
Jesus... Pretty, pretty... little Jesus. Oh, and he's got two
little teeth... Oh, how lovely. Mine hasn't yet got all his
teeth... He's been a little poorly, over the last month, but
he's better now... Here he is, look, sleeping like a little
angel... (*She calls him by name*) Mark! He's called Mark,
you know. Look how he's sleeping. Oh, my pretty little
one! You're pretty too, my little Mark... You know, it's
true what they say – we mothers always think that our own
babies are the prettiest of all... They might have some little
defect, but we never see it.
   You know, I love this little creature so much that if they
were to take him away from me, I would go crazy! When I
think of the terrible fright I had this morning, when I went
to the cradle and found it empty, full of blood, and my baby
nowhere in sight... Luckily, though, it wasn't true...
It was only a dream. I knew it was a dream, because a little
later I woke up, and I was still under the influence of the
dream, and I was so desperate that I almost went out of my
mind! I went out into the courtyard, and I began to curse
God: 'God, awesome in your heartlessness,' I shouted,
'You ordered this slaughter... you wanted this sacrifice in
exchange for sending down your Son: a thousand babies
killed for the sake of one of yours: a river of blood for a
cup! You should have kept him with you, this Son of yours,
if he was going to cost us poor souls such a mighty sacrifice.

Ah, but in the end you too will see what it means to die of heartbreak, the day when your own son dies! In the end, you too will understand what a mighty and awesome affliction you have visited on mankind for all eternity. No father on earth, no matter how wicked, would ever have had the heartlessness to impose such a thing on his own son.'

There I was in the yard, shouting these curses, as I say, when suddenly I looked round, and there, in the sheep pen, in among all the sheep, I discovered my baby, crying... I recognised him instantly, and took him in my arms, and began to cry, along with him. 'I ask your pardon, merciful Lord, for those bad words I shouted... I didn't mean them... It was the Devil, yes, it was the Devil who put them into my mouth! You, Lord, who are so good, you saved my son...! And you have made it so that everyone takes him for a little lamb; and even the soldiers don't realise it, and they let me go. I shall have to be careful when Easter comes, though, because then everybody starts killing lambs the way they've been killing babies today. The butchers will come to me looking for him, but I shall put a bonnet on his head, with all ribbons in it, and everyone will think that he is a baby. But right now I must make sure that nobody recognises him as a baby... In fact I shall take him out to pasture, and I shall make him eat grass, so that everyone thinks that he really is a sheep... And anyway, it will be easier for my son to get by as a sheep than as a man in this wretched world!'

Oh, he's woken up. Look, Madonna, my little Mark... Isn't he pretty... The little flower! (*The* WOMAN *draws her shawl aside and shows the* MADONNA *the lamb. The* MADONNA *shudders*) Oh, Madonna, do you feel ill? Cheer up, don't cry, because the worst is over, and everything will turn out alright, you'll see... Just have faith in Providence, which helps us all!

CHORUS: Lord, who art so full of pity that you make crazy those who are not capable of escaping from their grief...

WOMAN: (*Cradling the lamb and singing*)
    Hushabye, lullaby,
    Mummy's pretty baby.
    The Madonna cradled
    While the angels sang,
    Saint Joseph slept standing,
    And Baby Jesus laughed,
    And Herod cursed,
    A thousand babies flew to heaven.
        Hushabye, lullaby.

THE MORALITY PLAY
OF THE BLIND MAN AND THE CRIPPLE

Introduction

Another piece which relates to the theme of dignity is the *Morality Play of the Blind Man and the Cripple*. This piece is

Photo 9: 'Moralité de l'aveugle et du boiteux'. Frontispiece of a seventeenth-century French broadsheet.

well-known throughout the European medieval theatrical tradition. Versions of it are found in many countries – one in Hainault in Belgium; more than one in France (photo 9); and a well-known version by Andrea della Vigna, in Italy at the end of the fifteenth century.

Anyway, at a certain moment, the blind man says: 'Dignity does not lie in straight legs, or eyes that see; dignity is not having an employer to subject you.' True freedom is the freedom of not having bosses – not only that I should be free, but that I should live in a world that is also free – where others do not have bosses either. Just imagine it – all this in around 1200-1300!

Naturally, we're not taught this kind of thing in school, because it is extremely dangerous to let children know that away back in the Middle Ages poor people had realised a few things... knew that they were being exploited...!

THE MORALITY PLAY
OF THE BLIND MAN AND THE CRIPPLE

THE BLIND MAN: Help me, kind people... Give me alms, because I am a poor unfortunate. I am blind in both eyes, which is perhaps a lesser evil, because if I were able to see myself, I would be overcome with pity for myself, and would go mad with despair.

THE CRIPPLE: Oh, kind-hearted people, take pity on me. I am reduced to such a state. Just the sight of my own body scares me to such an extent that I would run away at top speed, were it not that I, poor cripple, am only able to move in this trolley.

THE BLIND MAN: Just think – I can't move around without forever banging my head on every pillar and post... won't somebody help me?

THE CRIPPLE: Just think – I can't get out of this hole, because the wheels of my little trolley are broken, and I shall end up dying of hunger here if someone doesn't come and help me.

THE BLIND MAN: Once I had a good dog as a companion…
but he ran off after a bitch in heat… At least I think it was
a bitch, but I can't be sure, because I can't see a thing,
me,… maybe it was some lousy rat of a dog or maybe a
scabby cat that caused my dog to fall in love.

THE CRIPPLE: Somebody help me… somebody help me…
Doesn't someone have four new wheels to lend me for my
little trolley? Lord God, I pray you, help to find me four
new wheels!

THE BLIND MAN: Whose is that voice, pleading with God
because he needs new wheels?

THE CRIPPLE: It is I, the cripple, whose wheels are broken.

THE BLIND MAN: Come over to me, on this side of the
street, so that I can see if I can help you… Or rather, no, I
can't see… not without a miracle… But anyway, let's see!

THE CRIPPLE: I can't come over to you… May God damn
all wheels in the world and turn them square, so that they
can no longer go rolling around.

THE BLIND MAN: Ah, if only I could find a way to get over
to you… Then you can be sure that I'd happily take you up
on my shoulders, all of you, apart from your wheels and
your little trolley of course! We two could then become
one… which would make us both happy. I would be able to
get around with the assistance of your eyes, and you could
get around with the aid of my legs.

THE CRIPPLE: Oh, that's an idea! You must have a mighty
brain, you! Full of wheels and cogs. I thank the Lord God
who has been so gracious as to lend me the wheels of your
brain to enable me to get around again and ask for charity!

THE BLIND MAN: Carry on talking, so that I can get my
bearings… Is this the right direction?

THE CRIPPLE: Yes. Keep going as you are. You're doing
well.

THE BLIND MAN: If I don't want to stumble, it would be
better if I came on all fours… There, am I still in the right
direction?

THE CRIPPLE: Move over to port a bit... No, not too much! You're moving off-beam. There... drop anchor and back up a bit... Good... Get out the oars, hoist the sail... line her up... Good. Now, full ahead.

THE BLIND MAN: What do you take me for – a galleon? When I get near you, give me your hand.

THE CRIPPLE: Right, I'm holding out both hands! Come on, come on, baby, come to mother... There you are... No... ! Don't move to the lee... steer to starboard... Oh my fine lifeboat...

THE BLIND MAN: Do I have you...? Is that really you?

THE CRIPPLE: Yes, it's me, my cock-eyed beauty... Let me hug you!

THE BLIND MAN: I'm dancing with joy, my dear cripple! Come on, I'll take you on board... Get up on my shoulders.

THE CRIPPLE: To be sure, I will... Turn around... Bend down... Now, lift! There we are.

THE BLIND MAN: Ouch, don't dig your knees into my ribs... You're hurting me...

THE CRIPPLE: I'm sorry... It's the first time I've ridden a horse, and I'm not used to it. Now look, you take care that you don't send me tumbling!

THE BLIND MAN: Don't worry, my friend, I've got you as firmly as if you were a sack of turnips. But you, make sure that you do your guide's work properly... Don't send me walking into cow-shit.

THE CRIPPLE: Don't worry, I'll look out. You wouldn't happen to have a piece of iron to put into your mouth, like a bridle, and a pair of reins that I could put around your neck, would you? That way it would be easier for me to guide you around.

THE BLIND MAN: What do you take me for – an ass?! Oh, what a weight you are! Why are you so heavy?

THE CRIPPLE: Lead on... ! Save your breath... Giddy-up! Gee up! Trot, my cock-eyed beauty. And pay attention.

When I pull your left ear, you turn to the left... and when I pull...

THE BLIND MAN: Alright, alright, I understand... I'm not an ass. Oh, by God, you're a heavy animal!

THE CRIPPLE: Me, heavy? I'm like a feather... A butterfly.

THE BLIND MAN: A lead butterfly! If I were to drop you, you'd make such a hole in the ground that, God's blood, water would run forth! Did you eat an anvil for your breakfast?

THE CRIPPLE: You must be crazy! It's two days since I last ate.

THE BLIND MAN: Yes, but I'll warrant it's at least two months since you last did a shit.

THE CRIPPLE: Don't talk nonsense. I take God as my witness... It's barely six days since I last performed my needs.

THE BLIND MAN: Six days?! At two meals a day, that makes twelve courses. By Saint Jerome, patron of all porters, I've taken on board a load of provisions sufficient for a year of famine. I'm sorry, but I'm going to have to off-load you here and now, and you will do me the honour of going and emptying your illegal load!

THE CRIPPLE: Stop. Do you hear that noise?

THE BLIND MAN: Yes, it's people shouting and blaspheming! What's making them shout like that?

THE CRIPPLE: Move back a bit, I'll try and see... Back up over there. Good. Now I can see him... They're taking it out on him... Poor creature... Poor Christ...

THE BLIND MAN: What poor Christ?

THE CRIPPLE: Him, Jesus Christ in person... the Son of God.

THE BLIND MAN: The Son of God? Which son?

THE CRIPPLE: What do you mean, which son?! The *only* son, ignoramus! A very holy son... And they say that he has done some amazing, miraculous things; he has cured the worst diseases, the most terrible illnesses known in the world. If you ask me, we'd best get out of these parts as fast as we can!

THE BLIND MAN: Get out? Why?

THE CRIPPLE: Because that thought doesn't fill me with joy. They say that if this Son of God even so much as passed by here, I would immediately be miracled. You too…! Just think, if both of us had the misfortune to be relieved of our infirmities! All of a sudden, we would be forced to go out and look for work so as to be able to survive.

THE BLIND MAN: Well, I think that we should go and see this saint, so that he can lift us out of our wretched condition.

THE CRIPPLE: Are you serious? You'll end up getting miracled, and then you'll die of hunger, because everybody will tell you: 'Go to work…'

THE BLIND MAN: Oh, it puts me into a cold sweat just to think of it…

THE CRIPPLE: 'Go to work, vagabond,' they will say. 'People who don't work should go to prison…' And that way you will lose that great privilege which we share with the lords and the masters, of collecting tithes. They use the tricks of the law, and we make use of pity. But both of us take our tolls from fools.

THE BLIND MAN: Let's go. We must avoid meeting this saint… I'd rather die. Oh mother! Let's go… Let's go at the gallop. Grab hold of my ears and lead me as far away as you can from this city! We'll even leave Lombardy… We'll even go to France, or to some other place this Jesus, Son of God, will never get to… I know, we'll go to Rome!

THE CRIPPLE: Calm down… Both of us will be safe and sound… There's no danger yet, because the procession accompanying the saint hasn't moved off yet.

THE BLIND MAN: What are they doing?

THE CRIPPLE: They have tied him to a column... And they're beating him... Oh, how they are beating, they're so worked up.

THE BLIND MAN: Oh, poor boy... Why are they beating him? What has he done to them, for them to get so worked up?

THE CRIPPLE: He has come to tell them about loving each other, about being equal, like so many brothers. But make sure that you don't get taken with compassion for him, because you'll run a great danger of getting miracled.

THE BLIND MAN: No, no, I'm not feeling compassion... That Christ doesn't mean anything to me... I don't know the man. But tell me, what are they doing now...?

THE CRIPPLE: They're spitting on him... Dirty pigs, they're spitting in his face.

THE BLIND MAN: And what's he doing... ? What is he saying, this poor holy son of God?

THE CRIPPLE: He's not saying anything, he's not speaking, he's not fighting back, and he doesn't even look angry with those wicked people...

THE BLIND MAN: And how's he looking at them?

THE CRIPPLE: He's looking at them with looks of pity.

THE BLIND MAN: Oh, dear boy... Don't say another word, because I feel my stomach turning, and a chill on my heart... I fear that it might be something related to compassion.

THE CRIPPLE: I too feel my breath catching in my throat, and my arms shaking... Let's go, let's get away from here.

THE BLIND MAN: Yes, let's go and shut ourselves in some place where you don't have to see unhappy things like this. I know... a tavern... !

THE CRIPPLE: Listen...

THE BLIND MAN: What?

THE CRIPPLE: That noise... It's getting nearer...

THE BLIND MAN: Do you suppose it's the holy Son arriving?

THE CRIPPLE: Oh, dear God! Don't scare me... We would be lost... There's nobody down by that column any more...

THE BLIND MAN: Not even Jesus the Son of God? Where have they all gone?

THE CRIPPLE: Here they are... Look at them all arriving in procession... We're ruined!

THE BLIND MAN: Is the holy man there too?

THE CRIPPLE: Yes, he's in the middle, and they've made him carry a heavy cross, the poor devil!

THE BLIND MAN: Don't wait around here getting all sorry for him... Hurry up instead and get me to some place where we can hide from his eyes.

THE CRIPPLE: Yes, let's go... Go to the right there... Run, run, before he can set eyes on us, this miraculous saint...

THE BLIND MAN: Ouch, I've twisted my ankle... And I can't move any more.

THE CRIPPLE: The devil take you! You have to choose this moment! Couldn't you look where you were putting your feet!

THE BLIND MAN: No, of course I couldn't look, because I'm blind and I can't see my feet! What am I saying, 'I can't see them'? Yes, I *can* see them... I see them! I see my feet... my two lovely feet! By the saints, with all their toes... How many toes? Five per foot... With toenails, big ones and small ones next to each other... Oh, I want to kiss you all, one by one.

THE CRIPPLE: You're mad... Behave yourself, or you'll tip me off... Oh, you've thrown me... Wretch! If I could only give you a good kicking... (*He gives him a kick*) Take that!

THE BLIND MAN: Oh, what a miracle... I can even see the sky... And the trees... And the women (*As if he can see women passing*) How beautiful the women are! ...Well, at least, some of them!

THE CRIPPLE: Hey, was that really me that gave you a kick? Let me try it again: Yes... Yes... Damn this day! I'm ruined!

THE BLIND MAN: Blessed be the holy son that has cured me! I see things that I have never seen in my life... I was a wretched animal to try and run away from him, because there is nothing in the world so sweet and joyful as he.

THE CRIPPLE: The devil take you, and him with you. I must have been really damned unfortunate to get looked at by that man full of love! I'm in despair! I'm going to end up dying with an empty belly... I'm going to end up eating these cured legs of mine, out of sheer anger!

THE BLIND MAN: Now I see it well – I was mad to have wandered off the straight and narrow path to take this dark road... I did not realise what a great prize it was to be able to see! Oh how beautiful the colours are! The eyes of the women, the lips... and the rest... How pretty the ants and flies are... and the sun... I can't wait for the night to come so that I can see the stars and go to the tavern to discover the colour of wine... Thanks be to God, son of God.

THE CRIPPLE: Oh poor me... Now I'll have to go and work for an employer, sweating blood in order to eat... Oh most wretched of wretches! I'm going to have to go and find me another saint who'll do me the favour of making me a cripple once again...

THE BLIND MAN: Miraculous son of God, there are no words either in Latin or in the common tongue which can describe your holiness. Like a river in full flow! Even under the weight of a cross, you still have such an excess of love as to give thought to the misfortunes of poor wretches like us...!

THE MARRIAGE AT CANA

Introduction

In the nineteenth century an Englishman by name of Smith published a book containing illustrations of a number of Italian religious festivals. This, for example, (photo 10) is a picture of a rite which is still performed in Sicily to this day — in Piana dei Greci, to be precise. Here we see Christ's entry into

Photo 10: 'Palm Sunday'. Popular print (nineteenth century).

Jerusalem — you can see him here under the palm branches, surrounded by revellers. The scene reminds one of Bacchus — Dionysus's descent into hell. Dionysus was a Greek god of Thessalo-Minoan origin, dating from some fifteen centuries before Christ. It is said that he so loved mankind that when a demon came to earth and stole the springtime (in order to carry it off to hell and enjoy it all for himself), Dionysus decided to sacrifice himself on mankind's behalf: he mounted a mule, went down to hell, and paid with his own life in order that humanity might have their spring back.

Anyway, fifteen centuries later we find Jesus Christ, coming to earth as a god and seeking to give mankind back their spring. That springtime was, as I have said, man's dignity — a theme that we shall return to later, in another of the pieces I shall perform. And at the heart of the Jesus story we find traces of Bacchus, the god of happiness — of drunkenness even — a jolly, boisterous kind of god.

There is, by the way, nothing unusual about this grafting of one god onto another; it is a familiar characteristic of popular religions.

So, the key character in this jongleur piece is a drunkard. He tells how he went to a wedding feast, and got drunk on wine that had been made by, actually created by, Jesus Christ. Jesus Christ becomes Bacchus; at a certain point he is even shown standing on a table and addressing the wedding guests: "Enjoy yourselves, people; get drunk; have a good time." The important thing is to be happy. Don't wait for heaven after you die, because heaven can be here on earth too. Exactly the opposite of what they ram down your throats when you're kids... that you have to suffer on earth... that it's a vale of tears... that not everybody can be rich, because some people are destined to be poor, and anyway your reward will come in heaven... so relax, and behave yourselves, and don't kick up a fuss... That's more or less the line of argument.

The philosophy that Jesus puts forward in this jongleur piece is quite the opposite. He says: "Get drunk, people... Go ahead, let yourselves go!"

This piece actually involves two characters: the drunkard and an angel. While the angel — or rather the archangel — tries to present the prologue of a religious performance piece, within the traditional style of the genre, the drunkard is bent on mischief. He wants to interrupt the show and tell of how he got magnificently drunk at the Marriage at Cana. The angel speaks in an aristocratic, elegant, polished Venetian dialect;

the drunkard on the other hand speaks in a strong rustic dialect that is crude and highly coloured. I perform this as a solo piece, but not because I'm an exhibitionist: we tried performing it with two actors, but we found it didn't work. You see, almost all these texts were written to be performed by one person. The jongleurs almost always worked on their own; we can see this from the fact that, in the text, things that happen tend to be indicated by the actor splitting himself between two parts, and by allusion, so that the full comic and poetic weight of the piece is heightened by the free play of imagination.

In this piece, you have to use your imagination. Not like when you're watching TV: in order to save you straining your brain, they feed you all the details, all the particulars, and you just sit there, mind half asleep... maybe have a little nap, maybe fart a bit... and the next day you're all fresh and ready for work, all ready to be exploited again.

So: when I'm on this side of the stage (*He points to stage-left*) I shall be the angel, with his fine, aristocratic gestures; when I am over there (*He points to stage-right*) I shall be the drunkard.

For as long as the angel is on stage, the image in photo 11 is projected onto the backdrop.

THE MARRIAGE AT CANA

ANGEL: (*To the audience*) Pay attention, kind people, and I shall tell you of a true story, a story which began...

DRUNKARD: I would like to tell you a story too, about a drinking session, a glorious binge...

ANGEL: Drunkard!

DRUNKARD: I want to tell you...

ANGEL: Silence... Not a word!

DRUNKARD: ...But I...

ANGEL: Silence... I am the one who's supposed to give the prologue! (*To the audience*) Kind people, everything that we are going to tell you will be true, utterly true, and is all taken from books and from the Gospels. Nothing presented here is created from imagination...

Photo 11: A Cimabue angel from Assissi (late fourteenth century).

DRUNKARD: I want to tell a story too, and mine is not imaginary either. I have just been on such a magnificent bender, such a binge, that never again do I ever want to get drunk again, lest I forget how magnificent it was. It was a bender like you've…

ANGEL: Drunkard!

DRUNKARD: I would like to tell…

ANGEL: No… You're not telling anything… Alright?!

DRUNKARD: Ah, but… I…

ANGEL: Ssssh… !

DRUNKARD: But I… No?

ANGEL: Kind people, everything that we are going to tell you is wholly true. Everything comes from books, and from the Gospels. The little imaginary material that we have added…

DRUNKARD: (*Very quietly*) I'll tell you about my wonderful binge afterwards…

ANGEL: Hey! Drunkard!

DRUNKARD: I wasn't doing anything… I only moved my finger.

ANGEL: Well *don't* move your finger!

DRUNKARD: But I don't make any noise with my finger!

ANGEL: You're making a noise… Brrrr!

DRUNKARD: How can I make a noise with my finger?! Alright! I'll do it with my brain… I shall think and think and think, and with my eyes… And they will understand…

ANGEL: No.

DRUNKARD: But I don't make any noise with my brain…

ANGEL: You do make a noise!

DRUNKARD: I make a noise with my brain? Heavens above! I must really be drunk! Holy Mary!

ANGEL: Don't breathe!

DRUNKARD: What, aren't I allowed to breathe? Not even through my nose? I shall burst!

ANGEL: Burst, then!

DRUNKARD: Ah, but if I burst, then I'll make a noise, eh?

ANGEL: Ssssh…!

DRUNKARD: But I…

ANGEL: Everything of what we are about to tell you is true, everything has come from books and from the Gospels. The little imaginary material that we have added…

The DRUNKARD *creeps up on the* ANGEL *and pulls out one of his feathers.*

DRUNKARD: (*Very quietly, miming making the feather fly*) Oh, what a pretty coloured feather!

ANGEL: Drunkard!

DRUNKARD: (*He starts, and mimes swallowing the feather. He coughs*) Eh… But…

ANGEL: Ssssh…!

DRUNKARD: Eh… But I… no…

ANGEL: Everything that we are going to tell you will be entirely true; everything comes from books and from the Gospels… (*The* DRUNKARD *creeps up on the* ANGEL *again, and pulls out other feathers. He mimes admiring them. He fans himself and struts about. The* ANGEL *notices*) Drunkard!

DRUNKARD: Eh…? (*Throwing the feathers in the air*) It's snowing!

ANGEL: Will you kindly leave the stage?!

DRUNKARD: I would quite willingly leave, if you would care to accompany me, because I am not capable of putting one foot in front of the other without falling down and banging my nose on the ground… If you would be so good as to accompany me, then I shall tell you about this beautiful drinking session I had…

ANGEL: I am not interested in your drinking session... Out! Out, or I shall kick you off the stage!

DRUNKARD: Ah? You'll kick me off?

ANGEL: Yes, I'll kick you off... Get out of here!

DRUNKARD: Kind people! Did you hear that? An angel who wants to kick me out... Me! An angel... (*Aggressively, turning to the* ANGEL) Come on, then, my big angel... Come and kick me off if you dare! Because I'll pull out all your feathers, like plucking a chicken! I shall pull out your feathers one by one, from your backside too... from your arse... Come on, my big chicken... Come on!

ANGEL: Help... Don't touch me! Help! Murderer... !

He flees.

DRUNKARD: Me, murderer? Did you hear that? He called me a murderer! I, who am so good that goodness pours out of my ears... and spills all over the floor, and you could almost slip on it... And how could I not be good, after that wonderful drinking session that I've been on? You know, I never imagined that today was going to end up so beautifully, because it began so wretchedly and miserably...

You see, I was invited to a wedding, a marriage, in a place near here, called Cana... Cana... In fact, in days to come they're going to talk of it: the Marriage at Cana. I was invited, as I say... I arrived, and there was all the whole table ready for the wedding feast, with all the food arranged on it... and nobody had sat down to eat yet. They were all standing up, and stamping around the place, and cursing.

There was the bride's mother. She was crying... There was the bride's father. He was banging his head against the wall, in a foul mood.

'But what's happened, what's happened?' I asked.

'Oh the shame of it...'

'Has the groom run off?'

'The groom is that fellow over there, swearing more than anyone.'

'Well, then, what's happened?'

'Oh the shame of it... We've just found out that an entire vat of wine, a barrel of wine that was prepared especially for the wedding banquet, has all turned to vinegar. We're in a right pickle!'

'Oh. Oh... All the wine turned to vinegar! How terrible! I've heard it said that a rained-on bride is supposed to be a lucky bride, but being rained on by vinegar would make her the kind of bad luck you'd want to keep away from...'

And everyone was crying and cursing, and the bride's mother was tearing her hair, and the bride was crying, and the bride's father was banging his head against the wall...

At that moment, a young fellow turned up, a certain Jesus, the one they've nicknamed... the 'Son of God'. And he wasn't alone, no! He was accompanied by his mother, whom they call the Madonna. A fine figure of a woman!!! They had been invited, and had turned up just a little late. Anyway, when this Mrs Madonna found out what a state everything was in, what with the wine being turned into vinegar and all, she went over to her son Jesus, son of God (and also of the Madonna) and said: 'You, my son, who are so good... you who do such wonderful things for everybody... see if you can manage to get these poor people out of the mess they're in.'

No sooner had the Madonna spoken to him, than all of a sudden everyone saw a sweet, sweet smile spread across Jesus' lips. His smile was so sweet that if you didn't watch out, it would make your kneecaps fall off and drop on your toes! What a sweet smile! When she finished talking, this young fellow gave his mother a kiss on the nose and said: 'Kind people, could I have twelve buckets full of good clean water?'

In a flash, twelve buckets arrived, full of water, and when I saw all that water all together at the same time, I felt a bit queasy. I felt like I was drowning, by heaven! Everyone fell silent, almost like being in church for the Sanctus, and this Jesus twirled his hands about a bit, snapping his fingers, and began to make signs over the water, the kind of signs that only sons of God make. I was standing a little bit away from the scene, because, as I said before, looking at water makes me nervous, and I wasn't even looking. I was just leaning to one side, all sad, and all of a sudden I caught a whiff in my nostrils of a smell that was unmistakably the aroma of crushed grapes...

You couldn't mistake it, it was wine! Heavens, what wine. They passed me a cup of it, and I put it to my lips and swallowed a drop. Heavens! Oh... Oh... Ye blessed in purgatory, what a wine! I had no sooner swallowed it when I got the taste; a bit bitter at the back, a bit sharp, almost spicy in the middle; it sent out a deep red sparkle, a glow, a wine without mould or froth, a wine of at least three years standing, a golden vintage! And it slips down your gullet, gurgles down to your stomach, spreads out a little, stays there for a bit, and then, wallop, comes rolling up again, up your gullet, in great waves, and the flavour hits your nostrils and spreads forth. A wine to stop a man in his tracks even if he were passing on a race-horse!

'It's spring,' he shouted. What a wine! And everyone began to clap Jesus. 'Well done, Jesus! You're divine!' And the Madonna! The Madonna, his mother, was beside herself with happiness and pride at having a son who was so clever in bringing forth wine from water. Within a very short time we were all drunk. There was the bride's mother, dancing; the bride was in festive mood too; the bridegroom was leaping about; the bride's father was still in front of the wall, in a wicked mood, banging his head against it... because nobody had told him!

Jesus got up on a table, and began pouring wine for everybody: 'Drink, good people, be happy, get drunk, don't save it till later, enjoy yourselves... !'

And then, all of a sudden, he remembered his mother: 'Oh holy mother! Oh Madonna! Mother, I forgot, excuse me! Here, here's a drop for you too; drink a bit yourself.'

'No, no thank you, my son, thanks all the same, but I cannot drink, because I am not used to wine. It makes my head spin, and afterwards I start saying silly things.'

'But no, mother, it can't do you any harm. It will only make you a bit happy! This wine can't do you any harm; it's a pure wine, this, a good wine... I made it myself!'

And just imagine, there are still some damned rabble going around saying that wine is a creation of the devil, and that it's a sin, and that it's an invention of the most diabolical order. But do you think that if wine had really been an invention of the devil, that Jesus would have given some to his mother to drink? To his very own mother? Because Jesus had so much love for his mother that even I don't have for all the grappa in this world! I'm sure that if God the Father, in person, instead of leaving it so late when he taught Noah this wonderful trick of crushing the grape and bringing forth wine, if instead, right from the start, he had taught Adam, even before Eve, then we wouldn't be in this wretched state of a world that we are in now. We would all be in Paradise! Your health! Because on that wretched day when the wicked serpent came to visit Adam with the apple in his mouth, and told him: 'Eat the apple, Adam! It's sweet and good... Apples are sweet and red!!', then all it needed was for Adam to have a good big glass of wine near him, and... whoosh... he would have given a good kick to every apple on earth, and we would all be happy in Paradise!

That was the dreadful sin, because fruit was not created to be eaten, but to be trodden and crushed; because from crushed apples you make a good cider; from crushed cherries you make good sweet grappa; and as for the grape, it would be a mortal sin to eat it! Because with the grape, you make wine. And I am sure that those who have been good and honest in their lives... for them, Heaven is going to be made all of wine!

What do you mean, that's blasphemy? No, I am not blaspheming! You know, I dreamt once that I was dead. One night I had a dream that I had died, and I dreamt that they came to take me away. They took me to a terrible place, where there were a lot of deep basins, and inside each basin there stood one of the damned – poor souls! They were submerged, standing up in a great sea of red liquid, which looked like blood. And I immediately began to cry: 'Oh God! I am in Hell!' Miserable wretch, sinner that I was! And while I was weeping, they took all my clothes off, and began to wash me, rubbing me down and cleaning me to such an extent, with hot and cold water, that I have never been so clean in all my life, not even at Easter!

Once I was good and clean, they put me into one of those big basins, with its red liquid. Glug... glug... glug... And that red liquid rose up to my lips. I shut my mouth, but one of the ripples... splosh... came back at me...: and went up my nose. Ooof! And I swallowed a great gulp. I was in Paradise... !!! It was wine, and immediately I realised that this wonderful invention had been created by God the Father, especially for the Blessed (because everyone there was Blessed) so that the blessed ones would not have to make too much effort, in the sense of having to lift up their glasses to drink every time, and then have to wait for them to be filled again. Instead, he took all the blessed ones, and immersed them all, right up to their ears, in huge glasses of wine, standing there, so that it came up to their lips, and all they had to do was open their mouths to say: 'Good morning, gentlemen,' and... glug... And I began to sing: 'My beloved is so fickle...' Glug... glug... Help... I'm drowning... Glug... What a lovely way to drown!!! Glug... Glug... Glug... Glug...

THE BIRTH OF THE JONGLEUR

Introduction

Here we have a picture (photo 12) of a drunkard, or rather a *jongleur* who is playing the part of a drunkard. This fresco dates back to around the year 1100. It comes from a little Romanesque church in Provence. It may be that he is acting precisely the piece that I've played tonight. At any rate, this piece appears in many languages and in different dialects. A version has been found even as far afield as Bavaria. The fact that *jongleurs* and their performances were even depicted on wall-paintings in churches reveals how important they were in their day.

I would now like to perform a new piece, which I have only played twice so far. Yesterday and the day before. I am still a bit nervous about doing it, because it is an extremely difficult piece to perform. It tells of the *Birth of the Jongleur*. The origins of this piece can be traced to Asia Minor, but the version that we know originates in Sicily. Sicily was linked to the East, not only by trade and commerce, but also by geographical and political factors, and thus by her culture. This was especially true in the 13th century, the period in which the piece which I am about to perform begins to be found in documented form.

There is another version in existence, which is rather older, although it is not possible to date it with precision. This version comes from my own part of the country (to be precise, from the area of Brescia-Cremona). The text as it was found was only a series of fragments. I had intended to reconstruct it, but I didn't have the courage to take it on. However, last year, I went to Sicily, and there, in the library at.Ragusa, thanks to a comrade who took us there, we were able to find the entire text, in Sicilian dialect. Extraordinary! The piece is incredibly violent. I even went so far as to learn it in Sicilian. But since the language would sound rather archaic and incomprehensible to today's ears, I have translated it into Lombard dialect, which you will understand rather better.

Photo 12: 'The drunkard'. Twelfth-century fresco from Provence.

What does this piece relate? We see a *jongleur*, explaining how, before he became a *jongleur*, he was a peasant, and that it was Christ who changed him into a *jongleur*. How did it happen that Christ gave him this new profession? It was because he used to own land, but a landowner tried to take the land away from him. I say no more, because there's not really much that I can add. The piece speaks for itself. Don't worry if at first you don't understand some of what I say. The sense, the gestures and sounds involved will help you. By my gestures and by the sounds of the piece, you will easily grasp the meaning of this tale.

THE BIRTH OF THE JONGLEUR

Kind people, gather round and listen. The jongleur is here! I am the jongleur. I leap and pirouette, and make you laugh. I make fun of those in power, and I show you how puffed up and conceited are the bigshots who go around making wars in which *we* are the ones who get slaughtered. I reveal them for what they are. I pull out the plug, and... pssss... they deflate. Gather round, for now is the time and place that I begin to clown and teach you. I tumble, I sing and I joke! Look how my tongue whirls, almost like a knife. Remember that. But I have not always been... Well, I would like to tell you how it was that I came to be.

I was not born a jongleur; I didn't suddenly turn up as I am now, with a sudden gust from the skies and, hopla, there I was: 'Good day... Hello.' No! I am the result of a miracle! A miracle which was carried out on me. Do you believe me? This is how it came about! I was born a peasant.

A peasant? Yes, a real countryman. I was happy, I was sad, I had no land. No! I worked as all of us work in these valleys, wherever I could. And one day I came by a mountain, a mountain all of rock. It was nobody's. I found that out. I asked people. 'No! Nobody wants this mountain!'

Well, I went up to its peak, and I scratched with my nails, and I saw that there was a little bit of earth there, and I saw that there was a little trickle of water coming down. So I began to scratch further. I went down to the river bank, and I wore my fingers to the bone bringing earth up onto this mountain. And my children and my wife were there. My wife is sweet, sweet and fair, with two round breasts, and a gentle way of walking that reminds you of a heifer as she moves. Oh, she is beautiful! I love her, and it gives me such pleasure to speak of her.

Anyway, I carried earth up in my own hands, and the grass grew so fast! Pfff... ! It grew of its own accord. You've no idea how beautiful it was! It was like gold dust! I would stick in my hoe, and pfff... a tree sprang forth. That earth was a miracle! A marvel! There were poplars, oaks and other trees everywhere. I sowed them when the moon was right; I knew what had to be done, and there, sweet, fine, handsome crops grew. There was chicory, thistles, beans, turnips, there was everything. For me, for us!

Oh, how happy I was! We used to dance, and then it would rain for days on end, and then the sun would blaze, and I would come, and go, and the moons were always right, and there was never too much wind, or too much mist. It was beautiful, beautiful! It was our land. This set of terraces was really beautiful. Every day I built another one. It was like the tower of Babel, beautiful, with all these terraces. It was paradise, paradise on earth! I swear it. And all the peasants used to pass by, saying:

'That's amazing, look what you've managed to bring forth out of this pile of rocks! How stupid that I never thought of that!' And they were envious. One day the lord of the whole valley passed by. He took a look and said:

'Where did this tower spring up from? Whose is this land?'

'It's mine,' I said. 'I made it myself, with these hands. It was nobody's.'

'Nobody's? That "Nobody's" is a word that doesn't exist. It's mine!'

'No! It's not yours! I've even been to the lawyer, and he told me it was nobody's. I asked the priest, and he said it was nobody's. And I built it up, piece by piece.'

'It's mine, and you have to give it to me.'

'I cannot give it to you, sir. I cannot go and work for others.'

'I'll pay you for it; I'll give you money. Tell me how much you want.'

'No! No, I don't want money, because if you give me money, then I'll not be able to buy other land with the money that you give me, and I'll have to go and work for others again. No, I don't want to. I won't.'

'Give it to me.'

'No!'

Then he laughed, and went away. The next day the priest came, and he told me:

'The land belongs to the Lord of the Valley. Be sensible, give it up. Don't play the fool. Beware, because he is a powerful, evil lord. Give up this land. In the name of God, be sensible!'

'No!' I told him. 'I won't.'

And I made a rude gesture at him with my hand. Then the lawyer arrived too. He was sweating, by heaven, when he came up the mountain to find me.

'Be sensible. There are laws... and you should know that you can't... that, for you...'

'No! No!'

And I made a rude gesture at him too, and he went away, swearing.

But the lord didn't give up. No! He began by coming on hunting expeditions, and he sent all the hares chasing over my land. With his horses and his friends, he galloped to and fro across my land, breaking down my hedges. Then one day, he set fire to all my land. It was summer; a drought. He set fire to the whole of my mountain, and burned everything, even my animals and my house. But I wouldn't leave! I waited, and that night it began to rain. After the rain, I began to clear up, and put the fence posts back in position, and replace stones, and bring up fresh earth, and water everything. I was determined, by heaven, that I wouldn't move from there! And I did not move!

But one day he arrived, along with all his soldiers, and he was laughing. We were in the fields, my children, my wife and I. We were working. He arrived. He got down from his horse. He undid his breeches. He came over to my wife, grabbed her, threw her to the ground, ripped off her skirt and... I tried to move, but the soldiers held me fast. And he leapt upon her, and took her as if she were a cow. And I and the children had to stand there, with our eyes bursting from our heads, watching... I moved forward, with a leap. I managed to free myself. I took a hoe, and I shouted:

'You bastards!'

'Stop,' my wife cried. 'Don't do it. That's all they want, that's exactly what they are waiting for. If you raise your stick, then they will kill you. Don't you understand? They want to kill you and take away your land. That's all they want. He is bound to defend himself. It's not worth taking your stand against him. You have no honour to defend. You're poor, you're a peasant, a country person, you cannot go thinking of honour and dignity. That is stuff for rich people, for lords and nobles! They are entitled to get angry if people rape their wives and daughters. But you're not! Let it be. The land is worth more than your honour, or mine. It is worth more than everything! I have become a cow, a cow for the love of you.'

And I began to weep, weeping and looking all around. The children were weeping too. And the soldiers, with the lord of the valley, suddenly went off, laughing, happy and satisfied. We wept, how we wept! We could not even look each other in the eye. And when we went into the village, they began throwing rocks and stones at us. They shouted:

'Oh you ox, you who don't have the strength to defend your honour, because you have no honour. You are an animal. The lord has mounted your wife, and you stood there, without saying a word, for a handful of earth. You wretch!'

And when my wife went around the village:

'Whore, cow!' they shouted after her. And then they ran off. They would not even let her go into church. Nobody would let her! And the children couldn't go out in the village without everyone picking on them. And nobody would even look us in the eye. My wife ran off! I never saw her again; I don't know where she ended up. And my children wouldn't look at me. They fell ill, and wouldn't even cry. They died. I was left alone, alone, with this land. I didn't know what to do. One evening, I took a piece of rope, and threw it over a rafter.

I put the noose around my neck, and said to myself:

'Right. Now I am going to end it all, now!'

I was just about to do it, just about to hang myself, when I felt a hand on my shoulder. I turned round, and saw a fellow with big eyes and a pale face.

He says to me: 'Could you give me something to drink?'

'I ask you, in heaven's name, is this really the moment to come asking somebody for something to drink, when he's just about to hang himself?'

I look at him, and see that he too has the face of a poor wretch. Then I look further, and see that there are two more men, and they too have faces full of suffering.

'Alright, I'll give you something to drink. And *then* I'll hang myself.'

So I go to get them something to drink, and I take a good look at them:

'Instead of something to drink, you people look as if you could do with something to eat! It's been days and days since I last cooked anything to eat... But anyway, if you want, there is food.'

I took a pan and put it on the fire to heat up some broad beans. I gave them some, one bowl apiece, and how they ate! I, personally, wasn't very hungry. 'I'll wait till they've finished eating,' I thought, 'and then I'll hang myself.' Anyway, while they were eating, the one with the biggest eyes, who looked like a right poor devil, began to smile. He said:

'That's a terrible story, that you're going to hang yourself. I know why you want to do it, though. You have lost everything, your wife, your children, and all you are left with is your land. Yes, I know how it is! But if I were you, I wouldn't do it.'

And he carried on eating. How he ate! Then, in the end, he laid aside the utensils, and said:

'Do you know who I am?'

'No, but I've got an idea that you might be Jesus Christ.'

'Well done! You've guessed correctly. And this is St Peter, and that over there is St Mark.'

'Pleased to meet you! And what are you doing in these parts?'

'My friend, you've given me something to eat, and now I'm going to give you something to say.'

'Something to say? What is this "something"?'

'You poor fellow! It's right that you have held onto your land; it is right that you don't want bosses over you; it is right that you have had the strength not to give in; it's right... I like you. You're a good man, a strong man. But you're missing something which is also right, and which you should have: here and here. (*He points to his forehead and to his mouth*) You shouldn't remain here stuck to your land. You should move around the country, and when people throw stones at you, you should tell them, and help them to understand, and deflate that great bladder of a landlord. You should deflate him with the sharpness of your tongue, and drain him of all his poison and his stinking bile. You must crush these nobles, these priests, and all those who surround them: notaries, lawyers, etc. Not only for your own good, for your own land, but also for those like yourself who don't have land, who have nothing, and whose only right is the right to suffer, and who have no dignity to boast of. Teach them to survive with their brains, not just with their hands!'

'But don't you understand? I am not able. I have a tongue which refuses to budge. I stumble over every word. I have no education, and my brain is weak and useless. How am I supposed to do the things you suggest, and go about speaking to other people?'

'Don't worry. You will now see a miracle.'

He took my head in his hands, and drew me to him. Then he said:

'I am Jesus Christ. I have come to give you the power of speech. And this tongue of yours will lash, and will slash like a sword, deflating inflated balloons all over the land. You will speak out against bosses, and crush them, so that others can understand and learn, so that others can laugh at them and make fun of them, because it is only with laughter that the bosses will be destroyed. When you laugh at the rulers, the ruler goes from being a mountain, to being a little molehill, and then a nothingness. Here, I shall give you a kiss, and that will enable you to speak.'

He kissed me on the mouth. He kissed me for a long time. And suddenly I felt my tongue dart about inside my head, and my brain began to move, and my legs began to move with a mind of their own, and I went out in the streets of the village, and began to shout:

'Gather round, people! Gather round! hear ye! The *jongleur* is here! I am going to play a satire for you. I am going to joust with the lord of the land, for he is a great balloon, and I am going to burst him with the sharpness of my tongue. I shall tell you everything, how things come and go, and how it is not God who steals! It is those who steal and go unpunished... it is those who make big books of laws... *They* are the ones... And we must speak out, speak out. Listen, people – these rulers must be broken, they must be crushed...!

Photo 13: 'The birth of the villeyn', from a fourteenth-century manuscript.

THE BIRTH OF THE VILLEYN

Introduction

Here we have a picture (photo 13) taken from a miniature. It shows a piece being acted out by a famous *jongleur*, Matazone da Caligano. Matazone is a nickname which means 'cheerful fellow' (as you see, *jongleurs*' nicknames are not always rude – there are exceptions). Caligano, or Carignano, is a village near Pavia. The local dialect, a dialect of what was then the territory of Pavia, is very easy for us Lombards to understand. And, in fact, I played this piece in Sicily one time, and everybody was able to understand it. Anyway, as you can see, up there we have an angel; here is the landowner, the lord, the lord of the land... and here we have the peasant, or, rather, the villeyn.

What's going on in this picture? It depicts the moment when the landowner is being presented with the first villeyn ever to have been created by the Holy Father. The story of this piece is as follows: After seven times seven generations of working the land, Man goes to the Holy Father and says: 'Listen, I can't stand it any longer. I'm working too hard. You must relieve me of some of my work. You promised me that you were going to make things a bit easier for me!' 'What do you mean?!' says the Holy Father. 'I gave you a donkey, a mule, a horse, an ox, to make life easier for you.' 'Yes, true, but it's still me who has to push behind the plough,' said Man. 'And it's still me who has to go and muck out the cowsheds, and it's still me who has to do all the lowliest jobs, like spreading dung on the fields, milking, killing the pig... I want you to create me someone who can help me in all this, in fact someone who can take my place, so that I can finally get some

rest!' 'Ah, so it's a villeyn that you want!' 'What's a villeyn?'
'It's exactly what you're looking for... But obviously, you
wouldn't know that, because I haven't created him yet! Come
on, let's go and create him now...' So, they go to see Adam.
No sooner does Adam see the Eternal Father arriving
together with another man than, hopla, he wraps his arms
round his ribs, and shouts: 'No, not again! I'm not giving up
another single rib!'

'Well, I suppose you're right too,' says the Eternal Father.
'But what am I supposed to do?' At that moment, a donkey
passes by, and the Eternal Father has an idea: he waves his
hand, and the donkey begins to swell up. It's pregnant.

Right: from this point I shall follow the original text. Here
we have the words of Matazone da Caligano. A printed text
exists, slightly different from the one which I am about to
perform, which has been reconstructed by putting together
various fragments, in order to give greater continuity and logic
to the piece.

THE BIRTH OF THE VILLEYN

The story goes, in an old book long since forgotten, that with
the passing of seven times seven generations from the sad
day of his expulsion from Paradise, Man was fed up and
beside himself with the amount of work that he had to do in
order to survive. He went to see God, personally. He began
weeping, and begged him to send someone to give him a hand
to do the work on his land, because he could no longer
manage it on his own. 'But don't you have donkeys and oxen
for that?' God replied. 'You are right, Lord God, but it is
always we men who have to stand behind the plough and push
it like wretches, and the asses aren't capable of pruning vines,
and no matter how carefully we teach them, they haven't yet
learnt to milk cows. All this labour is making us old before our
time, and our women are fading away... They're worn out by
the time they reach twenty.'

God, who is so good to all, when he heard these things, was
seized with compassion. He sighed, saying: 'Well, I am going

to create for you a two-legged creature who will come and relieve you of this suffering'. He went straight away to Adam: 'Listen, Adam, I come to ask you a favour: lift up your shirt, because I need to take another of your ribs, to use it for an experiment.'

But when Adam heard this, he began to weep: 'Lord, have pity on me, because you have already taken one rib in order to create my wife, the treacherous Eve... If you take yet another rib, I won't have enough left to keep my stomach in, and all my innards will fall out like a gutted chicken.'

'You're right too,' God murmured, scratching his head. 'What am I supposed to do?'

At that moment, a donkey was passing, and God had a sudden idea; when it comes to ideas, God is a veritable volcano! He waved his hand at the ass, and the ass promptly swelled up. After nine months, the beast's belly was swollen to bursting point... Suddenly a loud noise was heard. The ass let out an enormous fart, and at that point out leapt the villeyn, all stinking.

(*Aside*) 'Oh, what a lovely nativity!'

(*Aside*) 'Shut up, you!'

At that moment, a tremendous storm broke, and the rains flooded down, washing over the ass's offspring. Then followed hail and a blizzard and thunder and lightning and all kinds of things, battering the villeyn's body, so that he would be in no doubt about the kind of life that was in store for him. As soon as he was properly clean, the Angel of the Lord came down and called to Man, saying:

'By order of God, you, from this moment, will be the boss, the greater one, and he, the villeyn, the lesser one. Now it is written and laid down that this villeyn shall live on coarse bread and raw onions, broad beans and boiled beans and spittle.

'He is to sleep on a straw pallet, so that he always remembers his status. Since he has been born naked, give him a bit of rough canvas, the kind they use for holding fish, so that he can make himself a nice pair of trousers. Breeches, which must have an opening down the middle, and with no laces, so that he doesn't waste too much time when he pisses.'

We could almost be dealing with today's employers, here! As I go round Italy doing these shows, I often find myself brought up against these cruder facts of life. For example, we were performing in Verona one time, and some girls turned up in the theatre, with posters that they hung around the walls. They were on strike. They were on strike because their employer had banned them from going to the toilet. In other words, one of them felt the need... 'Excuse me, may I...?' 'No... No!' They were all supposed to go to the toilet at 11.25 sharp: the bell rings, and you do a wee. And anybody who doesn't feel the need at that precise moment, too bad; they have to wait till the next time.

These women were on strike in order to obtain the privilege of doing a wee when they felt the urge. I don't know how the story finished up... but maybe the most grotesque incident was at the Ducati plant in Bologna, a very large factory, world-scale – a major plant, in short. So, what happened there? The bosses of this particular factory decided to cut down the time allowed to workers for going to the toilet. Some people would stay in there for four minutes, some for as long as seven minutes, and the employers had had enough! They argued with the trade unions, and there was a tremendous struggle, and after a while they decided: 'Two minutes and thirty five seconds are more than sufficient for a person to fulfil their bodily needs...' Now, put like that it sounds almost reasonable. A person would think: 'Well, they must have carried out studies, they must have consulted technicians and experts etc.' But I can assure you, believe me, to do it in that time would be a record!

Two minutes and thirty-five seconds: a record! And these days, the Ducati workers don't just go to the toilet... they go into training at home first. If you don't believe that this is a record, try it for yourself. Take a couple of interesting books, wait for a good day, put on a nice record of soothing Hawaiian music (it's very helpful in this connection...) and, as you will see, IT CAN'T BE DONE! And it particularly can't be done when you're neurotic about clocks that go tick-tock, tick-tock. Yes! Because in every toilet at the Ducati factory there is a timing mechanism! As soon as you go in, it starts, tick-tock, tick-tock. But the truly grotesque part of the situation is still to come. How do you know when your time has run out? Obviously, you would imagine that the worker goes into the toilet cubicle (*He mimes going into a toilet*) and tick-tock, tick-tock... he takes a deep breath... (*He takes a deep breath*) ...like when you're about to dive into a cold swimming pool... and then (*He mimes*) tick-tock... tick-tock... PEEEEEP! (*A whistle*).

Now, it's logical that if the gadget is going to go off, it means that there must be a button under the toilet seat. No? That way, when you sit on the seat, it pushes down the button and sets off the timing mechanism. But the employer knows that the worker is pretty smart. Given half a chance, he'll try to avoid actually sitting on the seat, and will balance on his toes, poised over the pan, so that he can stay in the cubicle for hours on end. 'Ah!' says the employer. 'Now I'm going to fix you.' So, the push-button is not fixed under the toilet seat at all, but works off the door-handle! In other words, as soon as the worker puts his hand on the door-handle, the electric switch trips, and it begins. Tick-tock... tick-tock. 'Damn these braces, I can't... Hell and damnation... The paper...' (*A whistle. Then, looking down into the pan*) 'Pardon the intrusion.'

So, you have to get into training. You have to arrive with your bowels well locsened and ready for action... The first thing to remember is that you should arrive without your trousers on. You should have your trousers already folded, on your shoulder... Actually, this can look quite stylish... like a sort of scarf... Your shirt should be tucked up, like a native dancing girl (*All this is mimed*) because otherwise it'll get in the way. And above all, don't suddenly stop and think: 'Oh God...' (*He tries to cover himself in front with his hands*) You must forget all that silly stuff about nudity being embarrassing.

A German academic by name of Otto Weininger has made some extraordinary studies of this question: this man discovered that it is only when you adopt an attitude of shame that others become aware of the fact that you are naked. It's logical. If you go around like this (*He mimes a person covering his genitals and his backside with his hands*), people will

immediately point at you: 'Ooh! A naked man!! Look,
Mummy, a naked man!' But if you free yourself of this idiotic
sense of shame, and just relax, then who's going to worry?
There you are, stark naked, happy, relaxed, walking down
the street, and people will say: 'Oh, look, a duke!'

So there you are, the worker must become a duke when he
goes to the toilet; and, in addition to learning how to match
the speed of the assembly line, he must also learn to handle
the time limits set by the toilet cubicle. These two aspects of
time and motion are different, but fundamental. (*He mimes a
worker going into a toilet cubicle and sitting down*) One...
two... three... A dance!

Anyway, let's get back to the story of the villeyn. The angel
hands the villeyn over to his new employer. Let's listen to the
angel's advice to the employer, regarding how to treat the
man.*

THE BIRTH OF THE VILLEYN

As his coat of arms
Give him a pick and shovel over his shoulder.
Ensure that he goes round barefoot all the time,
For he will not complain.
In January give him a pitchfork over his shoulder
And send him to muck out the cowsheds.
In February send him to sweat in the fields, breaking the
    soil.
Don't worry if he gets sores round his neck,
If he's full of cuts and callouses,
Because your horse will benefit from it,
No longer will it be troubled by midges and dung flies
Because the flies will all go and live in the villeyn's house.
Tax everything that he does,
Tax him even when he shits.
At carnival time allow him to dance,
And even sing, let him enjoy himself,
But not too much, because he must not forget
That he exists in this world in order to labour.

*Translator's note: In the original, line endings rhymed.

In March too make him go barefoot.
Let him prune your vine when it has rust.
In the month of April
He should stay in the sheep-pen,
Sleeping with the sheep,
And let him sleep with open eyes,
Because the wolf is hungry!
If the hungry wolf is looking for something to eat,
Then let him take the villeyn, for I shall not complain.
In May, send him to cut the violet-strewn grass
But make sure that he does not get distracted,
Running after pretty girls.
And as for the girls, they are pretty and buxom.
What matter if they are peasants,
Bring them, to play and dance with you for the whole
     month.
Then, when you tire of them,
Give them to the villeyn to marry,
Give them in marriage already pregnant,
Which will save them from having to work.
In June, you must send the villeyn
To pick cherries from the trees,
As well as plums and peaches and apricots,
But first, so that he doesn't eat all the best ones,
Make him eat dry bread, which will block up his bowels.
In July and August,
When the burning heat is on us,
Slake his thirst.
Give him vinegar to drink
And if he gets angry and swears,
Do not worry that he has sinned:
Because the peasant, be he good or evil,
Is anyway destined to Hell.
In the month of September,
Let him relax,
Send him to harvest the grapes.
But make sure that he works hard at the wine-treading,
So that he is too tired to go and get drunk.
In fine October, have him kill the pig,

And as a reward let him have its entrails,
But not all of them,
Because some are good for making skins for sausages.
Leave the villeyn with blood-sausages,
Which are poisonous and noxious.
Your good, solid hams
You should leave in the hands of your villeyns –
Leave them the hams to salt.
Then have them bring them
To your house, which will give you a handsome feed.
In November, and then in December,
Make sure that the cold does not harm him,
Keep your peasant warm –
Send him to cut wood,
And make sure that he goes back again and again,
And that each time he comes well-loaded,
Because in this way he will not catch cold.
And when he comes near to the fire,
Send him packing,
Send him out of doors,
Because a fire will only make him soft.
If it is pouring with rain outside,
Tell him to go to Mass,
Because in church he will find shelter,
And he can pray,
Pass his time praying,
Because anyway it won't do him any good.
Because, anyway, he won't win salvation,
Because the peasant doesn't have a soul,
And God cannot listen to him.
And how could a stupid peasant hope to have a soul,
Given that he was born from an ass, blown out by a fart?

I would like to pause for a moment on one detail of this story:
the question of the soul. As Matazone says: 'You, villeyn, you
cannot have a soul, because you were born of an ass.' Well,
this is virtually telling him to accept his condition, to not
accept the soul, inasmuch as the soul provides a pretext for

one of the greatest blackmails ever perpetrated against mankind. We find this sentiment in Bonvesin de la Riva, in his *Dialogue Between the Soul and the Body*: 'Thank the Lord, Soul, that you do not have a backside, because, if you did, I would give it a good kicking: you are like lead to me; I cannot fly, because you weigh me down.'

Now, why this rejection of the soul? Because it is one of the greatest blackmails that the bosses can use against us. In a moment of desperation, one might come to the point of saying: 'So what do I care, let's have at least a minimum of dignity. I am going to stab that bastard boss of mine!' So then the boss, or rather the boss through the medium of the priest, comes along and says: 'No! Stop! Do you want to ruin yourself? You have suffered all your life, and now, shortly, you are going to die. You have the possibility of going to heaven now, because Jesus Christ told you that since you are the last among men you shall enter into the kingdom of heaven... And now you want to ruin everything? Think what you're doing, don't get rebellious! And wait for the after-life. I, for my part, am damned! I, for my misfortunes, am a boss. And what did Jesus Christ say about me? He said: "You will never enter into the kingdom of heaven. You are like the camel which will never pass through the eye of a needle." You see the con? Obviously, I, as employer, have to make my own little Paradise here on earth, and it's for that reason that I keep you down and rob you and grind you down. To be sure, I even rob you of your soul, it's true! I want my little Paradise here and now; it may be small, but I want it all for myself; and I want it for all the time that I am here on earth. You are lucky, though! You will have everything. You will have Paradise! You will only get it after death, it's true, but you will have it for all Eternity!'

THE RESURRECTION OF LAZARUS

Introduction

Now let us move on to the miracle of the Resurrection of Lazarus.

This piece was regarded as the *pièce de resistance* among virtuoso *jongleurs*, because in it the *jongleur* has to act out something like 15 different characters in succession, and only indicates the character changes with his body. He does not vary his voice at all; everything is done by gesture. This kind of piece requires the performer to play it a bit by ear, according to the responses of laughter, silence, etc that he gets from the audience. In effect, it is a basic framework which then gives a possibility for improvisation. The principle theme of this piece is a satirisation of everything that passes for the 'moment of mystery'. This is achieved by playing out an event which, among the people, passes for a 'miracle'. The satire is aimed at the miracle-mongers, the magicians, the conjurors' art of the miraculous, which is an underlying feature of many religions, including Catholicism. The piece deals with the way in which miracles are presented as supernatural happenings, which must have been performed by God. At the origins of these miracle stories, the principal notion is that of God's love and sympathy for the people, for mankind.

Here, though, the story of the miracle is told from the standpoint of the people. The scene is set as if it were a show about to be performed by a great conjuror, a magician, somebody who is able to do extraordinary and vastly entertaining things. Here there is no hint of the religious content which is supposed to lie behind the miracle.

In a cartoon wall-painting in Pisa cemetery, there is a portrayal of the Resurrection of Lazarus. (A cartoon is the original sketch which precedes the final stage of a fresco; in this case the fresco had been removed for restoration, and the well-preserved cartoon was revealed). Lazarus does not even

Photo 14: 'The resurrection of Lazarus', drawing by Dario Fo, based on a fresco in Pisa cemetery.

figure in the scene. One's attention is concentrated wholly on the crowd, on the people – almost like a theatre audience – struck with amazement. Their gestures express their marvel at the miracle under way. Within the picture, which is itself grotesque (almost as if theatre and figurative representation were going hand in hand) there is an added element of the grotesque. We find one of the characters (photo 14) dipping his fingers into the purse of a spectator standing near him. He is taking advantage of the miracle, of people's amazement and sense of wonderment, in order to steal their money!

THE RESURRECTION OF LAZARUS

'Excuse me. Is this the graveyard, the cemetery where they're going to perform the Resurrection of Lazarus?'

'Yes, this is the one.'

'Ah, good.'

'One moment... That'll be ten pence, to get in.'

'Ten pence?'

'Well, alright, let's make it two.'

'Tuppence?! Why, in hell's name?!'

'Because I am the guardian of the cemetery, and all you people coming in here are going to wreck the place. You'll ruin my hedges and trample my grass, and I must be recompensed for all the trouble and damage that you're going to cause. Two pence, or you won't see the miracle.'

'Alright! You don't miss a chance, do you! There you go!'

'Two pence for you others as well. And I don't care if you've got children... I don't care. They're here for the show too, aren't they? Well, alright... half a penny. Hey, you, wretch! Down off that wall! Cunning devil, he wants to see the miracle for free! He should pay, no? Two pence... No, no, you did *not* pay before. That'll be two pence for you too, tuppence to get in...'

'Pretty crafty that one, making money out of miracles. Anyway, now I'll have to find where Lazarus is. His name must be on his tomb! The last time I came to see a miracle here, I spent half a day waiting around, and then they ended up doing the miracle right over the back there! And I had to stand here like an idiot watching from a distance. But this time I've taken the trouble to find out the fellow's name in advance, and I'm going to look for it on the tomb. I'll be in the front row this time! Lazarus... (*Hunting around*) And I'll put myself... Lazarus... I'll put myself right next to the tomb, and that way I'll see everything... Lazarus... But then even if I do find the tomb with Lazarus written on it, I can't read, so I won't know, will I! Still, I suppose I'll just have to guess. I'll stand here. I didn't do so well last time, but let's hope it goes better this time.'

'Who's that pushing? No, don't start pushing! I got here first, and I'm having the front position! I don't care if you are only little! Little people should come first thing in the morning and reserve themselves a position. Pretty clever, eh? He's little, so he wants to get in front! Supposing we were to stand in order of height? The little ones in front, and the big ones behind! Then the little ones would all turn up afterwards, and it would be as if they'd got here first! Stop pushing, you're going to push me into the tomb! For heaven's sake! I don't care. Get back. Eh? Oh! Now the women are pushing as well!'

'Hasn't he arrived yet? Isn't it time for the miracle?'

'Isn't there someone here who knows this Jesus Christ, who could go and get him to hurry up, because we're all here, waiting? After all, you can't wait for miracles for ever, eh?! They should set a timetable and stick to it!'

'Chairs! Who wants chairs! Chairs for hire, ladies! Two pence per chair! Make sure that you've got a seat, ladies, because when the miracle happens and the Holy Man brings Lazarus back to life, and he starts talking, and singing, and moving around, then you'll get a fright; you'll see his eyes glistening and gleaming, and you'll faint. You'll finish up falling backwards and banging your heads on a rock, and you'll end up dead! Dead! And this Holy Man only does one miracle per day! Chairs for hire! Only two pence!'

'I see, you only think about making money, do you, eh?'

'So, doesn't anybody want to…?'

'Don't push! I don't care…!'

'Stop climbing up on the chairs! Ah, pretty clever! Do you see that? The little fellow has climbed up on a chair now!'

'And don't lean on me, because I'm right on the edge of the grave, and…'

'Is he coming? Hasn't he arrived yet?'

'Sardines! Tasty sardines! Tuppence a time! Very tasty! Freshly grilled! Lovely sardines! Sardines to raise the dead! Two pence!'

(*Calling him over*) 'Sardines… give a couple to Lazarus, to prepare his stomach!'

'Shut up, blasphemer!'

'Behave yourselves.'

'He's coming! He's coming! Here he is!'

'Who is? Where?'

'Jesus!'

'Which one is he?'

'The dark one? Ugh! He looks pretty mean!'

'No! That's Mark!'

'Is Jesus the one behind?'

'Which one, the tall one?'

'No, the little one.'

'The lad?'

'Yes, the one over there with the little beard.'

'Oh, but he's only a young lad, for goodness sake.'

'Look! The whole lot of them are with him.'

'Oh, look, there's John! I know that John... (*Calling to him*) John! Jesus! What a nice fellow that Jesus is!'

'Oh! Look! The Madonna's there too! There's his whole family. But does he always go round with all these people? Hey...!'

'Well, they won't let him go around on his own, on account that he's a bit crazy!'

(*Calling to him*) 'Jesus?! What a nice fellow. He winked at me.'

'Jesus! Jesus! Do us the miracle of the loaves and the fishes like you did last time. They were really good!'

'Shut up! Blasphemer, behave yourself!'

'Silence! Get down on your knees. He's made a sign for everyone to go down on their knees, because we have to pray.'

'Where's the tomb?'

'Eh...? It's that one over there.'

'Oh, look! He's told them to lift off the tomb cover.'

'Ooooh... !'

'Shut up!'

'On your knees, on your knees. Come on, everyone down on your knees!'

'No, not me! I'm not going down on my knees, because I don't believe, I'm not a believer.'

'Oh, look at that!'

'Shut up!'

'Let me see.'

'No! Get down from there, down off that chair.'

'No! Let me get up there, because I want to see!'

'For goodness sake! Look! They've lifted the tombstone, and there's the corpse inside. There he is, it's Lazarus, and what a stink! What is that vile smell?'

'Good heavens!'

'What is it?'

'Shut up!'

'Let me look!'

'He's full of worms, and what a stink! Goodness! He must have been dead for at least a month, and he's all coming apart. Oh, what a rotten corpse they've landed him with! What a lousy trick! I'm sure he's not going to be able to manage it this time, poor devil!'

'There's no way he can do it, never! Impossible for anyone to bring *that* back to life. He's all gone rotten! What a joke! Lousy bums! They told him that the man had only been dead for three days! It must be a month at least! What a sight! Poor Jesus!'

'I say he can still do it, though! This man is a holy man, and he can do the miracle even when the body has been rotting for a month!'

'I say that he can't do it!'

'Do you want to bet?'

'OK, let's have a bet!'

'Right! Two pence! Three pence! Ten pence! What do you want to bet?'

'Shall I keep the money? Trust me! Here we all trust each other, don't we? Alright, I'll look after the money!'

'Behave yourselves! Now, pay attention! Everyone on your knees, and silence!'

'What's he doing?'

'He's beginning to pray.'

'Quiet, eh!'

'Hey there, Lazarus, rise up!'

'Ha, ha, you might as well tell him to come out and sing as well, because the only things that are going to come out are the worms that are in him! Rise up, indeed!?'

'Quiet! Look, he's risen up onto one knee!'

'Who? Jesus?'

'No! Lazarus! Heavens, look!'

'Nooo... ! It's impossible!'

'Let me see.'

'Oh, look! He's moving, he's moving, he's on his feet, come on! Oh, he's fallen! Now he's moving again, he's on his feet.'

'A miracle! Oh, a miracle. Oh Jesus, sweet creature that you are, and to think that I didn't believe in you!'

'Well done, Jesus!'

'I've won the bet. Let's have the money. Hey, don't mess about...'

'Well done, Jesus!'

'My purse! They've stolen my purse! Stop, thief!'

'Jesus, well done!'

'Stop, thief!'

'Well done, Jesus! Well done, Jesus...!'

'Stop, thief!'

BONIFACE VIII

Introduction

And now we come to Boniface VIII. Boniface was Pope in the days of Dante Alighieri. Dante was well acquainted with the man: his hatred of him was such that he consigned him to Hell in his *Inferno* even before he was dead. Somebody else who hated him, albeit a little differently, was the Franciscan monk, Jacopone da Todi, an active and militant member of the Poor Brotherhood; in other words, in today's parlance, an extremist. He was tied up with the movement of poor peasants, particularly in the region where he lived. In breach of one of the laws enacted by Boniface VIII (who, by the way, was a crook of the first order), Jacopone had uttered the following verse: *Ah! Bonifax, che come putta hai tràito la Ecclesia.* In other words, 'Boniface, you who have reduced the Church to a whore!'

Boniface, obviously, was very taken with Jacopone: when he finally managed to get his hands on the monk (who, incidentally, was an extraordinary man of the theatre), he threw him into jail, and forced him to remain seated, in this position (*He demonstrates*), with his arms spread and his feet tied, for five long years. Chained in his own excrement. And they say that after five years, when Jacopone was finally released from prison after the death of this Boniface, the poor friar, even though still a young man, was no longer even able to walk: he was literally bent double, and that's how he got around. Then, a year and a half later, he died. They tried to stretch him out in his coffin, but it proved impossible. Every time they stretched him out... Creeeak... he simply folded up as before. In the end, they had enough, and buried him sitting upright!

However, he wasn't the only one with an abiding hatred of the Papacy. Gioacchino da Fiore, who lived well before the times of St Francis (who was more or less the father of all heretical movements within the church), argued along the following lines:

'If we want to bring dignity to the church of Christ, we must destroy the Church. The great beast of Rome, the mighty monster of Rome. And in order to destroy the Church, it is not enough for us to bring down the walls, the roofs and the belfries; we must also destroy those who rule it: the Pope, the bishops and the cardinals.'

A fairly radical point of view!

Anyway, the Pope of that period immediately sent a hundred or so armed troops to visit him. They went looking for him on the mountain where he lived, and thanks to an informer they found his cave. But, unfortunately for them, they arrived only to find him dead; still warm, but dead nonetheless. He had died two minutes before they arrived. We don't know whether he died from fright at seeing the soldiers arriving, or just because he was a bit mischievous and wanted to upset them. I suspect it was the latter: Gioacchino da Fiore had a wicked sense of humour.

Here we have an extremely realistic portrayal (photo 15) of Boniface VIII. We see him using the monk Segalello da Parma as a chair to sit on. Segalello of Parma was a member of the 'Sackcloth' order of monks, so called because they dressed in sackcloth. Another extremist, in the language of today's newspapers...

So, this particular extremist, whom we see here providing a seat for the Pope, was one of those who demanded that the Pope and Church should be poor, extremely poor, and that all their wealth should be handed over to the poor of the world. In Segalello's words: 'The dignity of the Church should be founded on the dignity of the poor.'

In other words, when the Church has within it a large body of people who are dying of hunger, then that Church has very little to be proud of. Incidentally, this fellow had an interesting nickname. The local people called him Segarello – little

wanker. Segalello was a member of an order that preached
absolute chastity, and he obviously got his nickname from the

Photo 15: 'Boniface VIII'. Reconstruction from a
    fourteenth-century codex.

fact that nobody ever saw him go with women. Anyway, this
monk with his jester's nickname used to go round stirring up
the peasantry:

'Good morning, my friends, what are you up to? Enjoying
yourselves? No? You're digging the earth? You're working! And whose is this land? Yours, I presume! No? It's not
yours? How can that be! You work the land and... But you
must gain the profits from it?! What profits? Ah... you take
such a low percentage? And what's that you say? The
owner keeps the rest for himself? The owner of what?! Of
the earth? Ha, ha, ha! The earth has an owner? Do you
really believe that in the Bible the land was handed over to
people so that they could own it...? Fools! Imbeciles! The
land is yours; they took it for themselves, and then they

gave it to you to work. The land who belongs to those who work it, don't you see?!'

Just imagine, in the Middle Ages, going round saying things like that: the land belongs to those who work it! You'd have to be raving mad to go round saying it even nowadays... so just imagine, in the Middle Ages! Anyway, they promptly arrested him and burned him at the stake, himself and his whole brotherhood of 'Sackcloth' Friars.

Only one got away. He was known as Fra' Dolcino, and he went off back to where he used to live, near Vercelli. But despite his narrow escape, far from staying quietly at home, he too decided to go round stirring up the peasantry. He took to the streets as a jester. He would go up to people and start:

'Hey, peasant! The land is yours. Take it! Fool, imbecile, the land belongs to those who work it...'

And the peasants of the Vercelli countryside (perhaps because he spoke their local dialect and they could understand him) looked at him and said: 'Hey... That Fra' Dolcino is a bit crazy! But what he says is pretty sensible! You know what, I've got a mind to keep this land for myself... No. Why don't we leave the land to the landowner, and instead I'll just keep the harvest.' So, from that day on, every time the landowners' henchmen arrived, the peasants used to stone them. And the peasants began to tear up their contract, which in those days was called the *angheria* – in other words, 'oppression'. That's right, the contract which existed between peasants and the landowners in the Middle Ages was called 'oppression'. Of course, in those days it only meant 'contract'; but anyway, the people soon began to see the true nature of this contract, and the word took on other meanings: the word that used to mean contract between peasant and landowner came to be synonymous with oppression.

So, the peasants were beginning to tear up this contract. But they realised that they could not hope to win on their own. So they began to organise together and unite all the peasants in the region. In addition, realising that in order to build their strength they would have to extend their organisation, they began setting up links with the waged workers – in other words, the small artisans – who were beginning to develop in large numbers in the Middle Ages. This led to the organisation of an extraordinary community: they called themselves the 'communards' (*comunitardi*).

These were the first commune-dwellers in our history; their organisation was built around the *credenza*, in other words, the food cupboard. In Italy, from north to south, the word *credenza* means the pantry, the place where we keep food in the house. This noun obviously derives from the verb *credere* ('to believe'), to believe in something. So, *credenza*, the food cupboard, from *credere*, to believe, to believe in the community. These forms of communes had already begun to exist in the 6th century AD. The first *credenza* which comes down to us through history is the *credenza* of the commune of Sant'Ambrogio; an enormous, giant food cupboard, with little doors and separate storage spaces in which the commune's food could be kept, in order to protect grain from the damp, and to feed the commune in periods of famine.

However, expectation of famine was not a major consideration in the distribution of the common wealth; everyone would gather, and the food was distributed to each according to their needs. Bear that in mind – to each according to their needs; not according to the work that each had put in.

This method of self-government was beginning to upset the landowners – particularly those who felt that they had been 'robbed' of their land. One in particular, the Count of Monferrato, organised a punitive expedition. Setting off with a gang of his henchmen, he managed to capture a hundred or so communards. He cut off their hands and feet. This was a style of the times. In Brittany, two hundred years previously, the nobles had done the same with their own peasantry. Anyway, minus their hands and feet, they were mounted on donkeys and driven to the city of Vercelli. This, in order that the communards should realise what happened to people who took too many liberties.

When the communards saw their own brothers in this sorry mutilated state, they did not sit down and weep. That same night they set off, and unexpectedly marched into Novara. They entered the city, and carried out a full-scale massacre of the Count's murderous thugs and assassins. In addition, they succeeded in convincing the local population to seek their freedom, and organise themselves too into a commune. The movement spread with incredible rapidity. Oleggio, Pombia, Castelletto Ticino, Arona, the whole northern area of Lago Maggiore, Domodossola, the area by Monte Rosa, the whole of Lago d'Otra, Valsesia, Varallo, Val Mastallone, Ivrea, Biella, Alessandria... In short, half of Lombardy and half of Piedmont was in a state of rebellion. The local nobility, the dukes and counts, did not know what to do. They sent an envoy to Rome, who went to see the Pope, shouting: 'Help, help, you must help us, in the name of God!'

Well, faced with this 'in the name of God', what was the Pope to do? 'Forsooth, in the name of God, I must help them...' Luckily for him – and luckily for the northern nobility – the Fourth Crusade was about to embark from Brindisi (this, by the way, is the Crusade about which we know nothing, because nothing is ever written about it, and you usually find that what is passed off as the 'Fourth' Crusade was in fact the Fifth). The Pope sent his envoy with a message for the crusaders: 'Stop, everybody. Sorry, I made a mistake. The infidels are not on the other side of the ocean – they're up north, in Lombardy, in the guise of rebellious peasants. Off you go, at once!'

So, after a long march, eight thousand men (almost all of them Germans) arrived in Lombardy. They joined up with troops of the noble families of Visconti, Modrone, Torriani, Borromeo and the Count of Monferrato – along with the Savoys, another noble family which was beginning to get under way in that period. The net result was a vicious massacre. They succeeded in cutting off three thousand communards on a mountain near Biella. Men, women and children. At one fell swoop, they slaughtered the lot of them, burned them, and slit their throats...

Needless to say, this history which I have briefly summarised for you, receives no mention in the history books used in our schools. This of course is quite natural. After all, who organises our education system? Who decides what is to be taught? Who has a material interest in not letting certain things be known about? The employers, the landowners and the bourgeoisie. For as long as we continue to allow them, it's obvious that they'll carry on doing what they consider to be correct. Can you imagine what would happen if they all suddenly went crazy and began telling the history of how, in the 14th century, in Lombardy and in Piedmont, there was a full-blooded revolution, during which, in the name of Jesus Christ, people began to set up communes in which all people were equal, everybody loved each other, and nobody exploited anyone else? What would happen? The children would get all excited, and start shouting: 'Long live Fra' Dolcino! Down with the Pope!' And, my goodness, this sort of thing cannot be allowed...!

Of course, I'm overstating the case, from my natural love of polemic. The truth is that in some of our better schools, this information can just about be found in the history books. Admittedly, only in footnotes. Footnotes which go something like this: 'Fra' Dolcino, a heretic, was burned alive in 1306, together with his woman friend.' You see? The children learn that Fra' Dolcino was a heretic. Probably because he had a woman friend!

Now I would like to perform the Boniface VIII sketch. It begins with an extremely ancient liturgical chant in Catalan, from the Pyrenees. During this chanting, the Pope dresses himself for a very important ceremony. You should bear in mind that Boniface VIII had a habit: that of nailing certain monks to the doors of the houses of the nobility in certain cities... by their tongues. You see, these 'Poor Brothers', who were linked with the Cathars and other heretical movements, had an unfortunate habit of going round speaking ill of the nobility. So the Pope grabbed them, and... whap...! (*He mimes the action of nailing somebody up by their tongue*) Not the Pope personally, of course, because he got upset at the sight of blood: he had men employed to do it... He wasn't one to keep such pleasures all to himself...

Another story is told about Boniface, which will give you an idea of the sort of man he was. He organised an orgy on Good Friday, 1301. Among the many processions taking place in Rome that day, there was one organised by the Cathars, who used their liturgical chanting in order to get a few underhand digs at the Pope. They said:

> 'Jesus Christ was a poor person. He went around without even a cloak. But there is a person who does have a cloak, and that cloak is full of precious stones. There is someone who sits on a throne made all of gold, while Christ walked with bare feet. Christ, who was God, the Eternal Father, came to earth to be a man; there is somebody who is not even a man, and who fancies himself so much as the Eternal Father that he has himself carried around on a litter.'

I ask you! Boniface, of course, who was pretty sharp, thought to himself: 'You see, they're picking on me! So? I'll show them what I think of them!' So he organised an orgy. On the very day of Good Friday. He summoned a number of prostitutes, a number of women from good families (which often meant the same thing), bishops and cardinals, and it appears that they all set about indulging themselves in some pretty low-life goings-on. To such an extent that all the courts of Europe were scandalised, including that of Henry III of England, who, according to chroniclers of the time, was a fairly gross king as kings go. In fact, they say that he used to amuse his barons during banquets by blowing out a candle with a burp at three metres distance! In fact, one of the chroniclers claimed – not that I personally believe him – that he was able to blow out candles with a kind of ricochet effect... He would aim his burp against a wall, and it would bounce off... (*He mimes*) Crash, bang, wallop! This of course is the English sense of humour, the subtleties of which we are not in a position to grasp. We just have to accept it for what it is, a bit like cricket.

BONIFACE VIII

He plays the part of Boniface VIII. He mimes the gestures of praying and chanting.

> On the Day of Judgement,
> An eternal King will come,
> He who has created everything,
> Fleshed in our mortal flesh,

     Verily he will come,
     From heaven, on the day…

He breaks off, turns to an imaginary CLERIC *and takes his mitre. He begins chanting again.*

     Thus the judgement will not be…
     A mighty sign will be given…

He mimes taking the mitre off his head.

Oh, this is really heavy! No, let's go… I must carry on…

He mimes taking another item of headgear.

Ah, this one will do.

He puts it on his head, and begins chanting again.

     On the Day of Judgement…

He breaks off.

The mirror…

He mimes looking at himself in the mirror.

It's crooked, you see! …The gloves!

He starts walking again, trying to get one of his gloves on. He chants.

     Thus the judgement will not be…
     A mighty sign will be given…

Where's the other one… ? Why only one glove? I've got two hands, you know! I haven't only got one hand… ! Am I supposed to cut the other one off?

He chants.

     The sun will fade in splendour,
     The earth will tremble with fear…

He gives an order.

The cloak, the big cloak…

He mimes taking a large, heavy cloak.

     On the Day of Judgement
     He will appear, who…

Oof, this is really heavy…!

He tries getting it around his shoulders. He beckons his ACOLYTES *to help him.*

He will appear, who created all things.

Push, all together, let's go...

His chant slows.

Come on! Are you going to get a move on? Why aren't you singing too?! Do I have to do everything myself? Sing, wear the cloak, wear the hat... Let's go! Now, stop a minute. Let's start again!

Still turning to the imaginary CLERICS.

And you, sing! Let's have...you, first voice...

He chants as if he is trying to get a particular CLERIC *to chant.*

　　　...created a-a-a-all things.

He continues, nodding his head in time.

　　　An eternal King will come...

Second voice!

He points to another CLERIC.

　　　Fleshed in our mortal flesh...

Third voice!

He turns to the first CLERIC.

　　　He will come for sure, from heaven...

He breaks off, fed up.

Out of tune!! Come on, let's all sing together.

He chants, his voice going into the high register. Then he stops abruptly.

　　　To bring the Day of Judgement...

Who trod on my cloak?!

He spins round, furious.

Was it you? You there – squeaker! Miserable wretch... He won't chant and he won't push... Right, let's go. Let's have the Alleluiah.

He breaks off, incredulous.

Don't you even know what the Alleluiah is? ...The Alleluiah is the twiddly bit that goes up and down in the middle. Right, let's go...

　　　On the Day of Judgement
　　　He will appear who has created everything

He trills his words and drags his cloak. He stops, exhausted.

Oh, what a lousy job, being Pope!

He gives a final heave, to get his cloak on.

> An eternal King will come,
> Fleshed in our mortal flesh...

Again he turns to a CLERIC.

The ring!

Still chanting, he slips the ring on. He admires it, and breathes on it as he warbles and trills.

Look how it sparkles!

He gives an order.

And the other ring. The big one... for my thumb...

He puts the ring on his thumb, and continues chanting.

> ...Will come for sure, from heaven

The crozier, my staff!

Shouting.

No, the staff... Not the one for beating people with. Get on with it. I want the one with the curly bit on top!

He indicates the curly top of the crozier. He starts chanting again.

> Will come for sure, from heaven...

Are we ready? Can we start? Eh? Let's go. Together. Don't push like that, wretch; do you want to send me sprawling in the mud? And you, deaf-ears, squeaker, watch out! Right. Let's mark time: two steps marking time before we go: One, two, *now*, the Alleluiah!

He chants.

> The babies who have not been born
> Will cry out from inside their mothers.
> Everyone will weep and cry.
> Help us, oh all-powerful God.

I'm in good voice today!

Hey! Where are you all going? Where are you off to? Where's everyone gone?! You can't just leave me here like this! I am the Pope! I am Boniface! I'm not just some old horse and cart driver...

Who is that? Who...? Who's that with the cross? Jesus? Ah, Christ! Jesus Christ... Look, look what a terrible state he's in! Now I see why they call him 'poor Christ'... Good heavens... Look at the state of him...

Damn! Let's get moving! I don't like looking at things like this.

He pretends to reply to a CLERIC *who has a different opinion.*

You say it would be better if I went over to him...? So that I can show people that I'm a good person, so that I can show myself helping to carry his cross... Well now, that would be a good idea. Everyone will applaud me, saying: 'What a good fellow that Boniface is' ...Alright, then, let's make them happy, these simpletons... Let's go.

He mimes taking his things off.

There you go, take the cloak... Take it... And the staff... I'd better go now. You won't believe this, but my legs are shaking... Hello Jesus, how are you? Jesus... Don't you recognise me? I am Boniface... Boniface... the Pope... What do you mean, who's the Pope?! You know, he's the shepherd, the one who follows on from St Peter, with all the others, at the end of the line... Don't you recognise me? Ah, it must be because of this big hat... Weeell, that was because it was raining... Anyway...

Turning to the CLERIC.

Come and take all this stuff off... And the ring! Don't let him see that I've got rings...

He mimes taking off all his frippery.

Don't let him see all this glittery stuff... He's got terrible fixed ideas, that one! A very odd character... Come on, take my shoes off... quick! He likes to see people with bare feet... Come on, quick! Give me something so that I can dirty myself... Some earth for my face.

He smears his face with mud.

Come on, dirty me all over. He likes people like this. What do you expect – he's crazy!

He turns to CHRIST.

Do you recognise me now? I am your son... Humble as I am,
I come before you. Jesus... Look, I kneel before you... I, who
have never kneeled before anyone; I, before whom... Jesus...
Jesus... For God's sake, pay attention for a moment! What is
this – he's ignoring me!! Let's have some manners, for
heaven's sake! As I was saying...

He stops, as if CHRIST *had interrupted him.*

Me... Me? What did you say? That I have killed monks? Me?
That I have done wrong? It's not true! This is gossip. These
are lies put round by malcontents, out of jealousy...

Pointing at him angrily.

I've heard a few things about you too, my friend, but I don't
believe them! My goodness, those are bad people, you
know...

He kneels down, in desperation.

Jesus, Jesus, look into my eyes. I love you and I have always
had nothing but good feelings for the monks...

He turns to the imaginary CLERIC.

Go and get me a monk, quickly!

To CHRIST.

I love them...

To the CLERIC.

Where are you supposed to go and find monks? Go to the
prison! It's full of them!

To CHRIST.

Jesus, I... Jesus, look, a monk, look, how splendid...

He mimes embracing the MONK *and kissing him, and turns
his face away in disgust.*

What a stink!

To CHRIST.

Jesus, let me help you carry your cross, because I am strong,
and you're getting tired... I am used to it... I'm an ox, you
know... I wear really heavy cloaks! Let me... Out of the way,
Cyrenian!

He mimes chasing off the CYRENIAN *and taking his place
carrying the cross.*

I'll help you... No, it's no trouble... No, don't push! Jesus, good...

He's sent flying headlong by a great kick.

Christ! Kicking me?! Me, Boniface! The Prince! Ah, right! Rabble...! Ne'er-do-well...! I tell you, if your father gets to hear of this... Wretch! Donkey of all donkeys! Listen, I don't mind telling you that it will give me great pleasure to see you nailed up; and this very day I am going to get myself drunk! I am going dancing... dancing! And I am going with whores!!! Because I, I am Boniface... I am a prince! Cloak, mitre, staff, rings... and everything! Look how they glisten... Rabble! I, I am Boniface! Sing!

He exits, triumphant, and strutting, chanting at the top of his voice.

On the Day of Judgement will appear
He who has created everything.
An eternal King will come,
Fleshed in our mortal flesh,
He will come from heaven for sure...

THE PASSION PLAYS

DEATH AND THE FOOL

In an inn, a number of layabouts are playing cards with the Fool.

FOOL: The Horse on the Ass, and the Virgin on the Lecher means that I take the lot. Ha, ha! You thought you were going to pluck me like a chicken, didn't you?! So what do you think of that, then?

He deals the cards.

FIRST PLAYER: The game's not over yet... Wait a while, before you start to crow.

FOOL: Not at all, I shall sing as I like... and dance. Oh, what lovely cards. Good evening, your majesty, Mr King, would you mind going and taking the crown off that ugly bastard friend of mine?

He slaps a card down on the table.

SECOND PLAYER: Ha, ha! You've come unstuck with your King, because now I cap him with an Emperor!

FOOL: Oh, oh, look what the Emperor has done! Alright, I'll cap you with this. (*He turns his back and puts his backside on the table*) And then, for good measure, I'll put down this Murderer, who will slaughter your Emperor like a pig.

FIRST PLAYER: And I've got a Captain, to arrest your Murderer...

FOOL: And I shall bring in War, so that your Captain has to go away.

SECOND PLAYER: And I'll lay Famine, Cholera and

Pestilence, which will end the War.

FOOL: Well, then you'd better take your umbrella, because I'm going to bring a storm... this storm... Psssss... Rain and flood!

He takes a mouthful from his glass, and sprays it over everyone in sight.

FIRST PLAYER: Oh, Matazone, you wretch, what are you, crazy?

FOOL: Of course I'm crazy, ha, ha... If *matto* means crazy, and you call me Matazone, then I must be crazy... And I win the card-game with my Flood, which washes away all pestilences.

LANDLADY: Do you mind stopping all this row, because there's people in the big room next door who're just going to sit down to eat.

FOOL: Who are they?

LANDLADY: I don't know... I've never seen these fellows in my inn before, in Emmaeus. They call them the Apostles...

SECOND PLAYER: Ah! Those are the twelve fellows who follow the one from Nazareth.

FOOL: Yes, Jesus. He must be the one in the middle there... Look, what a pleasant fellow! Hello, Jesus of Nazareth... Hello, there. Enjoy your dinner! Did you see that? He winked at me... What a lovely fellow!

THIRD PLAYER: Twelve and one makes thirteen... Oh, thirteen of them sitting down to eat... That's bound to bring bad luck!

FOOL: Well, seeing that they're mad...! Wait a minute, and I shall say a spell to keep away the evil eye. (*He sings*) Thirteen at table to eat does not bring bad luck; evil eye, stay away, as I touch this bum!

He pinches the LANDLADY's *backside.*

LANDLADY: Behave yourself, Matazone, because you'll make me spill all this hot water.

FIRST PLAYER: Hot water? What are they going to do with that?

LANDLADY: I think they're going to wash their feet.

SECOND PLAYER: Wash their feet before eating? Hey, they really are crazy! Matazone, you should go and join them, because they're the right sort of company for the likes of you.

FOOL: You've said it, you're right. I'll win this game, and with the money that I win off you, I'll go into the big room, and drink it all away with them. And you won't be able to come – you can't join the madmen, because you're all sons of bitches and crooks.

They shuffle the cards.

THIRD PLAYER: Come on, let's start. Play your hand, because I'm really looking forward to seeing how you think you're going to win.

FOOL: While we're on the subject of crooks, what ever happened to the Fool that I had among my cards?

SECOND PLAYER: Someone give him a mirror, so that he can look at himself. Then you'll find the face of your Fool.

FIRST PLAYER: Don't waste time, let's get on playing… (*He plays a card*) A Knight with his sword.

SECOND PLAYER: A Queen with her sceptre.

FOOL: The Witch with her goat…

THIRD PLAYER: The Innocent Child.

FIRST PLAYER: God Almighty.

FOOL: Justice and Reason.

SECOND PLAYER: The Trickster and the Lawyer.

THIRD PLAYER: The Executioner and the Hanged Man.

FOOL: The Pope and the Popess.

FIRST PLAYER: The Priest giving Mass.

SECOND PLAYER: A Good and Happy Life.

THIRD PLAYER: Death in black and white.

SECOND PLAYER: All my cards are gone. My dear Fool, you have lost.

FOOL: How can that be! How could I lose?

FIRST PLAYER: How could you lose? Because, my dear, idiotic Fool, you don't know how to play. Let's have you now. Out with your money!

FOOL: You hunchbacked horror! You've stripped me completely, and just think, I was sure that I had that card here, the card of Death. I know I had it here somewhere.

At the back of the stage, DEATH *appears: a fair-skinned woman, with her eyes circled in black.*

SECOND PLAYER: Oh, Mother, who is that?!

The FOOL *has his back to* DEATH. *He is intent on counting out his money.*

THIRD PLAYER: The Witch...! Death!

Everybody except the FOOL *exits, running.*

FOOL: Yes, Death! There you are... I *did* have it! Goodness, it's turning cold... Where have you all disappeared off to? This cold is enough to chill you to the bone. Shut that door! (*He barely notices* DEATH) Good day. All the windows are shut... Where on earth can this freezing cold be coming from? (*He sees* DEATH *standing there*) Good day, good evening, good night, madam. Excuse me. (*He gets up to leave*) Since my friends have all decided to leave... (*He has forgotten his money on the table*) Were you looking for somebody? The landlady is there in the big room, serving the Apostles, and taking them a basin to wash their feet in. If you want to join them, feel free, don't stand on ceremony. Oh, my teeth are chattering!

DEATH: No, thank you. I prefer to wait here.

FOOL: Alright. Would you like to sit down? Take this chair. It's still warm, I warmed it up myself! Excuse my asking, madam, but now that I see you from close up, I have a feeling that we've met somewhere before.

DEATH: That is impossible, for people who meet me meet me only once.

FOOL: Ah yes? Only once? And you have a slightly foreign way of speaking. It sounds a bit Tuscan. Or Ferrarese? Or Roman? Or from Sicily? Or maybe Cremona? Because the Cremonese are more foreign than anyone, even more foreign than the people of Lodi, who are foreigners even in their own town! Anyway, madam, I hope you won't mind my saying so, but you look a bit down in the dumps, a little pale in the face, compared with the last time we met.

DEATH: Are you saying that I look pale?

FOOL: Yes. I hope I haven't offended you?

DEATH: No, I have been pale for all time. Pallor is my natural colour.

FOOL: Naturally pale, eh? Ah, that's who you look like! You're the spitting image of that picture on the playing card!

DEATH: True. I am Death.

FOOL: Death? Ah, so you're Death? Oh, what a combination! Death! Well, pleased to meet you... I am Matazone, the Fool.

DEATH: Aren't you afraid?

FOOL: Me, scared? No. I am a Fool, and everyone knows that, just like in the Tarot cards, the Fool has nothing to fear from Death. On the contrary, he goes looking for her, to marry her, because, joined together, they can beat any other card, even the card of Love!

DEATH: If you're not afraid, then how come your leg is all trembling?

FOOL: My leg? Ah, that's because this isn't my own leg. I lost my own leg on the battlefield... and so I took another one from a Captain, who had been killed, and his leg was still alive and moving, like the tail of a freshly killed lizard.

Anyway, I cut his leg off, and I stuck it on in place of my own, stuck it on with spit. There you are, look, you can see that it's not mine... It's longer than the other one by about a span, and it makes me limp. Hey! Behave yourself, Captain's leg! Because you shouldn't be afraid of such an illustrious and noble madonna... Let's have you!

DEATH: That is very kind of you, to call me an illustrious madonna.

FOOL: Oh, believe me, I'm not just standing on ceremony. As far as I'm concerned, I swear it, you really are illustrious, and very nice too. And I'm very glad that you came here looking for me, because I like you. So much so that I would like to buy you a drink, if you'll permit me.

DEATH: Willingly! Did you say that you liked me?

FOOL: Certainly! I like everything about you, your scent of chrysanthemums, and the paleness of your face, because, where I come from, we have a saying: 'A woman with a skin the colour of whitewash is a woman who will never tire of making love.'

DEATH: Oh, you're making me all bashful, Fool – for so you are! Nobody has ever made me blush like this before.

FOOL: Go ahead and blush, because you are a pure and virgin lady. It is true that you have embraced many men, but you only embrace them once... And none of those was worthy of coming to lie next to you, because none of them values you or bears you a sincere and honest love.

DEATH: It is true, nobody values me!

FOOL: That is because you are too modest, and you don't blow your own trumpet or bang your drum to announce your arrival, for all that you are Queen, Queen of the World! I drink to your health, Queen!

DEATH: The health of Death? I can't make out whether you're just mad, or a poet!

FOOL: Both. Because every poet is a fool, and every fool a poet. Drink, my pale lady, because this wine will give you a bit of colour.

DEATH: Oh, how good the wine is!

FOOL: And how could it not be good? It is the same wine that the Nazarene is drinking in the big room next door, and he's a man who really knows about wine! He's a big connoisseur, that one!

DEATH: Which one of them is the fellow from Nazareth?

FOOL: The young one sitting in the middle, the one with the big shiny eyes.

DEATH: Oh, he's a fine looking fellow, and so sweet.

FOOL: Yes, he's a fine man, but I hope you're not trying to make me jealous. You're not going to do me the discourtesy of leaving me, to go with them? Because then I would burst into tears.

DEATH: So, you rogue, you're trying to flatter me, eh?

She removes her black veil.

FOOL: Me? Flatter? Flatter a lady whom not even popes or emperors can conquer? (DEATH *reveals herself; she has blond hair*) Oh, how beautiful you are, with that golden hair. I would happily gather all the flowers on earth and cover you with them, all over, a great heap, and then I would dive in and find you under that heap, and I would strip you of those flowers... and of everything else too!

DEATH: My dear Fool, these words are making me all hot and flustered, and I must say, I'm sorry, because I would have been glad to remain in your company, and then to take you away with me.

FOOL: Wasn't that the reason you came? To take me away with you? Ah! So you didn't come for me... Ha, ha! And to think that I thought... Ah, how ridiculous. Oh well, I've really enjoyed our conversation. I'm really happy... Ha, ha!

DEATH: Now I see that you are a liar, and that you were only pretending to love me, so that you could get on the right side of me, out of your fear of me... of Death...

FOOL: No, my pale Lady, you don't understand. I am happy because you didn't come to me for any particular reason, because you didn't just stay in my company because you had a job to do, drawing out my final breath. You stayed with me because you like me, isn't that so? You find me a pleasant fellow, don't you, pale lady? But, what's happening? What are those tears welling up in your eyes? Oh, come on, that's too much. Death, crying! Have I offended you?

DEATH: No, not offended me. You have only softened my heart. I am crying because I am sorry for that boy Jesus, who is so sweet, because he is the one that I am supposed to take away to die.

FOOL: Ah, so you came for him? For Christ? Well, I'm sorry too. Poor lad, with that well-meaning face of his. And what illness is going to carry him off? A stomach illness? A heart disease? A disease of the lungs?

DEATH: Cross sickness...

FOOL: Cross sickness...? You mean that he's going to be nailed up? Oh, poor Christ, why couldn't you be called something else! Listen, pale Lady, do me a favour. Let me go and warn him, so that he can prepare himself for this terrible suffering.

DEATH: It is pointless you warning him, because he knows already. He has known it since the day he was born, that one day he would be stretched on the cross.

FOOL: He knows it, and still he stays there, chatting, and smiling happily with his friends? Oh, he must be even more crazy than me!

DEATH: It is true, what you say... And how could he not be crazy, he who so loves mankind, even those who are going to take him to the cross, even Judas who will betray him!

FOOL: Ah, so it will be Judas? That fellow with the Judas face over there, the one at the corner of the table. I might have known it! Wait while I go and give the wretch a smack round the ear and spit in his eye.

DEATH: Leave him be. It's not worth it, because you would have to spit in all their eyes, because when the time comes, they will all turn their backs on him.

FOOL: All of them? Even Saint Peter?

DEATH: He will be the first, and will betray him thrice thereafter. Come on, let's not sit here thinking about it. Pour me a glass of wine, because I want to get drunk, and escape from this sadness.

FOOL: Better to have a happy Death! So: let's drink and chase off the gloom. Fine pale lady, come and let's be merry. Take off your cloak, so that I can see your arms, the colour of the moon... Oh, how beautiful they are... And undo your jacket in front, because I want to feast my eyes on those two silver apples, that look like the stars of Diana.

DEATH: No, please, Fool, I am still a maid and a virgin, and you're putting me to shame, because no man has ever touched me naked!

FOOL: But I am not a man, I am a Fool, and Death would not be committing a sin to make love with a Fool, with a crazy lunatic such as me. Don't be afraid, because I shall turn out all the lights, and leave only one burning, and we shall go and dance some pretty steps that I shall teach you, and I shall make you sing with sighs and amorous swoonings.

MARY HEARS OF THE SENTENCE
IMPOSED ON HER SON

Mary is with Joanna, and meets Amelia in the street.

AMELIA: Good day, Mary... Good day, Joanna.

MARY: Good day, Amelia, are you going shopping?

AMELIA: No, I already did my shopping this morning... I've
got something I have to tell you, Joanna.

JOANNA: Tell me. Excuse me a moment, Mary.

They move to one side, and talk excitedly.

MARY: Where are all these people going? What's happening
down there?

JOANNA: It must be somebody's wedding...

AMELIA: Yes... It's a wedding... That's just where I'm
coming from now.

MARY: Oh, Joanna, let's go and look, because I love
weddings. Is the bride young? And who is the bridegroom?

JOANNA: I don't know... I think it must be somebody from
out of town.

AMELIA: Let's go, Mary. Let's not waste time with
weddings, let's go home, because we still have to put the
water on the stove for the stew.

MARY: Wait, listen. They're cursing!

JOANNA: Oh, they must be swearing because they're
happy...

MARY: No, it sounds as if they're really angry. They're
shouting: 'Sorcerer!' Yes, there it is again. I can hear it

clearly. Listen. Who are they taking it out on?

JOANNA: Oh, now I think about it, it isn't a wedding at all; they are taking it out on somebody they discovered last night, dancing with a goat, which turned out to be the Devil.

MARY: Ah, so that's why they're calling him 'Sorcerer'.

JOANNA: Yes, that must be it... But let's not delay, Mary. Let's go home, because you shouldn't look at things like that, because you might get the evil eye on you.

MARY: There's a cross sticking out over the people's heads! And look, another two crosses!

JOANNA: Yes, those other two are for two thieves...

MARY: Poor people... Are they going to crucify all three...? Just think of their poor mothers! And to think that she, poor woman, probably doesn't even know that they are killing her son.

Enter MARY MAGDALENE, *running.*

MARY MAGDALENE: Oh Mary! Your son Jesus...

JOANNA: Yes, yes, she knows it already. (*Aside*) Shut up, you fool.

MARY: What do I know already? What's happened to my son?

JOANNA: Nothing... What should have happened to him, you blessed woman? It's only that... Ah, didn't I tell you? Oh, how forgetful of me... It completely went out of my head, to tell you that he, your son, told me that he wouldn't be home to eat at noon, because he had to go into the mountains to tell parables.

MARY: Is that what you too came to tell me?

MARY MAGDALENE: Yes, that's it, Madonna.

MARY: Thank the Lord... You arrived in such a hurry, dear girl, that I took a terrible fright... I began to imagine all kinds of terrible things... How silly we mothers are sometimes... we get all worried over nothing!

JOANNA: Yes, how stupid of her, coming running like crazy, just to tell you something so trivial.

MARY: Alright, Joanna... Don't start shouting at her now... After all, she was good enough to come and give me the message. I thank you, young lady... What's your name? I seem to know you...

MARY MAGDALENE: I am Magdalene...

MARY: Magdalene? Which Magdalene? The one who...

JOANNA: Yes, she's the one... The prostitute. Let's leave, let's go home, because it's best that we're not seen with people like her. It gives a bad impression.

MARY MAGDALENE: But I don't work any more.

JOANNA: That must be because you can't find any dirty men to get your hands on... Leave us, hussy!

MARY: No, don't chase her off, poor girl... If my beloved Jesus has faith enough in her as to send her to give me a message, it's a sign that she's seen the error of her ways, isn't it, Magdalene...?

MARY MAGDALENE: Yes, I'm more sensible now.

JOANNA: You really believe that? The truth is that your son is too good. He lets himself be overcome by pity, and everyone takes advantage of him! He's always surrounded by a crowd of ne'er-do-wells, people without work or skills, starvelings, wretches and whores... like this one!

MARY: Joanna, those are wicked words! My son always says that it is for them, above all others, for them, the wretched and the lost, that he came into this world, in order to give them hope.

JOANNA: Alright, agreed. But don't you understand that it creates a bad impression. People start talking behind your back... Just think, with all the proper people that there are in this town, the gentlemen and the ladies, the doctors, the nobles... And he, with his gentle, wise and learned ways, could command immediate respect, and would be honoured, and could get help if he needed. But no, my goodness; he goes and takes up with lousy rogues!

MARY: Listen how they are shouting, and laughing... But I can't see the cross.

JOANNA: Leaving aside the fact that it would also be better if he stopped always talking ill of bishops and priests... because they don't forgive such things lightly!

MARY: There they are again, the three crosses...

JOANNA: One day they're going to make him pay for all that... They'll find some way of doing him harm!

MARY: Do harm to my son? Why? Because he is so good. Doesn't he help everyone, even those who don't ask? And everybody likes him! Listen, they've started sneering and jeering again... One of them must have fallen down. Everyone likes my son, don't they...

MARY MAGDALENE: Yes, I like him too, a lot!

JOANNA: Oh yes, everybody knows the way that you like him, the way that *you* like Mary's son!

MARY MAGDALENE: I have more love for him than I would have even for a brother! And now...

JOANNA: Now... ! What about before, then!?

MARY: Joanna, stop tormenting the poor girl... What's she ever done to you...? Can't you see that she's upset? Why are they shouting so much? And so what if this young girl had the kind of love for him that normal women have for men that they like...? Well? Isn't my son a man too, as well as being God? He has the eyes, the hands, the feet of a man... He is a man all over, even down to his pain and happinesses! So, it'll be up to my son to decide... And he will know the right thing to do, when the time comes, if he decides to get married. As far as I am concerned, anybody whom he chooses, I shall cherish as if she were my own daughter. And I hope that this day comes soon... Because he's already thirty-three, and it's time that he started raising a family... Oh, what a horrible noise they're making with all that shouting down there, and how black that cross

is! I would so much like to have his children running
around the house... to play with, and cradle... I know a lot
of lullabies... I would really spoil them, and tell them
stories, the kind of stories that always have a happy ending!

JOANNA: Yes, but that's enough standing here and
dreaming, Mary... Come along, because at this rate we
won't even be in time to prepare the evening meal.

MARY: I'm not hungry... I don't know why... I've a bit of
stomach cramp... I'm going to have to go down there, to
see what's going on.

JOANNA: No, don't go... That sort of scene just makes
people sad. You'll feel heartbroken all day. Your son
won't like it. At this very moment, he could be at home
waiting for us, starving hungry.

MARY: But he sent a message to say that he wouldn't be
home!

JOANNA: He might have changed his mind. You know what
children are like. You wait at home for them, and they
don't come... And then they always turn up when you least
expect them! And you have to be there, all ready, with the
food on the stove.

MARY: Yes... you're right. Would you like to come as well,
Magdalene, and share a bowl of soup?

MARY MAGDALENE: I'd love to, if it's no trouble.

VERONICA *crosses the stage*.

MARY: What has happened to that woman, with that
bloodied towel that she's carrying...? Good woman, have
you hurt yourself?

VERONICA: No, not me... It was one of those that they've
got down at the crosses, the one they're calling 'Sorcerer'...
He's not a sorcerer, though. He's a holy man, a saint, for
sure, because you can see it from his sweet eyes... I cleaned
his bloody face for him...

MARY: Oh, you kind woman...

VERONICA: ...with this towel, and a miracle happened... He left the imprint of his face on the towel. It could almost be a portrait.

MARY: Let me see.

JOANNA: Don't, Mary. Curiosity is not good for you.

MARY: I'm not curious... I just feel that I must see it...

VERONICA: Alright, I'll let you see it. But first, you must cross yourself... There, he's the Son of God!

MARY: Oh, my son! Oh, it's my son!

She runs off, in desperation.

JOANNA: Now look what you've done... Wretched woman!

VERONICA: But I didn't realise she was his mother!

THE FOOL BENEATH THE CROSS,
LAYING A WAGER

Onstage, the FOOL, SOLDIERS *and four* CRUCIFIERS.
They hang up a sheet, behind which JESUS *is made to undress.*

FOOL: Come on, Ladies! You ladies who love this Christ, come and feast your eyes on him... Come and see your dear one all naked as he undressed... Two pence for a look... Come on, Ladies! He looks almost good enough to eat! They say that he was the Son of God. To me he looks the same as any other man, just the same! Two pence for a look at him, Ladies! Doesn't anyone want to take up my offer – only two pence? Well, it's a holiday today, so I'll cut my prices... Come along you, I'll let you look for free... Oh, what a miserable face... Come here. It's a chance not to be missed... Aren't you that Mary Magdalene who was so much in love with him that, when you couldn't find a towel to dry his feet, you dried them with your hair? Well, so much the worse for you; because now the law says that here in this place of sin we are to dress him, dress him in a little apron that'll make him look like a ballerina!

Is the chief player ready? Pull up the cloth so that we can start the show! Scene One: the Son of God, a gentleman knight... See his crown! He's going a-jousting. He'll be riding a fine horse made out of wood... And so that he does not fall off, we are going to nail him to the saddle... by his hands and feet!

CHIEF CRUCIFIER: Stop clowning around and come here to give us a hand... Put a rope round his wrists, one on either side, so that we can stretch him out properly... But leave his palms free, so that we can get the nails in. I'll hammer the right one in, and...

FIRST CRUCIFIER: And I'll do the other. Throw me a nail... I already have a hammer.

SECOND CRUCIFIER: Oh, what an ugly great nail! Let's have a bet. I bet that I can hammer it right home with seven blows.

FIRST CRUCIFIER: And I shall do it in six. We bet?

SECOND CRUCIFIER: Agreed. Right, you two, move aside, so that we can put the wings on this Angel, so that he can fly up into the sky, like Icarus.

THIRD CRUCIFIER: All heave together... Together, I said! You're tipping him off. Gently, so that he stays in the saddle, this knight of ours... Over to me a little... Right! I'm right on the mark now.

SECOND CRUCIFIER: I'm not, though. You've made the holes too far apart... Hey, you, pull! Go on! What's the matter, did you eat cheese for lunch? A bit of effort!

FIRST CRUCIFIER: You say 'a bit of effort', but we'll end up by tearing the ligaments in his shoulders and elbows.

THIRD CRUCIFIER: Don't worry... They're not your ligaments! Pull! A bit of effort!

JESUS *groans with pain; the* WOMEN *groan in chorus, and in counterpoint*

FIRST CRUCIFIER: Oh, did you hear that crack?

SECOND CRUCIFIER: Yes... horrible, wasn't it! It sends shivers down your spine. But at least he's stretched out to the right length. Now I'm over the hole too.

FIRST CRUCIFIER: Right. Keep the tension on the rope. You, raise the hammer, and we'll start off together.

SECOND CRUCIFIER: Mind you don't bang your thumbs!

The others laugh.

THIRD CRUCIFIER: Open your paw. I promise I won't tickle you... Oh, just look at that hand! Look at his life-line. It's so long that you'd think that this light was going to live for at least another 50 years... That's what you get for believing in old wives' tales, you!

SECOND CRUCIFIER: Shut your mouth and raise your hammer.

FIRST CRUCIFIER: I'm ready.

THIRD CRUCIFIER: Right, let's go. Give the first blow... (*A thud*) Ohioa ahh! To make a hole in his palms!

CHIEF CRUCIFIER: (*In counterpoint with* CHRIST's *screams*) Oooh! He's trembling all over. Calm down. Now the second blow: Ohaioaohh! To spread the bones a bit.

Ohoh And now he's spitting blood.
Give the third blow.
Ohahiohoh
This nail will deflower you.
Ohoh you who have never had a woman.
The fourth is a present from the soldiers
Ohahiohoh
Whom you told not to kill
Ohahiohoh!
And to love their enemies like brothers.
Ohahiohoh
The fifth is from the bishops in the synagogue
Ohahiohoh!
Who you said were false and damned.
Ohahiohoh!
The sixth is a present from the rich
Ohahiohoh!
Who you said could not go to heaven
Ohahiohoh!
When you told them about the camel.
Ohahiohoh!
The seventh blow is from the impostors
Ohahiohoh!
Whom you told that it didn't matter if they prayed
Ohahiohoh!
Because the Lord would ignore them.

FIRST CRUCIFIER: I've won! You owe me a drink. Don't forget it.

SECOND CRUCIFIER: Let's drink to the health of this gentleman and his misfortunes! How are you, your majesty? Do you have your steed well in hand? Right, let's off to the jousting, but without shield or lance this time!

CHIEF CRUCIFIER: Have you released the rope from his wrists? Well done, my barons... Now, tighten this belt around his chest, because we don't want him falling on us as we hoist him up, this champion of ours! Then, once we've got his feet nailed down, we'll remove it.

SECOND CRUCIFIER: Come here all of you... Spit on your hands, because now we've got to hoist up our greasy pole! Come over here with that rope, and hook it over the crossbeam... And you too, Matazone. Climb up on top of the ladder so that you can be ready to hold it.

FOOL: I'm sorry, I can't help you: that fellow has never done anything to harm me.

SECOND CRUCIFIER: Oh rubbish... He hasn't done anything to us either: we're just crucifying him to pass the time, ha, ha! And they're giving us ten pence a head for the trouble... Come on, give us your hand, and then afterwards we'll do you the honour of playing a game of dice with you.

FOOL: Ah well, if it's for a game of dice, then that's a different matter. Look, I'm on the ladder already... You can begin!

FIRST CRUCIFIER: Bravo! Everyone ready to begin? Right, let's go... Please, all pull together, one long pull at a time. I'll give you the rhythm.

Ho, let's pull – Ehiee
Up this ship's mast – ohoho
On it, as a banner – ohoh
We've stuck a fool – ohoho

Ho let's pull – Ehiee

Up this big greasy pole – ohoho
With Christ in the crow's nest – ohoho

Ho, what a pole – Ahaaa
It pierces the sky – ohoho
It rains blood – ohoho
Our father weeps – ohoho

Be merry, be merry – Ohee
For we have found that brave lad – ohoho
Who made himself a slave – ohoho
In order to clothe us anew – ohoho

Stop. That'll do. I think that's good and firm. Right, now get the dice out so that we can play.

They play at dice, and at Tarot, and the FOOL *wins Christ's tunic, and the* CRUCIFIERS *pay.*

FOOL: If you want all your money back, I'll let you have it willingly, including the necklace, and the ring. Look. And I'll throw this in too.

FIRST CRUCIFIER: And what do you want in exchange for all this stuff?

FOOL: That man...

SECOND CRUCIFIER: Christ?

FOOL: Yes. I want you to let me take him down from the cross.

CHIEF CRUCIFIER: Alright, wait till he's dead, and he's all yours...

FOOL: No. I want him now, while he's still alive.

FIRST CRUCIFIER: Oh, you must be the fool of all fools! Do you want all us four to end up, up there, in his place?

FOOL: No, you needn't worry that anything's going to happen to you. All we have to do is put someone else up there, of about the same build, and nobody will notice the change... because anyway people look much the same when they're crucified.

FIRST CRUCIFIER: That's true enough... Stripped like that he looks like a fish on a griddle...

CHIEF CRUCIFIER: That's as may be. But I don't agree. Anyway, who did you have in mind to put in his place?

FOOL: Judas!

CHIEF CRUCIFIER: Judas? You mean the one who...

FOOL: Yes, that treacherous apostle who hanged himself in despair from the figtree behind the hedge fifty yards down the road.

CHIEF CRUCIFIER: Hey, get a move on, hurry up, let's go and strip him, because he must still have those thirty pieces of silver in his pocket.

FOOL: I wouldn't bother, if I were you... Because he threw them away into a thicket right away.

CHIEF CRUCIFIER: How do you know?

FOOL: I know because I went and picked up that money, piece by piece. Look how my arms got scratched in the process!

CHIEF CRUCIFIER: I'm not interested in your scratches. Let's see the money. Oh! And it's all silver! Look how splendid! How heavy! And what a chinking sound...

FOOL: Alright. You can keep them. These are yours too, if you'll do that swap. I'm ready.

CHIEF CRUCIFIER: So are we.

FOOL: Right, so go and get that hanged Judas at once, while I work out how to get Christ down.

FIRST CRUCIFIER: And what if the Centurion arrives and finds you in the middle of taking Christ off the cross?

FOOL: You tell him that it was my idea, and that I'm a Fool. And that you're not guilty. But don't stand there wasting time. Go!

CHIEF CRUCIFIER: Yes, yes, we're going. And let's hope that these thirty pieces of silver bring us good luck.

FOOL: Good. That's all done, then! I can hardly believe it. I'm so happy. Jesus, hold fast... Salvation is at hand... I'll take the pincers... Here they are... You'd never have thought, would you, Jesus, that a Fool would have come to save you! Ha, ha! Wait a minute while I fasten this belt around you... Don't worry that I'm going to hurt you. I'll bring you down as gently as a bridegroom brings his bride... and then I'll put you over my shoulder, because I'm as strong as an ox, me... And away we go! I'll take you down to the river; there I've got a boat, and with four strokes we'll be across the river. And before day breaks, we'll be safe and sound in the house of a friend of mine, who is a doctor and will give you medicines and cure you within three days. You don't want that? You don't want my sorcerer friend? Alright, then we'll go to the ointment-doctor, who's also a man I know and trust. No? You don't want me to un-nail you?

I see! You think that with these holes in your hands and feet, and with your muscles all torn, the way they've left you, you won't be able to get around any longer, or fend for yourself. You don't want to have to be reliant on others in this world? Am I right? What? It's not even for that reason? It's for the sacrifice? What do you mean, for salvation? For redemption...? What are you talking about...?! What? Oh, poor soul... you're feverish... Look at how you're shivering... Alright, but for the moment I'm taking you down. I'll cover you with this tunic... Now, if you don't mind my saying, you're as stubborn as a mule... You don't want to be rescued? You really want to die on this cross? Yes? For the salvation of man?

Oh, I can't believe it... And they call *me* the Fool, but you beat me by a long chalk, Jesus, my friend! And there I was, breaking my back to win that game of cards, all night, just to have this satisfaction... But by the grail, you are the Son of God, no? That's right, isn't it? I'm not mistaken, am I? Well, then, seeing that you are the Son of God, you know what's going to be the result of you dying here on the cross... I am not God, nor am I a prophet... but the Pale

Lady told me this morning, between her tears, how it's all going to end up.

First of all, they're going to model you all in gold, from head to foot. Then they'll carve your iron nails. All out of silver. Your tears will become sparkling diamonds; and your blood that is now flowing all over the place, they will turn into a stream of shiny rubies. All this they will do to you, you who have shouted yourself hoarse, telling them of poverty. In addition, they'll go putting this pain-bearing cross of yours all over the place: on shields, on banners of war, on swords to kill people as if they were calves, killing in your name, you, who cried aloud that we are all brothers and that we should not kill each other. You've already had one Judas, haven't you? Well, rest assured that the Judases will swarm like ants, betraying you, working to cut your balls off.

Believe me, it's not worth the effort! You don't believe me? So, who's going to be any different? The blessed Francis... and then Nicholas... St Michael Cut-the-cloak... Dominic... Catherine and Clare. Yes, alright, I'll accept that. But these are only a handful, in comparison with the number of rogues... and that handful will end up being treated in just the same way that they've treated you, after they've persecuted them in their lifetime. Say that again... sorry, I didn't catch it. Even if there were only one... Even if there were only one man on the whole earth worthy of being saved, then your sacrifice will not have been in vain... Oh no! Now you really are the chief of all Fools! You're a complete lunatic asylum! The only time I liked you was when you turned up in church and all the traders were there, and you began to beat them all with a big stick. Oh, that was so good to see. *That* should be your job, not dying on the cross for people's salvation! Oh Lord, Lord... I'm going to cry... But I'm crying with anger.

CHIEF CRUCIFIER: Hey, Matazone, you wretch! Haven't you got him down yet? What have you been doing up till now? Sleeping?

FOOL: No, I haven't been sleeping! I've just changed my mind. I don't want to un-nail this Christ after all. It's better that he stays on the cross.

CHIEF CRUCIFIER: Oh, wonderful! And now I suppose you'll want all that gold and silver back... Oh, what a crafty devil! You sent us off to act as porters, to bring this hanged Judas, just so as to make fun of us! Well, no, my dear Matazone. If you want the stuff back, you're going to have to win it back at Tarot! Only on that condition do you get it back!

FOOL: No, I don't want to play. You can keep it all... the money, the gold, the earrings, because I shall never gamble again as long as I live. I won tonight, for the first time, and that's enough for me... Even for just one man who is worthy... it would be worth dying on a cross?! Oh, but you're mad... The Son of God is mad!

Take a stick and beat, beat, all those who trade in church, thieves, swindlers, impostors and rogues. Out with them! Beat them, beat them!

THE PASSION:
MARY AT THE CROSS

WOMAN: See – his mother's coming – the blessed Mary. Run and stop her. Don't let her see him hung up and crucified like a skinned goat, running with blood like a flowing fountain, like a mountain of melted snow in spring, because of the great nails that they've driven into the flesh of his hands and feet, driven right through the bone.

CHORUS: Don't let her see him!

But she will not stop. She runs along the path in despair, and the four of us cannot hold her.

MAN: If four of you cannot hold her, try five, or six... She must not see this son of hers, his body all twisted like the root of an olive tree eaten by ants.

OTHER WOMAN: Hide the Son of God, cover his face, so that his mother doesn't see who he is... We shall tell her that the man on the cross is someone else, a stranger... That it is not her son...

WOMAN: I think that even if we covered the Son of God all over with a white sheet, his mother would still recognise him... It would need only a finger sticking out, or a lock of his hair, because all that was made by her, by his mother.

MAN: She's coming... The blessed Mary has come... It would be more merciful by far to kill her with a knife, rather than let her see her son! Give me a stone. I shall stun her with a blow, so that she falls down and does not see...

OTHER MAN: Be quiet. Move aside... Oh, poor woman, you whom they call blessed... And how can she be blessed with this decoration of four nails that they have hammered and driven into that bleeding flesh, something you would not even do to a poisonous lizard or a bat?

WOMAN: Be quiet! Hold your breath, for now you will hear this woman scream and scream, as if grief had torn her in two, poor wretch; a pain like seven stab wounds, enough to burst her heart asunder.

MAN: Stay there. Don't say a word… At least let her weep a bit. Let her scream! Let her give vent to the pain that is choking her!

OTHER WOMAN: Listen to that silence. Listen to the din of it. There's no point blocking your ears. Say something, say something, Mary… Oh, please!

MARY: Give me a ladder… I want to climb it, to be near to my loved one. My loved one… Oh, my fine, pale, dying son. Don't worry, my beloved, because now your mother is here! What have these murderers, these butchers done to you? These God-forsaken animals? Coming and doing this to my son! What did this big silly boy of mine ever do to you, for you to hate him so much, for you to do such terrible things to him… But I shall make you pay for this, one by one! Oh, you will pay, even if I have to go to the ends of the world to find you. Animals! Beasts! Wretches!

CHRIST: Mother, don't shout, mother.

MARY: Yes, yes. You're right. Forgive me, my dear one, for this outburst and for the angry words I spoke. It was just my grief at finding you here, stained with blood and stripped, kicked, beaten and hung on this cross… with holes in those delicate, fine hands and feet… the feet that I made… the feet that now drip blood, drop by drop… Oh, it must hurt so!

CHRIST: No, mother, don't worry. I promise you, I don't feel pain any more. it has passed. I don't feel anything; go home, mother, go home, please…

MARY: Yes, we'll go home together. I'll come up and bring

you down. I'll pull out your nails, gently, gently. Give me
a pair of pincers... come and give me a hand... help me,
someone!

SOLDIER: Hey, woman, what are you doing up on that
ladder? Who gave you permission?

MARY: That's my son that you have crucified... I want to pull
his nails out, and take him home with me...

SOLDIER: Home? You're in a hurry! But he's not yet run out
his time, holy Virgin, he's not yet well seasoned! Rest
assured that the moment he draws his last breath, I'll give
a whistle, and you can come and take this young fellow of
yours, all packed up and ready to go... Alright? Come
down, now...

MARY: No, I'm not coming! I'm not going to leave my son all
on his own, to spend the night in this place, dying, all on his
own. And you can't do this to me. Because I'm his mother!
I am his mother!

SOLDIER: Alright, Mrs Mother-of-him, now I've had
enough. Now I'm going to have to bring you down the way
we get apples off a tree. Do you want to see how? I give a
good shake to this ladder, and you'll come down with a
thud, like a big ripe pear.

CHRIST: No! Soldier, as you are a good man, I pray you. Do
to me as you will... shake the cross so that it lacerates the
flesh of my hands and my bones, but please, I pray you,
don't harm my mother...

SOLDIER: Did you hear that, my good lady? And what am I
supposed to do now? For me it's all the same: either you
come down from that ladder, and fast, or I am going to
shake the cross.

MARY: No, no... For pity's sake... wait. I'm coming down.
Look, here I am, down already.

SOLDIER: So you finally got the message, woman... And
don't look at me with those burning eyes. It's not my fault
if that young fellow decides to jump up, spread his arms

and hang there... No, don't think that I don't feel sorry. I know your pain. The glisten of bloody tears that are now falling from your eyes shows the pain and grief of a mother! But I can't do anything to help. I have my orders. This sentence must be carried out. I have been sentenced to make sure that your son dies, or otherwise I'll end up nailed there myself, with those very same nails.

MARY: Oh kind soldier, gentle soldier, take this; I make you a gift of this silver ring... and of these golden earrings... Take them and keep them in exchange for a favour that you can do me.

SOLDIER: What favour is that?

MARY: Let me take water and a rag to clean the blood off my son, and let me give him a bit of water to dampen his lips, all shrivelled with thirst...

SOLDIER: Is that all you want?

MARY: I also ask you to take this shawl and go up on the ladder and put it round his shoulders, under his arms, so as to help him as he hangs there from the cross...

SOLDIER: Oh lady, you do your son a disservice. Do you really want to keep him alive and living, so that he has to suffer all this terrible pain? In your shoes, I would try and help him die as soon as possible!

MARY: Die? Is my sweet one going to have to die, then? His hands, dead, his mouth, dead, and his eyes... and his hair, dead? Oh, they have betrayed me...!

Oh Gabriel, you young man, you with your sweet face, with your voice like a seductive viol, you were the first; you betrayed me like a trickster: you came to tell me that I would be queen... and blessed... happy, blessed among all women! Look at me! Look at me! See how I am reduced. I end up as the last among women!

You knew it, you knew it... When you brought me the 'annunciation', when you moved me with emotion and left me this child flowering in my belly, and I thought that I was going to be Queen of that fine throne! Queen, with a gentle son, a knight, with two spurs, these two great nails, banged into his feet! Why didn't you tell me this before my dream? Oh, you can be sure, I would never have let myself conceive, never, even if God the Father in person had come, instead of this pigeon, this dove, this Holy Ghost, come to wed me...

CHRIST: Mother, has your grief turned you mad, that you blaspheme so? That you say things without knowing what you say? Take her home, brothers, before she collapses with her grief.

MAN: Let us go, Mary. Make your son happy. Leave him in peace.

MARY: No. I shall not! Forgive me... Let me stay here close to him, and I won't say another word against his father. Or against anyone. Leave me... be so kind!

CHRIST: I have to die, mother, and it is hard. I have to let myself go, mother, and use up the breath that keeps me alive... But with you here tormenting your heart, mother, I can't... It just makes it harder...

MARY: I want to help you, my dearest one. Oh, don't make me go! Why can't we both die together, mother and son, so that they can put us, locked into an embrace, into one tomb?

SOLDIER: I told you before, lady! There is only one way to make him happy: kill him at once. If you want to hurry it up and take that lance leaning over there, we soldiers will pretend not to see, and you must run up under the cross and stick the point into him with all your strength, stick the lance right into his belly, right in, and then, in a moment, you will see Christ die. (*The Madonna faints*) What's the matter? Why did she faint? I never even touched her!

MAN: Lay her out... do it gently... and give her room to breathe...

WOMAN: Let's have something to cover her with... she's shivering with the cold...

OTHER MAN: I left my cloak at home…

MAN: Move aside there… Help me to lay her out…

OTHER MAN: And now be quiet and let her recover.

MARY: (*As if in a dream*) Who are you, up there, young man, I seem to know you. What is it that you want from me?

WOMAN: She's talking in her sleep, she's confused… she's having visions…

GABRIEL: I am Gabriel, the Angel of the Lord. I am he, oh Virgin, the herald of your solitary and delicate love.

MARY: Go spread your wings, Gabriel. Return to the radiant joys of Heaven, for there is nothing for you on this vile earth, in this tormented world. Go, so that you do not soil your wings, with their feathers coloured in gentle colours… Don't you see the mud… and the blood… dung and filth…? It's like a sewer… Go, so that your delicate ears are not burst asunder with this desperate crying, the pleading and weeping that arises on all sides. Go, so that you do not sear your bright eyes looking at sores and scabs and boils and flies and worms creeping forth from torn bodies of the dead.

   You are not used to this, because in Paradise you have no wailing and lamentation, or wars, or prisons, or men hanged, or women raped. In Paradise there is no hunger, no starvation, nobody sweating with work, wearing themselves to the bone, no children without smiles, no women out of their minds with grief, nobody who suffers to pay the price of original sin. Go, Gabriel, go, Gabriel.

GABRIEL: Grief-stricken woman, whom suffering has struck even in her belly, now I understand clearly… Now that this torment has seized you, seeing the young Lord God nailed up… at this moment, I too understand, just like you…

MARY: You understand, just like me, just like me? Gabriel, did you bear my son in your swelling belly? Did you bite your lip so as not to scream with pain while giving birth to him? Did you feed him? Did you give him the milk from your breast, Gabriel? Did you suffer when he was sick with fever, when he was down with measles, and did you stay up all night comforting him when he was crying with his first teeth? No, Gabriel? Well, if you didn't go through all that, then you cannot speak of sharing my grief at this moment...

GABRIEL: You're right, Mary... Forgive my presumption. I said it because my heart is breaking within me. I, who thought that I was above all suffering. But I come to remind you that it is just this, your song, this lament without a voice, this plaint without sobs, this, your sacrifice, and the sacrifice of your son, which will tear apart the heavens, and which will enable men for the first time to enter Paradise!

APPENDIX

Different cultures might produce different versions of Mistero Buffo. *This edition therefore includes a section from Stuart Hood's own Lallans translation, taken from* The Resurrection of Lazarus.

He's comin. He's comin. He's here.
Wha is he? What ane is he?
Jesus!
What ane?
The wan wi the black face? I dinna like the way he glowers.
No, no. That yin's Mark.
The yin ahint?
The big yin?
No, the wee yin.
The hauflin?
The ane wi the baird ana.
He luiks like a hauflin tae me, dammit if he disna.
Luik! There aa there!
Hey John. I ken him — John. John! Jesus. A real nice face, Jesus.
Luik! there's the Madonna as weel. There's aa his kith and kin. He's aye got them aa wi him.
They dinna let him gae about alane — he's no richt i the heid.
Jesus! Oh I like that yin. He gied me a wink anna!
Jesus, Jesus, dae that miracle wi the laifs and the fishes like that ither time whan they were that guid.
Whaur's the tomb?
Eh? — it's yon ane there.
Oh luik, he's tauld them tae tak aff the muckle stane.

No, I'll nae get down on my knees. I dinna haud wi that.
  That's great.
Wheesht!
Lat me see!
No, get affen that chair!
No, lat me up. I need tae see.
Jesus. Luik. They've taen up the muckle stane. There's the
  deid man, he's in there — it's Lazarus stinkan. Feech!
What's that awfa stink?
Christ!
Whit's wrang?
Wheesht!
Lat me see!
He's fou o wurms — o creepie-crawlies. Feech! He maun
  hae been deid a month — he's a fa'in apairt. That's a fine
  thing they've dun tae him. Tae Jesus. It's nae joke. I fear
  he'll no manage this time, pair thing.
I'm sure he'll no manage it, he canna dae it! There's nae
  wey he cin mak him come oot. He's stinkan rotten.
  That's a fine thing — tellin him he wasna deid mare nor
  three days! It's a month an mair. That's a fine like thing.
  Puir Jesus!
I say he'll manage aa the same, that yin's a haily man at cin
  dae the miracle even if they've been stinkan for a month
  and mair.
And I say he canna.
Will ye wager?
I'll wager anna!
Richt than! Saxpence! A sheelin. Fitever ye like.
I'll haud them. Dae ye trust me? He dis. We aa trust each
  ither. Fine than, I'll tak the money.
Richt than, tak tent though. Doun on yer knees, aabody.
Fit's he daein?
He's there prayin.
Wheesht will ye?
Hey there, Lazarus, git up noo.
Oh, he cin haud forth and he cin sing if he likes — aa at'll
  come oot is the worms he's fou o.
Git up, I bid ye!

Wheesht! he's up on his knees.
Wha? Jesus?
No! Lazarus. God, luik at that.
Get awa wi ye it's nae possible.
Lat me see.
Luik, luik — he's waukin, he's fa'en doon. He's staunan!
  On his twa feet.
A meeracle! Oh, it's a meeracle anna. Oh Jesus, ye're a
  great ane and I didna believe.
Weel duin, Jesus.
I hae won the wager. Gie's the money. Dinna try ony tricks
  wi me!
Weel duin, Jesus.
My purse, they've stawn my purse. Thief!
Weel duin, Jesus.
Thief!
Weel duin, Jesus. Jesus! Weel duin! Thief...

Accidental Death of an Anarchist

translated by Ed Emery

Characters

INSPECTOR BERTOZZO
MANIAC
CONSTABLES
INSPECTOR IN THE SPORTS JACKET
SUPERINTENDENT
MARIA FELETTI

Translator's note

This is the third version of *Accidental Death...* to be published by Methuen Drama. The previous editions (Belt and Braces, and Cummings/Supple) were both heavily adapted from the original text. In this translation I have chosen to stay close to Fo's original, maintaining the original references.

I have also, by the way, avoided the over-use of Very Rude Words, which may or may not be characteristic of the constabulary world-wide, but which are not characteristic of Dario Fo.

There is by now a tradition with the staging of Fo's plays: theatre companies take the original texts and adapt the political and cultural references to suit their own circumstances. You are invited to use your own imagination and creativity accordingly.

ED EMERY

Prologue

We wish to make it clear that the dialogue in this play is based on a reconstruction of authentic documents from the Pinelli case. There was no need to invent any of the situations that you will find represented here.

> *There is no greater equaliser than the stupidity of men –*
> *especially when those men have power.*

A point worth noting:

At the moment that the anarchist was about to plunge from the window down onto the pavement where Pinelli had fallen, there was a group of journalists present, from various major Milan-based newspapers. These journalists were coming from a press conference that had been taking place at police headquarters.

ACT ONE

Scene One

An ordinary room at central police headquarters. A desk, a filing cabinet, a cupboard, a few chairs and a coat-stand on which are hanging a dark overcoat and a black hat. There are also a typewriter, a telephone, a window, and a door on either side of the stage. On-stage, INSPECTOR BERTOZZO *and a* POLICE CONSTABLE *are engaged in interrogating a man: the* MANIAC.[1]

INSPECTOR BERTOZZO: (*As he flicks through a pile of paperwork, he turns to the* MANIAC, *who is seated, calm and relaxed*) Ha, so this isn't the first time you've passed yourself off as someone else! Here it says that you've been caught twice posing as a surgeon, once as a captain in the bersaglieri... three times as a bishop... once as a marine engineer... in all you've been arrested... let's see... two plus three, five... one, two... three... eleven times in all... So this makes the twelfth.

MANIAC: Correct. Arrested twelve times... But I must point out, Inspector, arrested, but never found guilty... My record is clean!

INSPECTOR BERTOZZO: Well... I can't imagine how you've managed to duck out of it every time... But I can assure you you're going to get a dirty record *this* time: you can count on it!

MANIAC: I know how you feel, Inspector: a spotless record just waiting to be sullied – it would make anyone's mouth water.

INSPECTOR BERTOZZO: Very funny... According to your charge sheet, you were arrested while passing yourself off as a psychiatrist, a lecturer, formerly teaching at the University of Padova... Trading under false pretences... You do realise that you could go to prison for that?

MANIAC: Certainly – false pretences perpetrated by a *sane* person. But I'm mad, Inspector: certified mad! Look, I've got my medical record, here: sixteen times in the nuthouse... and always for the same reason. I have a thing about dreaming up characters and then acting them out. It's called 'histrionomania' – comes from the Latin *histriones*, meaning 'actor'. I'm a sort of amateur performance artist. With the difference that I go for 'Théâtre Vérité' – my fellow performers need to be real people, but people who don't realise that they're in my plays. Which is just as well, 'cos I've got no money and couldn't pay them anyway... I applied to the Arts Council for a grant, but since I don't have political backing...

INSPECTOR BERTOZZO: You had the nerve to charge two hundred thousand lire for a single consultation...

CONSTABLE: (*Standing behind the* MANIAC) Jesus!

MANIAC: A reasonable rate for any self-respecting psychiatrist... Sixteen years studying before you qualify!

INSPECTOR BERTOZZO: Sure, but when did *you* ever study psychiatry?

MANIAC: Sixteen years I've studied... Thousands of lunatics like myself... day after day... And at night too! Because, unlike your normal psychiatrist, I slept with them... Often as not, three to a bed, because there's always a shortage of beds these days.

Anyway, feel free to check. I think you'll find that my diagnosis for the poor schizophrenic I was arrested for was spot-on.

INSPECTOR BERTOZZO: Your two hundred thousand lire was pretty spot-on too!

MANIAC: But Inspector, I had to... it was for his own good!

INSPECTOR BERTOZZO: Ah, for his own good, eh? So a big bill's part of the cure?

MANIAC: Sure! If I hadn't stung him for two hundred thousand, do you really think the poor bastard, and more particularly his family, would have been satisfied? If I'd asked for a mere fifty thousand, they'd have thought: 'He can't be a lot of use. Maybe he's not a real professor. Must be newly qualified...' But this way, it knocked them sideways and they thought: 'Who is this man? God Almighty?' And off they went, happy... They even kissed my hand... 'Thank you, Professor...' Kissy-kissy-kissy.

INSPECTOR BERTOZZO: I'll say this – you run a good line in patter!

MANIAC: It's true, though, Inspector. Even Freud says: 'Be you sick, be you ill, the best cure is a big fat bill – for the patient *and* for the doctor!'

INSPECTOR BERTOZZO: Now, let's take a look at your visiting card... (*He shows the card*) If I'm not mistaken, it says here: Professor Antonio Rabbi, psychiatrist. Formerly lecturer at the University of Padova... Come on, now, talk your way out of that one...!

MANIAC: First of all, I really am a lecturer... I teach drawing, actually... Decorative, free-hand, I do evening classes at the Church of the Holy Redeemer...

INSPECTOR BERTOZZO: I'm impressed, my compliments! But it says here: 'Psychiatrist'!

MANIAC: Well done – but after the full stop! Are you familiar with the rules of grammar and punctuation? Read it properly: Professor Antonio Rabbi. Full stop. Then there's a capital P. Psychiatrist! Now look, you can't tell me it's going under false pretences to say: 'psychiatrist.' I presume you're familiar with the grammar of the Italian language? Yes? Well in that case you should know that if a person writes 'archaeologist' it doesn't mean he's studied – it's like saying 'stamp collector', 'vegetarian', 'chronic arthritic'...

INSPECTOR BERTOZZO: Yes, but what about this: 'Formerly lecturer at the University of Padova'?

MANIAC: I'm sorry, now *you're* the one trading under false pretences: you just told me that you knew the rules of grammar and punctuation, and now it turns out that you can't even read properly...

INSPECTOR BERTOZZO: I can't even *what*...?!

MANIAC: Didn't you see the comma after the 'formerly'?

INSPECTOR BERTOZZO: Oh yes... You're right. I didn't notice it.

MANIAC: So you didn't notice it! You didn't notice it, and just for that you'd send an innocent man to prison?

INSPECTOR BERTOZZO: You're really mental, you know... What's a comma got to do with anything?

MANIAC: Nothing, for someone who knows nothing about grammar...! I think you should come clean – I want to see your school reports... Who was responsible for promoting you... (*The* INSPECTOR *tries to interrupt him*) Let me finish...! Remember, the comma is the key to everything! If there's a comma after the 'formerly', the whole meaning of the phrase changes.

The comma indicates a pause for breath... a brief hiatus... because 'the comma always indicates a change of intentionality.' So it goes like this: 'Formerly', and here we could do with a sarcastic sneer, and if you want to add an ironic chuckle, all the better! 'Formerly...' (*He grimaces and gives a high-pitched laugh*) 'Lecturer at the University, another comma, of Padova...' It's like it's saying: 'Come on, what do you take me for... Pull the other one... Only an idiot would fall for that!

INSPECTOR BERTOZZO: So I'm an idiot, am I?

MANIAC: No, you're just a bit short on grammar... I could give you lessons if you like. Do you a decent price... I say we start straight away... there's a lot of ground to make up. Recite me a list of the personal pronouns.

INSPECTOR BERTOZZO: Will you stop pissballing about! I think we can all agree that you've got performance mania, but I'd say you're just pretending to be mental... I'd lay money you're as sane as me!

MANIAC: Hmm, I don't know about that. Mind you, being a policeman does funny things to the brain... Let's have a look at your eye, a moment.

He presses down his lower eyelid with his thumb.

INSPECTOR BERTOZZO: Will you stop that! Let's get on with your statement!

MANIAC: I could type it myself, if you like, I'm a qualified typist, forty-five words a minute...

INSPECTOR BERTOZZO: Stay right where you are or I'll have the handcuffs on you!

MANIAC: You can't! Straitjacket or nothing. I'm mad, and if you put handcuffs on me... Article 122 of the Penal Code states: 'Any public official applying non-clinical or non-psychiatric instruments of restraint on a psychologically disturbed person, thereby resulting in a worsening of his condition, commits a crime punishable by five to fifteen years imprisonment, and loss of pension and rank.'

INSPECTOR BERTOZZO: Read up on the law, have we?!

MANIAC: Know it inside out. Studied it for twenty years!

INSPECTOR BERTOZZO: Where did you study law?

MANIAC: In the nuthouse! Very good for studying, you've no idea! There was a paranoid clerk to the court who gave me lessons. A genius, he was! I know it all. Roman law, Italian law, ecclesiastical law... The Justinian code... the Frederican... the Lombard... the Greek Orthodox... the lot! Try me with a few questions!

INSPECTOR BERTOZZO: No thank you. Can we get on. It

says nothing in your CV about your being a lawyer!

MANIAC: Ah, no, I'd never want to be a lawyer. Defence never was my style. Too passive. I prefer sitting in judgement... handing down sentences... coming down like a ton of bricks! I'm one of yours, Inspector. You can call me Antonio, if you like.

INSPECTOR BERTOZZO: You just watch your step... I've had enough of you taking the mickey.

MANIAC: Alright, alright...

INSPECTOR BERTOZZO: Now this might be interesting. Have you ever passed yourself off as a judge?

MANIAC: No, unfortunately. Chance never arose. I'd love to, though: best job in the world! First of all, they hardly ever retire... In fact, just at the point when your average working man, at the age of 55 or 60, is already ready for the scrapheap because he's slowing down a bit, losing his reflexes, your judge is just coming into his prime. A worker on the line's done for after the age of fifty – can't keep up, keeps having accidents, chuck him out...! Your miner has silicosis by the time he's 45 – get rid of him, quick, sack him before he sues for compensation! Same goes for the bank clerk, after a certain age he starts getting his sums wrong, starts forgetting the names of the bank's clients, can't tell a discount rate from a mortgage rate. Off home, you... move along, son... You're past it...! For a judge it's quite the opposite: the more ancient and idio... (*He corrects himself*) ...syncratic they are, the higher they get promoted, the classier the jobs they get! You see them up there, little old men like cardboard cutouts, silly wigs on their heads, all capes and ermine... with two pairs of glasses on cords round their necks because otherwise they'd lose them... And these characters have the power to wreck a person's life or save it, as and how they want: they hand out life sentences like somebody saying: 'Maybe it'll rain tomorrow...' Fifty years for you... Thirty for you... Only twenty for you, because I like your face! They make the law and they can do what they like... And they're holy too...

Don't forget, in Italy you can still be done for slander if you say nasty things about judges… In Italy… and in Saudi Arabia! Ah, yes, yes… The judge is the job for me – what a role! What wouldn't I give to be able to play a judge just once in my life? An Appeal Court judge would be lovely! 'Your Honour… this way please… silence in court… please be upstanding for the judge… Oh dear, lost our marbles, have we, Sir? I'll let you know if I find them…'

INSPECTOR BERTOZZO: Right. Now are you going to stop this nonsense? You're doing my brain in. Sit down! Right there. And shut up.

He pushes him towards the chair.

MANIAC: (*Reacting hysterically*) Hands off or I'll bite!

INSPECTOR BERTOZZO: What do you mean, bite?

MANIAC: You. I'll bite *you*. On the neck *and* on your gluteus maximus! Nyung…! And piss-all you can do about it. Article 122b: 'Provocation and violence towards a person of diminished responsibility.' Six to nine years, with loss of pension!

INSPECTOR BERTOZZO: Sit down, or I'm going to lose my temper! (*To the* CONSTABLE) And what are you doing standing there like a prat? Sit him down!

CONSTABLE: But he bites, sir!

MANIAC: Precisely. Grrr! Grrr! …And I should warn you, I've got rabies. Got it from a dog… A rabid mongrel who took off half my bum. He died, I survived. Survived, but I'm still infected: grrr grrr! Woof, woof!

INSPECTOR BERTOZZO: That's all we bloody needed – not only is he away with the mixer, he's got rabies too! Right, are we going to take your statement or not? Come on, be a good chap! Then I'll let you go… promise…!

MANIAC: Oh no, don't throw me out, Inspector. I feel safe here with you… I feel protected, somehow! Life's so dangerous out there on the street… People are so horrible… Driving around in their cars, hooting their horns, screeching their brakes… And going on strike! Then you've got trams and subway carriages with their doors shutting all of a sudden… Squish…! Keep me here with you… I can help you get confessions out of your suspects… And subversives… I know how to make nitroglycerine suppositories…!

INSPECTOR BERTOZZO: Right. Shut! Up!

MANIAC: Inspector, either you let me stay here with you, or I'm going to throw myself out of the window… What floor are we on? The third…? One short, but it'll do. I'm going to jump, and when I'm down there, splattered on the pavement, groaning in my death agony… because I assure you it won't be an easy death… I'll groan and I'll scream and I'll tell the journalists that it was *you* who threw me out. Here we go!

He runs to the window.

INSPECTOR BERTOZZO: (*He tries to stop him*) Please! Stop it! (*To the* CONSTABLE) Put the catch on that window!

MANIAC: Alright, then, I'll throw myself down the stairwell.

He runs to the door.

INSPECTOR BERTOZZO: Oh for God's sake! Now I've *really* had enough! Sit down! (*He pushes him onto a chair, and then addresses the* CONSTABLE) You, lock the door… take the key and…

MANIAC: …throw it out of the window…

The CONSTABLE *goes towards the window, in a daze.*

INSPECTOR BERTOZZO: Yes, throw it… NO… Put it in the drawer… close the drawer… take the key out…

The CONSTABLE *moves mechanically, doing as instructed.*

MANIAC: …put it in your mouth and swallow it!

INSPECTOR BERTOZZO: No, no, no, NO…! *Nobody* gives me the run-around! (*To the* CONSTABLE) Give me that key. (*He opens the door to show the* MANIAC *out*) Get out, go, leave…! And throw yourself down the stairs if you want… Do what you like… Get out, or I'll be the one going crazy!

He pushes him out of the room.

MANIAC: No, Inspector… Have a heart… Don't push like that…

INSPECTOR BERTOZZO: Get out! (*Having finally succeeded in getting rid of the* MANIAC, *he closes the door*) Oh, at last!

CONSTABLE: Don't forget, Inspector, you've got a meeting with Dr Bellati, and we're five minutes late already.

INSPECTOR BERTOZZO: Eh? What time is it? (*He looks at his watch*) Oh for God's sake! That imbecile has left me so's I don't know if I'm coming or going… Come on, we'd better get a move on…

They leave the room. The MANIAC *peeks in at the other door.*

MANIAC: Yoo-hoo, Inspector… Can I come in? Don't be angry. I've only come back to pick up my papers… Not talking to me, eh? Oh come on, no hard feelings… Pax… Well, look at that, not a soul in sight. I'll just have to help myself… (*He does so*) Medical record… visiting card… Oh look, here's my charge sheet too…. Too bad, tear it up, there you go, nice knowing you. (*He picks up more papers*) Another charge sheet. Who's this one? (*He reads*) 'Burglary…' A trifle, a trifle… You're free! (*He tears it up*) And what did you do? (*He reads it*) 'Taking and driving away… insulting behaviour…' Rubbish… Off you go, son, you're free! (*He tears it up*) Free, the lot of you! (*He pauses to read one of the sheets*) No, not you… You're an arsehole… You can stay… You're going to do time! (*He places the sheet in a prominent position on the desk and then opens the cupboard, which is bulging with files*) Nobody move… the Day of Judgement has arrived! Amazing! Would these all happen to be charge sheets? How would it be if I put a match to the lot of them…? (*He pulls out a* *cigarette lighter and is about to set fire to a bundle of papers when he reads the title page*) 'Judge's Report on the Death of the...' (*The he reads the label on another bundle*) 'Judge's Decision to Adjourn the Inquest of...'

Just at this moment, the phone rings. The MANIAC *answers it.*

Hello, Inspector Bertozzo's office... Who's calling? No, I'm sorry, I can't get him for you if you won't tell me who's calling... Well fancy that... the Inspector... Himself in person?! I don't believe it! Oh come on! What a pleasure... Inspector Defenestra...! No, nothing, nothing... And where are you calling from? Oh, of course, how silly of me, from the fourth floor... Where else? Anyway, what do you want with Bertozzo? No, he's busy at the moment, so you'll have to tell me. What's that? A High Court judge is being sent up specially from Rome...? If you ask me, he's being sent up to re-open the case of the death of the anarchist. Sure – it must be because Rome's not happy with the way the original inquest was put on hold when the judge adjourned it. That's what you've heard as well? Oh, it's only a rumour... I thought as much... First it suits them to a T, and then they have second thoughts... Of course, of course, they're responding to the pressure of public opinion... Do me a favour! When did they ever give a damn for public opinion... Exactly, and here's Bertozzo, laughing like a drain. (*He moves the phone away slightly and laughs*) Ha, ha! And making rude gestures... Ha, ha! (*He pretends to call over to* BERTOZZO) Bertozzo, our friend on the fourth floor says it's all very well for you to start cackling, you're not stuck in the middle... But he and his boss are in deep shit... (*He pretends to be* BERTOZZO *laughing*) Ha, ha... He's suggesting that you'd best keep your heads up! Ha, ha... No, this time it's me who's laughing! Frankly, I'd be very happy to see your boss the Superintendent up to his neck in it... Yes, I mean it sincerely, and you can tell him I said so... Inspector Anghiari – that's me, by the way – would be *delighted*... And so would Bertozzo, listen to him laughing. (*He holds the phone away from him*) Ha, ha! You hear that...? And who cares if they flush you down the pan... Yes, you can tell him that too: Anghiari and Bertozzo couldn't give a shit! (*He lets out a tremendous raspberry*) Prrruttt. Yes, it was Bertozzo who did the raspberry. Alright, no need to get hysterical...! Good man, we'll talk about it when we meet. So, what was it you were wanting from Bertozzo? What documents? Yes, you tell me, and I'll write them down. The copy of the judge's reasons for putting the anarchist's inquest on hold... Fine, I think we can provide that... And the copies of the statements... yes, yes, it's all here in the archive... Oh yes, quite right, you're going to have to start doing your homework... you and that ex-concentration camp commandant boss of yours... If the judge who's coming is even half as much a stickler for procedure as they say... Know him? Of course I know him! His name's Malipiero, Judge Malipiero. Never heard of him? Well, you will. As it happens, he spent time in a concentration camp during the War – on the receiving end... You should ask your boss, maybe he remembers seeing him there. OK, I'll get the stuff to you right away.

See you... Wait, wait! Ha, ha, Bertozzo just said something really funny... You won't blow a fuse if I tell you, will you? You sure? Alright then, I'll tell you. He said... Ha, ha... by the time this visiting judge's finished with you, they'll probably give you a nice posting down in the South somewhere, Vibo Valentia in Calabria, maybe... where the police station only has one floor and the inspector's office is in the basement... Ha, ha... you get it? In the basement! Ha, ha! Ha, ha, you like that? You didn't like it? OK, save it for another day. (*He listens to the voice on the phone*) Fine, I'll tell him straight away. Bertozzo, the soon-to-be-Calabrian inspector [2] at the other end of the line tells me when he catches up with the pair of us, he's going to give us a punch on the nose! Roger, message received, prrruttt (*A raspberry*) from both of us, over and out!

The MANIAC puts down the phone and returns to rifling through the papers.

'To work, your Honour, because time is getting short.' God, I've come over all hot flushes! If I manage to persuade them that I really *am* a High Court judge... if they don't tumble me... it'll be a cracker! Let's see now, first of all, find a walk... (*He tries a walk with a slight limp*) No, that's the clerk of the court. (*He tries another*) Arthritic, but dignified! There, not bad, with a bit of a crick in the neck... like a retired circus horse... (*He tries it, but then decides against it*)

No, I think I'd prefer the 'palais glide', with the little twitch at the end. (*He tries it*) Not bad! And the 'wobbly knee'? (*He tries it*) Or maybe a stiff knee, grasshopper style. (*He tries it. Short sharp steps, rocking from heel to toe*) What about the glasses... No, no glasses. The right eye closed a bit... there, that's right, slight squint when reading, man of few words... a bit of a cough: cough, cough! No, no cough... How about a twitch? Hmmm, we'll see how it feels come the time. A bit of a smoothie, maybe, nasal tone, jovial sort: 'No! My dear Superintendent, you're going to have to stop that, you're no¹ running a concentration camp now, you know – you should remember that once in a while!'

No, I think I'd prefer something different: cold, detached, short-shrift, bit of a drone, slightly shortsighted, gloomy sort... has glasses, but only uses one lens: like so.

He tries this out, as he sorts through a few papers.

Well, look at that! Brilliant! Just what I was looking for! Hey, calm down, son... Back in character, if you don't mind! All present and correct? Let's see: the judge's reasons for adjourning the inquiry into the anarchist's death... Ha, and here's the police report into the anarchist group in Rome, the one that was run by the male dancer... Very good!

He places all the documents in his bag. He goes over to the coat-stand and puts on the black overcoat and the dark hat that are hanging there. Re-enter INSPECTOR BERTOZZO. *He doesn't recognise him in this guise, and is momentarily taken aback.*

INSPECTOR BERTOZZO: Hello, can I help you? Are you looking for someone?

MANIAC: No one at all, Inspector. I've just come back to get my papers...

INSPECTOR BERTOZZO: What – you again? Get out!!!

MANIAC: Please, just because you're in a bad mood, no need to take it out on me.

INSPECTOR BERTOZZO: Get out!

He pushes him towards the door.

MANIAC: Oh for God's sake! You're all neurotic in here! First there was that lunatic who's going round looking for you, to smash your face in.

INSPECTOR BERTOZZO: (*This stops him in his tracks*) Who's that? Who's going round looking for me?

MANIAC: A character in a white roll-neck. [3] Hasn't he given you a smack in the gob yet?

INSPECTOR BERTOZZO: A smack in the gob?

MANIAC: That's what he said, I said.

INSPECTOR BERTOZZO: Listen, I think I've wasted enough time with you. Would you do me a favour? Piss off, and don't come back!

MANIAC: What, never, never, never? (*He mimes blowing him kisses. The* SUPERINTENDENT *reacts irritatedly*) Take my advice – next time you meet the Inspector from upstairs, you'd best duck!

He exits. INSPECTOR BERTOZZO *gives a great sigh of relief, and then goes over to the coat-stand. He sees it is empty.*

INSPECTOR BERTOZZO: (*Running after him*) Huh – the bastard! He goes round pretending to be mad, and then he steals your overcoat...! Hey, you! (*He stops the* CONSTABLE, *who enters at this moment*) Quick, get after that head-case... the one who just left... he's gone out with my coat... and my hat... and probably my briefcase too... That's right, that was mine too! Quick, before he gets away!

CONSTABLE: At once, Sir... (*He goes to the door, but then stops. He speaks to someone outside the door*) Yes, Sir, he's in his office.

INSPECTOR BERTOZZO: (*He rummages around to find the sheets that were torn up by the* MANIAC) Where the hell have those charge sheets gone?

CONSTABLE: Inspector Bertozzo, the Inspector from the Special Branch upstairs would like a word with you.

INSPECTOR BERTOZZO *raises his head from the desk, gets up, and goes over to the door.*

INSPECTOR BERTOZZO: Hello, there...! I was talking about you just a moment ago, with some nutter, who said... Ha, ha, can you imagine it... He said the next time you see me, you're going to give me... (*From outside the door we see a rapid movement of somebody's arm.* BERTOZZO *receives a punch in the face, which sends him reeling as he completes his sentence*) ...a smack in the gob!

He falls to the ground. The MANIAC *peers in through the opposite door and shouts:*

MANIAC: I told you to duck!

Blackout. A musical interlude: a march in the style of the 'Entry of the Clowns'. This continues for as long as is necessary to change the scene.

Scene Two

The lights come up, and we find ourselves in an office which is very similar to the previous one. The furniture is more or less the same, although arranged differently. On the wall at the back of the stage hangs a large portrait of the Italian President. There is also a large window, which is wide open. On stage are a CONSTABLE, *and the* MANIAC, *who is standing facing the window, with his back to the door. After a moment, enter the* INSPECTOR FROM THE FOURTH FLOOR. *He is wearing a sports jacket and a roll-neck sweater.*

SPORTS JACKET: (*Murmuring to the* CONSTABLE *standing at the door*) What does he want? Who is he?

CONSTABLE: I don't know, Sir. He came sweeping in here like he was God Almighty. He says that he wants to talk with you and the Superintendent.

SPORTS JACKET: (*He is continuously massaging his right hand*) Wants to talk, does he? (*He goes over to the* MANIAC) Good morning, I gather you want to see me.

MANIAC: (*He looks him up and down, coolly, and barely moves his hand to raise his hat*) Good morning. (*He watches curiously as the* INSPECTOR IN THE SPORTS JACKET *continues massaging his hand*) What have you done to your hand?

SPORTS JACKET: Er, nothing... Who are you?

MANIAC: Nothing, eh? So why do you keep rubbing it? An affectation, is it? Or is it a nervous tic?

The INSPECTOR IN THE SPORTS JACKET *becomes impatient.*

SPORTS JACKET: Could be... I said, with whom do I have the pleasure...?

MANIAC: I knew a bishop once who used to rub his hand like that. A Jesuit.

SPORTS JACKET: Are you suggesting...?

MANIAC: (*Ignoring his reply*) You should see a psychiatrist. When people keep rubbing their hands like that it's a sure sign of insecurity... guilt complex... and a lousy sex life. Do you have problems with women, perhaps?

SPORTS JACKET: (*Losing his temper*) Right! That'll do!

He bangs his fist on the desk.

MANIAC: (*Referring to his gesture*) Impulsive! There's the proof! Tell me the truth – it isn't a tic at all, is it...? You've just given someone a right-hander, haven't you? Come on – own up!

SPORTS JACKET: What d'you mean, 'own up'? Would you

mind telling me who you are? And among other things, you might care to remove your hat!

MANIAC: You're right. (*He removes his hat with studied slowness*) I hope you don't think I was being rude, keeping it on... It's just that you've got the window wide open... and I have a real problem with draughts. Don't you? Would you mind if we closed it?

SPORTS JACKET: Yes I would!

MANIAC: Oops, sorry I spoke! Pleased to meet you. Professor Marco Maria Malipiero, first counsel to the High Court...

SPORTS JACKET: (*Taken aback*) Oh I see...

MANIAC: (*Ironically, aggressively*) What do you see?

SPORTS JACKET: Nothing, nothing.

MANIAC: Precisely... (*Once again aggressive*) You see nothing! Who was it told you that I was supposed to be arriving to take a second look into the business of the anarchist's death?

SPORTS JACKET: (*In a tight spot*) Well, actually... I...

MANIAC: I'd like the truth, please... I get terribly upset when people lie to me... I have a tic too, see... here in my neck, and when people lie to me, look, it starts to twitch.... look, see? So, did you know I was coming, or didn't you?

SPORTS JACKET: (*Swallowing nervously*) Yes, I did know... But we weren't expecting you so soon... actually...

MANIAC: Of course – and that's precisely why the Supreme Court decided that I should come up early... We too have our informants, you know. And so we've caught you on the hop, eh? Does this worry you?

SPORTS JACKET: No, no, of course not...(*The MANIAC points to the nerve twitching in his neck*) ...Oh, alright, yes, it does... (*He shows him to a chair*) Sit down, please... Can I take your hat for you...? (*He takes it, but then has second thoughts*) Or maybe you'd prefer to keep it...?

MANIAC: No, no, help yourself, it isn't mine anyway.

SPORTS JACKET: Eh? (*He goes towards the window*) Would you like me to shut the window?

MANIAC: Not at all. Don't put yourself out on my account. I wonder, would you mind calling in the Superintendent... I'd like to start as soon as possible.

SPORTS JACKET: Certainly... But wouldn't it be better if we all went to his office. It's a bit more comfortable.

MANIAC: I'm sure it is. But it was in this office that the unfortunate business with the anarchist happened, wasn't it?

SPORTS JACKET: Yes, it was.

MANIAC: (*Flinging his arms open*) Well, then!

He sits down and takes a number of documents from INSPECTOR BERTOZZO's *briefcase. He also has another, enormous bag with him, from which he pulls an assortment of odds and ends: a magnifying glass, a pair of tweezers, a stapler, a judge's wooden gavel and a copy of the Penal Code. Over by the door the* INSPECTOR IN THE SPORTS JACKET *is talking quietly to the* CONSTABLE.

MANIAC: (*As he continues putting his papers in order*) If you don't mind, Inspector, I'll have no whispering while I'm here. Out loud, please!

SPORTS JACKET: I'm sorry. (*Turning to the* CONSTABLE) Ask the Superintendent to join us at once, if he can.

MANIAC: And even if he can't.

The INSPECTOR IN THE SPORTS JACKET *corrects himself.*

SPORTS JACKET: Yes, even if he can't.

CONSTABLE: (*He exits*) Yessir...

SPORTS JACKET: (*For a moment he watches as the* JUDGE *orders his papers and pins a number of sheets up on the side wall, on the flaps of the shutters, and on the cupboard. All* *of a sudden he remembers something)* Oh yes... The statements! (*He picks up the phone and dials a number*) Hello, get me Bertozzo... Where's he gone? Upstairs to see the Superintendent?

He replaces the handset, then picks it up again to dial another number. The MANIAC interrupts him.

MANIAC: Pardon my interrupting, Inspector...

SPORTS JACKET: Yes, your honour...?

MANIAC: This Inspector Bertozzo that you're so concerned about, would he maybe have something to do with the re-opening of the anarchist's inquest?

SPORTS JACKET: Yes... no... I mean, well, since he's the one with all the paperwork...

MANIAC: We don't need it... I have everything we need here, so why bother getting a second copy?

SPORTS JACKET: Well I suppose we could do without.

From off-stage we hear the angry voice of the SUPERINTENDENT. He comes flying into the office with CONSTABLE following close behind looking embarrassed.

SUPERINTENDENT: What exactly did you mean by that, Inspector, to come to your office if I can, and even if I can't?

SPORTS JACKET: I'm sorry, Super... It's just that since...

SUPERINTENDENT: Just that since be damned! You're getting too damn big for your boots, d'you know that? What's more, I'm not at all amused by your insolent style of behaviour... Especially when it comes to punching your colleagues in the face!

SPORTS JACKET: But Superintendent... Didn't Bertozzo tell you about the raspberry and his moronic joke about one-storey police stations in Calabria?

The MANIAC pretends to be sorting out his paperwork. He suddenly ducks beneath the edge of the desk, and then re-emerges.

SUPERINTENDENT: Raspberries!! Look, let's not start behaving like children. We need to keep on our toes... we're in the hot seat now. (*The* INSPECTOR IN THE SPORTS JACKET*signals to him desperately, in an attempt to shut him up*) ...with all these bloody journalists running round making insinuations... telling lies... and don't try to shut me up, because I believe in speaking my mind and I don't care who... (*The* INSPECTOR IN THE SPORTS JACKET *gestures towards the* JUDGE, *who pretends to be absorbed in something else*) Ah, yes...! And who's this, for God's sake?! A journalist? Why didn't you tell me...

MANIAC: (*Without raising his eyes from his paperwork*) No, Superintendent, don't worry, I'm not a journalist... There won't be any nonsense like that, I can assure you.

SUPERINTENDENT: I'm very glad to hear it.

MANIAC: This young man here, who, in my opinion, is rather too irritable for his own good, and who, as I gather from your conversation, also appears to be allergic to raspberries... (*Confidentially, taking him aside*) A word of advice, Superintendent... speaking as a father: this boy needs a good psychiatrist... You should take him to see this friend of mine... He's a genius. (*He hands him a visiting card*) Professor Antonio Rabbi... ex lecturer... watch out for the comma...

SUPERINTENDENT: (*Not knowing how to disengage himself*) Thank you, but if you'll allow me, I...

MANIAC: (*Suddenly changing tone*) Certainly I'll allow you... Sit down, and let's get started... By the way, did your colleague tell you that I...

SPORTS JACKET: Oh, I'm sorry, I forgot... (*To the* SUPERINTENDENT) This gentleman is Professor Marco Maria Malipiero, first counsel to the High Court...

MANIAC: I wouldn't insist on the 'first'... Let's just say 'one of the first'!

SPORTS JACKET: As you wish.

SUPERINTENDENT: (*Having difficulty recovering from the* *shock*) Your Honour... I really don't know...

SPORTS JACKET: (*Coming to his help*) His Honour the Judge is here to re-open the inquiry into the case of the ...

SUPERINTENDENT: (*In an unexpected reaction*) Oh of course, of course, we were expecting you!

MANIAC: You see, you see what a straightforward man your superior is? He prefers to play his cards openly! Learn from him! Another generation, another school, I would say!

SUPERINTENDENT: Another generation...!

MANIAC: Actually, if you don't mind my saying so, there's something very, how can I put it, familiar about you... As if we've met before somewhere... years ago. You wouldn't happen to have been in charge of some concentration camp during the War, would you?

SUPERINTENDENT: (*Stammering*) Concentration camp...?

MANIAC: No, no, of course not, what am I saying?! A man like yourself running a concentration camp? Unheard of! So, let's get down to business. (*He thumbs through his papers*) Right, now, according to these statements... On the evening of the... the date's immaterial... an anarchist, a railway shunter by profession, was right here in this room, being interrogated as to whether or not he had been involved in the bomb attack at the Milan Bank of Agriculture, which caused the death of sixteen innocent civilians. And here we have your precise words, Superintendent: 'There was strong evidence pointing in his direction'! Was that what you said?

SUPERINTENDENT: Well, yes, but that was only right at the start, your Honour... Later on...

MANIAC: We'll stick with the 'right at the start' for the moment... One step at a time. So, at about midnight, the anarchist was 'seized by a raptus' – these are still your words – he was seized by a 'raptus' and went and threw himself to his death from the window. Now, what is a 'raptus'? Bandieu says that a 'raptus' is a heightened form of suicidal anxiety which can seize even people who are psychologically perfectly normal, if something provokes them to extremes of angst, in other words, to utter desperation. Correct?

SUPERINTENDENT *and* **SPORTS JACKET:** Correct.

MANIAC: So we need to find out who or what it was provoked this anxiety, this desperation. I suspect that the best way would be if we do a reconstruction. Superintendent, the stage is yours.

SUPERINTENDENT: Me?

MANIAC: Yes, go ahead: would you mind re-enacting your famous entrance?

SUPERINTENDENT: I'm sorry, what famous…?

MANIAC: The one that brought about the 'raptus'.

SUPERINTENDENT: Your honour, there must be a misunderstanding here. It wasn't me who did the entrance, it was one of my officers…

MANIAC: Tut, tut, tut, it's not very nice to pass the buck to your subordinates. In fact I find it rather naughty… Come on, now, play your part…

SPORTS JACKET: I think I should explain, your Honour, it was just one of those tricks of the trade that the police occasionally use, to put pressure on a subject to confess.

MANIAC: Who asked your opinion? I was speaking with your superior! You should learn some manners. From now on, you only speak when spoken to… Understand? And now, Superintendent, I'd like to see you doing that entrance.

SUPERINTENDENT: Oh alright. It went more or less like this. Our anarchist suspect was sitting there, right where you're sitting now. My colleague – er, I mean, I – came in somewhat brusquely…

MANIAC: Well done!

SUPERINTENDENT: And I went for him!

MANIAC: That's what I like to hear!

SUPERINTENDENT: My dear railway shunter, not to mention subversive... You'd better stop making fun of me...

MANIAC: No, no... Stick to the script, please. (*He waves the statements*) No censorship here, if you don't mind... That wasn't quite what you said!

SUPERINTENDENT: Well, I said: 'Have you quite finished taking the piss?'

MANIAC: Well done. And then what did you say?

SUPERINTENDENT: We have evidence to prove that you were the one who planted the bombs at the station.

MANIAC: What bombs?

SUPERINTENDENT: (*In a lower tone, more discursive*) I'm talking about bombing on the twenty-fifth...

MANIAC: No, no, use the same words you used that evening. Imagine that I'm the anarchist railwayman. Come on, let's have you: 'What bombs?'

SUPERINTENDENT: Don't play dumb with me! You know very well what bombs. The ones you planted on the train at the Central Station eight months ago.

MANIAC: Did you really have this evidence?

SUPERINTENDENT: No, but as the Inspector was explaining just now, the police use these ploys every once in a while...

MANIAC: Aha... Shrewd move!

He slaps the SUPERINTENDENT *on the back, much to his surprise.*

SUPERINTENDENT: But we had our suspicions... Since the suspect was the only anarchist railwayman in Milan... there was a good chance it was him...

MANIAC: Absolutely – I agree... crystal clear. Since it's obvious that the bomb on the railway must have been planted by a railwayman, by the same logic we can say that the bombs at the Law Courts in Rome were planted by a judge, the bombs at the Monument to the Unknown Soldier were planted by a soldier, and the bomb at the Bank of Agriculture was planted by either a banker or a farmer, take your pick... (*He turns nasty*) Do me a favour, gentlemen... I'm here to conduct a serious inquiry, not to play cretinous word-games! So let's get on with it! Here it says: (*He reads from a sheet of paper*) 'The anarchist seemed unaffected by the accusation, and was smiling incredulously.' Who made that statement?

SPORTS JACKET: Me, you honour.

MANIAC: Well done. So he was smiling... But it also says here – and this is word for word what you said at the time: 'Undoubtedly one element in his suicidal crisis had been the fear of losing his job, of being sacked.' So? One minute he's smiling incredulously, and the next he's terrified? Who was it terrified him...? Who was it hit him with the bombshell that he was about to lose his job?

SPORTS JACKET: Er, well I, er...

MANIAC: Now look, please, there's no need to play coy with me. I know you're not running a girls' school here... I don't see why, when every police force in the world comes down like a ton of bricks, you have to be the only two going gently-gently. Don't you ever watch the police crime serials on TV? It's your absolute *right* to carry on like that. Of course it is!

SUPERINTENDENT and **SPORTS JACKET:** Thank you, your honour!

MANIAC: Don't mention it. Anyway, I realise it can be hard for you: you say to an anarchist: 'Things are looking pretty bad for you... Let's hope your employers don't find out you're an anarchist... Know what I mean? Otherwise bang goes your job on the railways...' And naturally he gets depressed... To tell the truth, anarchists are very attached to their jobs... Basically they're just petty bourgeois... attached to their little creature comforts... regular income every month, Christmas bonus, pension, health insurance, a peaceful old age... Believe me, there's no one like your anarchist for planning for his old age... I'm referring to your present-day anarchists, of course... your wishy-washy anarchists, not the real anarchists of yesteryear, the ones who were 'hounded by persecution from one country to the next...' Speaking of persecution, Superintendent...? Oh no, my goodness, what am I saying?! Anyway, to recapitulate, you put the anarchist in a state of terminal depression, blacken his day for him, and he throws himself out...

SPORTS JACKET: If you'll allow me, your Honour, it didn't happen straight away... There's still my contribution to come...

MANIAC: Ah yes, Inspector, you're right... First of all you went out. Then you came back in again... And after a dramatic pause, you said... Come on, Inspector, let's have your lines... Imagine that I'm the anarchist again...

SPORTS JACKET: Right, fine. (*He goes out of the door, and comes back in, playing his part*) 'I've just had a phone call from Rome... I've got a bit of news for you: your friend – sorry, your *comrade* – the dancer, has confessed... He's admitted that he was the one who planted the bomb at the bank in Milan.'

MANIAC: Was this true?

SPORTS JACKET: Of course not.

MANIAC: And how did our railwayman take this?

SPORTS JACKET: Badly, in fact. He went white as a sheet, asked for a cigarette... lit it...

MANIAC: And threw himself out of the window.

SUPERINTENDENT: No, not straight away, actually...

MANIAC: But you did say 'straight away' in the first version, didn't you?

SUPERINTENDENT: Yes, I did.

MANIAC: What's more, you yourself told the newspapers and the TV that before his tragic gesture, the anarchist was 'in a tight spot'. Was that what you said?

SUPERINTENDENT: Yes, 'in a tight spot'.

MANIAC: And what did you go on to say then...?

SUPERINTENDENT: That his alibi, that he had spent the afternoon of the bombing playing cards in a bar by the Canal, had collapsed.

MANIAC: And that therefore our anarchist was *also* strongly suspected of the bombing at the Milan bank, in addition to the trains. And you ended your statement by saying that the anarchist's suicide was an 'obvious admission of guilt'.

SUPERINTENDENT: Yes, Sir.

MANIAC: And you, Inspector, were announcing to all and sundry that there was proof that he was a villain and a hardened criminal. But just a couple of weeks later, Superintendent, you issued a statement to say – here it is – (*He shows him a piece of paper*) that 'naturally' – I repeat, 'naturally' – there was no such evidence against our poor railwayman. Am I right? So that he was completely innocent. And you, Inspector, even went as far as to say: 'The anarchist was a good lad.'

SUPERINTENDENT: Yes, fair enough... We'd made a mistake...

MANIAC: Of course, of course... We all make mistakes... But if I might say so, you went right over the top: first you arrest an innocent citizen more or less at random, then you abuse your powers by detaining him beyond the legal limit, and then you go and traumatise the poor man by telling him that you have proof that he's been going round planting bombs on railways; then you more or less deliberately terrorise him that he's going to lose his job; then you tell him that his card-playing alibi has collapsed; and then comes the *coup de grâce* – you tell him that his friend and comrade in Rome has confessed to the bombings in Milan. In other words, his best friend is a mass murderer. Thereupon he becomes terminally depressed, observes that 'this is the death of anarchism', and throws himself out of the window!

I mean, are we crazy or what? If you ask me, when you give a person the run-around like this it's no wonder he gets seized by a 'raptus'. No, I'm sorry, in my opinion you are all extremely guilty! I regard you as totally responsible for the anarchist's death – you should be charged at once with having driven him to suicide!

SUPERINTENDENT: You can't be serious, your honour! You said it yourself, our job is to interrogate suspects, and if we want to get them to talk, every once in a while we have to use tricks and ploys, and sometimes psychological violence...

MANIAC: But here we're not dealing with 'once in a while'. This was continuous, premeditated violence. To start with, did you or did you not have proof that this poor railwayman had lied about his alibi? Answers, please!

SUPERINTENDENT: No, we didn't have specific proof... But...

MANIAC: I'm not interested in 'ifs' and 'buts'! Is it or is it not the case that at this precise moment there are two or three old age pensioners right here in Milan who could have corroborated the anarchist's alibi?

SPORTS JACKET: It is.

MANIAC: So you lied, on TV and in the papers, when you said that his alibi had collapsed and that there was a whole pile of evidence against him? It seems that you don't only use your tricks and traps and porky-pies to get suspects to confess – you're quite happy to foist them onto an unsuspecting public too! Where did the information come from, that the anarchist dancer had confessed?

SPORTS JACKET: We made it up.

MANIAC: Well, how very creative! You should take up writing, you two. And you'll probably get the chance, believe me. Plenty of time to write, in prison.

So, feeling a bit knocked out, eh? Well, I think I should add that down in Rome they have a stack of evidence of major procedural irregularities having been committed by the pair of you. You're done for: the Ministry of Justice has decided that you must be made an example of, and that you must be dealt with with the full severity of the law, so as to restore the public's lost faith in the police.!

SUPERINTENDENT: What? I don't believe it!

SPORTS JACKET: How could they...?

MANIAC: It's true, I'm afraid: your careers are in tatters! Blame it on politics, friends! At the start you served a useful function: something had to be done to stop all the strikes... So they decided to start a witch-hunt against the Left. But now things have gone a bit too far... People have got very upset about the death of our defenestrated anarchist... they want someone's head on the block, and the government's going to give them – *yours*!

SUPERINTENDENT: Ours?!

SPORTS JACKET: That's right!

MANIAC: There's an old English proverb that says: 'The Lord of the Manor set his mastiffs on the peasants... The peasants complained to the King, so the Lord of the Manor went and killed his dogs, to make amends.'

SUPERINTENDENT: And you really think...

MANIAC: Well, who am I, if not your executioner?

SPORTS JACKET: What a poxy job!

SUPERINTENDENT: I've been set up... and I know who did it... Ha, he's going to pay for this!

MANIAC: I'd say a lot of people are going to be very happy to see you two get your come-uppance...

SPORTS JACKET: They'll make mincemeat of us! Can you imagine the headlines? The humiliation... the sniggering... the jokes behind our backs...

SUPERINTENDENT: Everyone turning their backs on us, pretending they don't know us... They won't even give us a job as car park attendants by the time we're finished!

SPORTS JACKET: What a bastard world!

MANIAC: No – what a bastard government!

SUPERINTENDENT: Your Honour, you're going to have to advise us. What do we do now?

MANIAC: How should I know?

SPORTS JACKET: Yes – what would *you* advise?

MANIAC: If I were in your shoes...

SUPERINTENDENT: Yes?

MANIAC: I'd throw myself out of the window!

SPORTS JACKET *and* **SUPERINTENDENT:** What?!

MANIAC: You asked my opinion... the way things are looking... rather than have to endure the humiliation... Take my advice, jump! Why wait? Wait for what? What's left for you in this lousy world? Call this living? Bastard world, bastard government... Bastard bloody everything! Jump!

He hauls them over to the window.

SUPERINTENDENT: No, your Honour, what are you doing? There's still hope!

MANIAC: There's *no* hope, you're done for... Understand...? Done for!! Jump!

SUPERINTENDENT *and* **SPORTS JACKET:** Help! No, stop...! Don't push!

MANIAC: I'm not pushing. You've been seized by a 'raptus'!

He forces them both up onto the window ledge and pushes them, trying to get them to jump. Enter the CONSTABLE *who had gone out at the start of the interrogation.*

CONSTABLE: What's happening, Sir?

MANIAC: (*Letting go of them*) Ha, ha, nothing. Everything's fine... Isn't it, Inspector? Eh, Superintendent? Come on, put the officer's mind at rest.

SUPERINTENDENT: (*He comes down, from the window-sill, shaking*) It's...er... alright... relax... It was only...

MANIAC: ...A 'raptus'.

CONSTABLE: A 'raptus'?

MANIAC: Yes. They were trying to throw themselves out of the window.

CONSTABLE: Them too?

MANIAC: Yes, but not a word to the press, eh!

CONSTABLE: No, sir.

SPORTS JACKET: It's not true, though – it was you, your Honour, you were trying...

SUPERINTENDENT: Exactly.

CONSTABLE: You were trying to throw yourself out, your Honour?

SUPERINTENDENT: No, he was doing the pushing.

MANIAC: It's true, it's true: I drove them to it. And they were in such a desperate state that they were almost ready to go... When a person is desperate, it takes practically nothing...

CONSTABLE: I know, sir!

MANIAC: And now look at them, they're still in a panic... Ooh, look at those long faces!

CONSTABLE: (*Excited at being brought into the conversation by the* JUDGE) Yes, Sir, up shit creek without a paddle, you might say...

SUPERINTENDENT: Constable!

CONSTABLE: I'm sorry, I meant, er, down the pan...

MANIAC: So flush the chain, and away we go...! Cheer up, gentlemen!

SUPERINTENDENT: It's all very well for you... If you were in our position... Do you know what, there was a moment just then when... I was actually almost about to throw myself out!

CONSTABLE: Throw *yourself* out, Sir? You yourself, personally?

SPORTS JACKET: Yes. Me too!

MANIAC: You see, you see, Superintendent – amazing, the effect of a 'raptus'! And whose fault would you say it was?

SUPERINTENDENT: Those bastards in the government... Who else? ...First they give you a free hand... 'Let's have a bit of repression, create a climate of subversion, the threat of social disorder...'

SPORTS JACKET: You bend over backwards for them, and then...

MANIAC: No, no, no... not at all... The fault would have been entirely mine!

SUPERINTENDENT: Yours? Why?

MANIAC: Because not a word of what I said was true! I made it all up!

SUPERINTENDENT: What do you mean? You mean to say that down in Rome they're not really out to get us?

MANIAC: Never even crossed their minds.

SUPERINTENDENT: And what about the 'stack of evidence' against us?

MANIAC: Doesn't exist.

SPORTS JACKET: And the business about the Ministry wanting our heads on the block?

MANIAC: All lies: they all love you, down in Rome. They think the sun shines out of your you-know-whats.

SUPERINTENDENT: You're not just having us on, are you?

MANIAC: Not at all! The government thinks you're entirely wonderful! And by the way, the English proverb about the lord killing his dogs? I made that up too. Whoever heard of a lord killing his dogs to satisfy a peasant? If anything, it'd be the other way round! And if a dog happened to die in the fray, the king would immediately send its owner a wreath and a telegram of condolence.

The INSPECTOR IN THE SPORTS JACKET *goes to say*

something. The SUPERINTENDENT *is nervous and tetchy.*

SPORTS JACKET: Unless I've got this wrong...

SUPERINTENDENT: Of course you've got it wrong... Leave this to me, Inspector...

SPORTS JACKET: Certainly, sorry, sir...

SUPERINTENDENT: I don't understand, your Honour, why you wanted to set us up like that...

MANIAC: Set you up? Not at all, it was just one of the 'tricks of the trade' which we visiting judges also like to use every once in a while, in order to demonstrate to the police that such methods are uncivilised, not to mention criminal!

SUPERINTENDENT: So you still think that when the anarchist jumped out of the window, it was because we drove him to it?

MANIAC: But you just said as much yourselves, a moment ago... when you panicked!

SPORTS JACKET: But we weren't even in the room when he threw himself out! Ask the officer, here!

CONSTABLE: It's true, your Honour. When he threw himself out, they'd just gone out!

MANIAC: That's like saying that if a man plants a bomb in a bank, and then goes out, he's not guilty, because he wasn't there when it went off! Ha! You run a fine line in logic here.

SUPERINTENDENT: But no, your Honour, there's been a misunderstanding... The constable was referring to the first version... but we're talking about the second.

MANIAC: Oh yes, of course... There's a bit of a rewrite, the second time round, isn't there.

SUPERINTENDENT: Well, I wouldn't exactly call it a rewrite... more like a correction.

MANIAC: Fair enough. Let's take a look at this 'correction'.

The SUPERINTENDENT *signals to the* INSPECTOR IN

THE SPORTS JACKET.

SPORTS JACKET: Well, we have...

MANIAC: Don't forget that here I also have your statements for the second version. Please, go ahead...

SPORTS JACKET: We've altered the time of our... what can I say... our ploy about the anarchist's alibi and so on...

MANIAC: How do you mean?

SUPERINTENDENT: Yes, well, you see, we stated that our session with the anarchist, when we tried to trick him, didn't happen at midnight, it happened at about eight in the evening.

SPORTS JACKET: Twenty-hundred hours, if you prefer...!

MANIAC: Ah, so you've brought the time of his flying lesson forward by four hours! A sort of super-summer-time, eh?

SPORTS JACKET: No, not the time of his fall. That still happened at midnight... the same as before. There were witnesses.

SUPERINTENDENT: Including the journalist who was down below in the courtyard at the time, you remember? (*The* MANIAC *indicates that he doesn't*) The one who heard him bouncing off the ledge and hitting the ground, and came running over... He took a note of the time it happened.

MANIAC: OK... so the terminal depression happened at eight o'clock and the suicide happened at midnight. So now what do we do with the 'raptus'? What I mean is, unless I'm mistaken, your whole version of the suicide is based on this 'raptus'...

Everyone concerned, from the judge who did the original inquest through to the Public Prosecutor, has always stressed that the poor devil threw himself out because of a... *sudden* 'raptus'... and now, hey presto, you've done away with the 'raptus'!

SUPERINTENDENT: No we haven't. Not at all.

MANIAC: Yes you have. We now have a gap of four whole hours between the moment when you, or your colleague, comes into the room and perpetrates this monstrous joke that 'we have concrete proof', and then the suicide. So where's my 'raptus' gone all of a sudden? After a gap of four hours, the anarchist would have had time to recover from a lot more than just your little porky pies... You could have told him that Bakunin was a supergrass for the police and the Vatican combined, and he'd have got over it!

SUPERINTENDENT: No, there *was* a 'raptus', but we just wanted to show that it couldn't have been caused by our feeding him false information... precisely because there was a gap of four hours between then and the time of his suicide!

MANIAC: Of course – you're right! That's brilliant... Well done!!!

SUPERINTENDENT: Thank you, sir.

MANIAC: So that way nobody is going to be able to lay the blame at your door! Alright, a few white lies were told, but they couldn't have been the reason for his death!

SPORTS JACKET: Exactly. So we're not guilty.

MANIAC: Congratulations! We still don't have the faintest idea why the poor wretch threw himself out of the window, but that doesn't matter! For the time being, the main thing is, you're innocent.

SUPERINTENDENT: Allow me to thank you again. I must admit, I was beginning to think that you had it in for us.

MANIAC: How do you mean?

SPORTS JACKET: That you'd made up your mind that we were guilty.

MANIAC: Oh my goodness, no... Quite the opposite. I realise that I have been rather provocative, but I only did to force you to come up with ideas that were sufficiently convincing for me to be able to help get you out of this mess.

SUPERINTENDENT: I'm really grateful to you… It is good to know that the judiciary is still a policeman's best friend!!!

MANIAC: You might even say 'collaborator'…

SPORTS JACKET *and* **SUPERINTENDENT:** Of course.

MANIAC: But you're going to have to collaborate too, if you really want me to get you out of this… and put you completely in the clear.

SUPERINTENDENT: Absolutely.

SPORTS JACKET: My pleasure.

MANIAC: Well, the first thing we're going to have to prove – absolutely irrefutably – is that during that four-hour gap the anarchist had lost all trace of his famous 'psychological collapse', as the inquest judge called it at the time.

SPORTS JACKET: Well, there's the statement by the officer here – and mine too – where we say that, after a moment's uneasiness, the anarchist relaxed again…

MANIAC: Do we have that in black and white?

SPORTS JACKET: Yes, I think so…

MANIAC: Oh yes, here it is – in the second version of the events… (*He reads*) 'The railwayman became more relaxed and said that he didn't have a good relationship with the ex-dancer.' Excellent! And let's not forget that our railwayman was very well aware that the anarchist group in Rome was choc-a-bloc with spies and police informers… I believe he himself had said as much to the dancer: 'The police and fascists are using you as a way of creating a climate of social disorder… Your group is full of paid provocateurs… who seem to be able to do what they like with you… and the Left's going to carry the can for all this…'

SPORTS JACKET: Maybe that was why they had a row?

MANIAC: Very possibly, and since the dancer seems to have ignored his warnings, maybe our railwayman was beginning to think that he was a police spy too.

SUPERINTENDENT: Ah yes, could be.

MANIAC: And therefore not worth worrying about. Case proven. The anarchist was happy!

SPORTS JACKET: In fact he was smiling... You remember – I said so, in the first version.

MANIAC: True, but unfortunately we have a small problem – in the first version you also said that the anarchist lit a cigarette, and that he was 'utterly dejected'.

SUPERINTENDENT: You're right, your Honour, that was *his* idea. I told him, I said: 'We're supposed to be police officers – leave the fancy screenplays to the movie-makers...

MANIAC: You know what I say? The only way to find a sensible solution to all this is to chuck it all in the bin and start over again.

SPORTS JACKET: You mean draw up a third version?

MANIAC: Not at all, not at all – just make the two we've already got a bit more plausible.

SUPERINTENDENT: I agree.

MANIAC: So, Rule Number One: What's said is said, and can't be unsaid. We have to take it as given that you, officer, and you, Superintendent (or someone acting on your behalf), played your little charade... that the anarchist smoked his last cigarette, and uttered his famous last words... But here's where the difference comes: he didn't throw himself out of the window, because it wasn't yet midnight, it was only eight o'clock in the evening.

SUPERINTENDENT: As in the second version...

MANIAC: And, as we know, railwaymen are very particular about time-keeping.

SUPERINTENDENT: So this gives us plenty of time to change his mood... and to delay his suicidal intentions.

SPORTS JACKET: Things were going swimmingly!

MANIAC: Yes, but how did this change come about? Time on

its own is not sufficient to heal certain wounds...
Somebody must have given him a hand... I don't know... a
kind gesture, or something...

CONSTABLE: I gave him a piece of chewing gum!

MANIAC: Well said. And you?

SUPERINTENDENT: Um, I wasn't there...

MANIAC: No, this is a very delicate moment, you must have
been there!

SUPERINTENDENT: Oh alright, I was.

MANIAC: Right, now, for a start, can we say that you were
both a bit *moved* by the state the anarchist had got into?

SPORTS JACKET: Yes. In fact I felt really sorry for him.

MANIAC: And might we also say that you, Superintendent,
were also sorry to see him feeling so bad...? You are, after
all, a sensitive sort of chap, are you not?

SUPERINTENDENT: Yes, I was ever so sorry... Sad, even.

MANIAC: Perfect! And I bet you couldn't resist going up to
him and putting your hand on his shoulder...

SUPERINTENDENT: No, I don't think so.

MANIAC: Oh come on, a fatherly gesture...

SUPERINTENDENT: Well maybe... I don't remember.

MANIAC: I'm sure you did! Please, tell me you did...!

CONSTABLE: He did, he did... I saw him!

SUPERINTENDENT: Fair enough, if he saw me...

MANIAC: (*Turning to the* INSPECTOR IN THE SPORTS
JACKET) You, on the other hand, gave him a friendly pat
on the cheek... like this.

He gives him a friendly pat on the cheek.

SPORTS JACKET: No, I'm sorry to disappoint you, but I
most definitely did not... No friendly pats on cheeks.

MANIAC: You do indeed disappoint me... And do you know

why? Because that man was not only an anarchist, he was a railwayman! Have you forgotten that? And do you know what this railwayman means? It's something that goes back to the childhood of every one of us. It means train sets – clockwork... electric... Didn't you ever have a train set when you were a kid?

SPORTS JACKET: Yes, I did... A steam train... With real steam... An armoured train, of course.

MANIAC: And did it go toot-toot?

SPORTS JACKET: Sure, toot-toot...

MANIAC: Wonderful! When you said 'toot-toot', I saw your eyes light up! Inspector, I just *know* that you felt affection for this man... because in your subconscious you connected him with your train set... If your suspect had been... a bank clerk, or something... you wouldn't have given him a second thought... But he was a railwayman... and you, I just *know*... you gave him a friendly pat on the cheek.

CONSTABLE: That's right, that's right – I saw him... He patted him on the cheek. Twice!

MANIAC: See...? We have witnesses! And what did you say as you were patting him on the cheek...?

SPORTS JACKET: I don't remember...

MANIAC: I'll tell you what you said: you said, 'Cheer up... don't look so miserable (and you called him by his name), you'll see, this won't be the death of anarchism!'

SPORTS JACKET: No, I don't think so...

MANIAC: Oh come now... for goodness sake... You *did* say it... Otherwise I'm going to get annoyed. My neck, look at my neck. Did you or did you not say it?

SPORTS JACKET: Oh alright, if it makes you any happier...

MANIAC: Well say it, then... I have to put it in the statement.

He begins writing.

SPORTS JACKET: Well, I said... 'Cheer up (*name of actor*), don't look so miserable... You'll see, this won't be the death of anarchism!'

MANIAC: Well done. And then you sang a song.

SPORTS JACKET: We sang a song…?

MANIAC: Of course… Because you were all in such a good mood… You were all friends, comrades, even… And you couldn't resist having a good sing. Let's see, what could you have sung? How about an anarchist song? 'Nostra patria è il mondo intiero', I imagine…

SPORTS JACKET: No, I'm sorry, your Honour, but we really can't go along with that, an anarchist sing-song…

MANIAC: Oh, you can't, eh? Well, you know what I say? At this point I give up! You can damn well sort yourselves out… It's down to you! I'll string together the facts that you've told me so far… and do you know what will come out – excuse the terminology – a big bloody mess! Yes, really! You say one thing, then you contradict it… First you give one version, then half an hour later, you give a completely different one… You can't even agree among yourselves. You tell the world's press, and, if I am not mistaken, the TV news as well, that 'naturally' there are no written minutes of your interrogation of the anarchist, because there wasn't time, and then all of a sudden, a miracle, we find that we have two or three – and all signed by his very own hand! If one of your suspects was to contradict himself one half as much as you have, you'd have had him hung, drawn and quartered by now!

Do you know what people are going to think of you? That you're a bunch of bent bastards and liars… Who do you think is ever going to believe you again? And do you know why people won't believe you…? Because your version of the facts, as well as being total bollocks, lacks humanity. Not a shred of fellow-feeling… You never ever let yourselves go… Let rip… Laugh, cry… Sing!

People would be happy to forgive all your cretinous blunders if they could only see two decent human beings behind it all – two policemen who, just for once, allowed their hearts to rule their heads, and agreed to sing the anarchist's favourite song with him... just to make him happy... 'Nostra patria è il mondo intiero...' It would bring tears to their eyes... They'd sing your praises, shout your names from the rooftops, hearing a story like that! So please, for your own sakes... Sing!!

He sings the song, quietly at first, and encourages the POLICEMEN *to sing. At first they are embarrassed, but then, one after the other, they join in.*

> Raminghi per le terre
> E per i mari
> Per un'idea lasciamo
> I nostri cari.

Come on, sing up! (*He puts his arm round their shoulders to encourage them*)

> Nostra patria è il mondo intiero...

Let's have a bit of oomph, for God's sake!

> ...Nostra legge è la libertà
> Ed un pensiero, ed un pensiero...
> Nostra patria è il mondo intiero...
> Nostra legge è la libertà
> Ed un pensiero
> Ribelle in cuor ci sta... [4]

The lights fade on the singers.
Blackout.

ACT TWO

Scene One

The stage is still in darkness. We hear again the song that ended Act One. The lights come up, and as they reach full intensity, the chorus ends in a descanted finale.

MANIAC: (*Clapping, hugging his fellow singers and shaking hands all round*) Well done, brilliant! I think we can say that we've done it. How could anyone possibly doubt that at that moment the anarchist was in an extremely good mood?!

SPORTS JACKET: I'd say he was probably even happy.

MANIAC: Of course he was! He felt at home. It felt like being in his anarchist group in Rome where, as we know, there were always more plain-clothes police than there were real anarchists.

SUPERINTENDENT: 'He emerged spiritually unscathed from the onslaught of our false accusations.'

MANIAC: So, no 'raptus'. The 'raptus' comes later. (*He points to the* INSPECTOR IN THE SPORTS JACKET) When?

SPORTS JACKET: Around midnight.

MANIAC: And what caused it?

SUPERINTENDENT: Well, I suppose the reason...

MANIAC: No, no, no, for goodness sake! You suppose

nothing... You're not supposed to know anything about it, Superintendent!

SUPERINTENDENT: *Why* am I supposed not to know anything...?

MANIAC: For the love of God, here we are, going to extraordinary lengths to get you out of this mess, to prove that you had nothing to do with the death of the anarchist... because you weren't even there...

SUPERINTENDENT: You're right, I'm sorry... I wasn't thinking.

MANIAC: Well you *should* be thinking, Superintendent... Pay attention... So, as Totò [5] said in one of his farces, 'At this time, the Superintendent was not in the station'! But the Inspector was.

SPORTS JACKET: That's true, I was. But I went out shortly afterwards...

MANIAC: Oh, here we go, passing the buck again. Now, there's a good chap, tell me what happened around midnight.

SPORTS JACKET: There were six of us in the room: four constables, myself, and a lieutenant from the carabinieri.

MANIAC: Oh yes, the one who then got promoted to captain.

SPORTS JACKET: That's the one.

MANIAC: And what were you doing?

SPORTS JACKET: We were interrogating the anarchist.

MANIAC: What, again? 'Where were you... what were you doing... don't get funny with me, son...!'

SPORTS JACKET: Not at all, your Honour... No, we were interrogating him jokingly...

MANIAC: You're kidding! Jokingly?!

SPORTS JACKET: No, really... Ask the officer, here...

He pushes the CONSTABLE *towards the* JUDGE.

MANIAC: No need to. It may seem incredible... (*He waves a* *sheet of paper*) ...but here it is, in the statement made to the judge who adjourned the inquest!

SPORTS JACKET: Certainly, and he never raised any doubts about it.

MANIAC: Ha, I can well believe it... But in what sense, 'jokingly'?

SPORTS JACKET: In the sense that we were being playful... We were interrogating him but trying to have a laugh at the same time.

MANIAC: I don't understand; were you playing Blind Man's Buff? Putting funny hats on? Blowing trumpets?

SPORTS JACKET: Well, we didn't quite go that far... But we were having a bit of a chuckle... A few jokes, a few gags...

CONSTABLE: That's right, we were having a laugh. You know, the Inspector might not look it, but he's got a terrific sense of humour... When he's on form some of his interrogations are hilarious... Ha, ha, he's terrific!

MANIAC: Now I understand why the government's decided to change your motto.

SPORTS JACKET: Change our motto?

MANIAC: That's what I said – the Ministry's already decided.

SUPERINTENDENT: They're going to change it?

MANIAC: Well, not so much change it as complete it... How does it go at the moment?

SPORTS JACKET: 'The police – at the service of today's citizens.'

MANIAC: Well, from now on it's going to be: 'The police – at the service of today's citizens – to give them a good laugh!'

SPORTS JACKET: Ha, ha, pull the other one, your Honour!

MANIAC: Not at all, I quite believe that you treat your suspects 'jokingly', as you say... I remember, I was in Bergamo at the time when they were interrogating the members of the so-called 'Monday Gang' – you

remember? – there was even a priest involved, and a
doctor, and the man who ran the chemist's shop… virtually
the entire village put on trial, and then found innocent.
Well, I was staying in a little hotel right near the police
station where the interrogations were taking place, and just
about every night I was woken up by shouting and
screaming. At first I thought it was the sound of people
being beaten up… but then I realised that they were
laughing. Yes – the suspects were laughing: 'Ha, ha, oh
Jesus! Stop it, ha, ha! Help, you're too much! Inspector,
stop it, I'll die laughing!'

SUPERINTENDENT: Joking apart, you do of course know
that every one of the officers involved, from the chief
inspector to the lowest constable, all went to prison for
that?

MANIAC: Yes. For comical behaviour liable to occasion a
breach of the peace, wasn't it? (*The* POLICEMEN *have
had enough of his joking*) No, no, I'm being serious. You
have no idea how many completely innocent parties move
heaven and earth just to get themselves arrested and
brought to this station! You think they're anarchists,
communists, autonomists, trade unionists… No, the truth
is, they're all just poor, sick manic depressives,
hypochondriacs, gloomy people, who disguise themselves
as revolutionaries just so's they can be interrogated by
you… and at last have a damn good laugh! Get a bit of
enjoyment, for once in their lives!

SUPERINTENDENT: I would say that you're not just making
fun of us, your Honour, you're taking the piss!

MANIAC: Goodness, no, I wouldn't dream of it…

SUPERINTENDENT: (*Rubbing his arms*) Would you mind if
I shut the window? It's turned cold all of a sudden…

MANIAC: Go ahead… You're right, it has turned a bit parky!

SPORTS JACKET: That's because the sun's just gone down.

Responding to a gesture from the INSPECTOR IN THE
SPORTS JACKET, *the* CONSTABLE *goes to shut the
window.*

MANIAC: Exactly. But on the evening in question, it appears the sun didn't go down.

SPORTS JACKET: What?

MANIAC: I said: on the evening when the anarchist threw himself out of the window, did the sun stay up? Are we to assume there wasn't a sunset?

The three POLICE OFFICERS *don't know what to make of this. They look at each other.*

SUPERINTENDENT: I don't understand.

The MANIAC *pretends to get annoyed.*

MANIAC: All I'm saying is that here we are, at midnight, in the middle of December, and the window was still wide open. In other words, it couldn't have been cold... And if it wasn't cold, that can only mean that the sun hadn't gone down... Or maybe it went down later than usual – one o'clock, perhaps, like Norway in July.

SUPERINTENDENT: Not at all. We'd just opened it to get a bit of fresh air in, hadn't we?

SPORTS JACKET: Yes, there was a lot of smoke.

CONSTABLE: The anarchist smoked a lot, you know!

MANIAC: So you opened the windows. And the shutters too?

SPORTS JACKET: Yes.

MANIAC: In December? At midnight, with the thermometer sub-zero, and a freezing fog...? 'Open the windows – who cares if we all die of pneumonia!' You must at least have had your coats on?

SPORTS JACKET: No, we were in our jackets.

MANIAC: Oh very sporty!

SPORTS JACKET: But it wasn't cold at all. Honestly!

SUPERINTENDENT: Quite mild, really...

MANIAC: Oh yes? That evening the weather forecast for the whole of Italy said that it was going to be cold enough to freeze the knackers off a polar bear, and you weren't cold... In fact it was positively spring-like! What do you have here – your own personal Gulf stream running through the drains under police headquarters?

SPORTS JACKET: Excuse me, your Honour, but I don't understand; a short while ago you told us you were here specially to help us, but instead all you've done is cast doubt on everything we say, poke fun at us and make us feel like shit...

MANIAC: You're right, maybe I have been overdoing it. But I feel like I'm doing doing one of those idiot puzzle games you get in kids' comics: 'Find the 37 mistakes made by Inspector Biggio Stupidoni.' I don't see how I'm supposed to help you. (*The* POLICE OFFICERS *sit there, dumb and disconsolate*) Alright, alright... no need to sit there looking like you're at a funeral – cheer up! I promise, no more joking. Total seriousness! So let's forget about all the earlier business...

SUPERINTENDENT: Good idea.

MANIAC: ...and let's concentrate on the nitty-gritty: the anarchist's jump.

SPORTS JACKET: I agree.

MANIAC: So, our anarchist, seized by this 'raptus' (in a minute we'll have to see if we can find a more plausible reason for this) ...suddenly gets up, takes a short run, and... wait a minute – which of you gave him a leg-up?

SPORTS JACKET: What do you mean, a 'leg-up'?

MANIAC: I mean, which of you stood next to the window with his fingers interlocked like so – to give him a good foot-hold – and then... Whee! Heave-ho, and out he goes!

SPORTS JACKET: Surely, your Honour, you're not implying that we...?

MANIAC: No, please, don't get me wrong... I was only wondering... after all, it is rather a high jump, with not much of a run-up, and without a little helping hand... I wouldn't want anyone to be able to suggest...

SPORTS JACKET: There's nothing to suggest, your Honour, I assure you – he did it all by himself...!

MANIAC: Did our friend perhaps have bouncy rubber heels?

SPORTS JACKET: No he did not...

MANIAC: Alright, so what do we have? On the one hand we have a man who stands about five foot feet tall, all on his own, with no help, and with no ladder handy... On the other, half a dozen police officers, only a couple of yards away, and one standing right next to the window, who were unable to stop him in time...

SPORTS JACKET: But it was all so sudden...

CONSTABLE: And you have no idea what a slippery customer he was... I only just managed to grab him by one foot.

MANIAC: Ha! You see, you see, my technique of provocation works! You grabbed him by one foot!

CONSTABLE: Yes, but his shoe came off in my hand, and down he went anyway.

MANIAC: Never mind. The important thing is that his shoe came off in your hand. That shoe proves irrefutably that you were trying to save him!

SPORTS JACKET: Irrefutably and incontrovertibly!

SUPERINTENDENT: (*To the* CONSTABLE) Well done!

CONSTABLE: Thank you, Super...

SUPERINTENDENT: Shush!

MANIAC: Just a minute... something doesn't quite fit here. (*He shows the* POLICE OFFICERS *a sheet of paper*) Did our suicidal friend have three shoes?

SUPERINTENDENT: Three shoes?

MANIAC: That's what I said. One ended up in the hands of this officer here... We have his statement to that effect, a couple of days after the event... (*He shows them the sheet of paper*) Look, here.

SPORTS JACKET: Correct, your Honour... He was interviewed by a journalist from *Corriere della Sera*.

MANIAC: But in this Appendix here, we're assured that as the anarchist lay dying on the pavement below, he still had both his shoes on his feet. This was witnessed by various bystanders, including a journalist from *L'Unità* and various other press people who happened to be passing.

SPORTS JACKET: Well, I can't imagine how that happened...

MANIAC: Neither can I! Unless this officer was very quick about it, and went rushing down to the second floor, stuck his head out of the window as the anarchist was coming past, put his shoe back on mid-flight, and then shot back up to the fourth floor just in time for the body to hit bottom.

SUPERINTENDENT: There, you see, you see, you're making fun of us again!

MANIAC: You're right... I couldn't resist it... I'm sorry. So, three shoes... Would you happen to remember if he was a tri-ped?

SUPERINTENDENT: Who?

MANIAC: Our suicidal railwayman... If it turns out he had three feet, that would explain why he had three shoes.

SUPERINTENDENT: (*Tetchily*) No, he was not a tri-ped!

MANIAC: Alright, no need to get ratty... Anyway, that's the least you'd expect of an anarchist!

CONSTABLE: That's true!

SUPERINTENDENT: Shut up, you!

SPORTS JACKET: Oh God, what a mess... We're going to have to find a plausible explanation, because otherwise...

MANIAC: I've got it!

SUPERINTENDENT: Let's hear it.

MANIAC: Here goes: obviously, one of his shoes was too big, so since he didn't have a handy insole lying around, he put another, smaller shoe on first, and then put the bigger one on, on top of it.

SPORTS JACKET: Two shoes on the same foot?

MANIAC: Yes. Perfectly normal... Remember galoshes? When people used to go round wearing rubber overshoes...

SUPERINTENDENT: Exactly. *Used* to.

MANIAC: No, but people do still wear them... And do you know what I say? I say that what the officer was left holding wasn't a shoe at all, it was a galosh.

SPORTS JACKET: No, that's impossible: an anarchist in galoshes...! Only conservatives wear galoshes...!

MANIAC: Anarchists can be terribly conservative, you know...

The phone rings. They all freeze. The INSPECTOR IN THE SPORTS JACKET *picks up the phone.*

SPORTS JACKET: Excuse me... Yes, what is it... Hang on a moment... (*To the* SUPERINTENDENT) It's the desk sergeant downstairs, he says there's a journalist at the main entrance asking to see you, Superintendent.

SUPERINTENDENT: Oh yes, I told her I'd see her today. She's the one from *L'Espresso* or *L'Europeo*, I don't remember which... Ask him if her name's Feletti.

SPORTS JACKET: (*Down the phone*) Is her name Feletti? (*To the* SUPERINTENDENT) Yes, Maria Feletti.

SUPERINTENDENT: That's the one... She wanted an interview. You'll have to ask her to come back another day. I'm busy today...

MANIAC: I wouldn't dream of letting you do that: I can't let you get yourself into hot water on my account.

SUPERINTENDENT: How do you mean?

MANIAC: I know that journalist – she's a mean lady... not the sort of person to get on the wrong side of... Very touchy!

She's quite capable of doing you a very nasty article... You really ought to see her!

SUPERINTENDENT: But what about your Inquiry?

MANIAC: It can wait. Haven't you realised yet that you and I are all in the same boat? And it's best to have people like that with us, not against us, believe me!

SUPERINTENDENT: Oh alright. (*Turning to the* INSPECTOR IN THE SPORTS JACKET) Have her sent up.

SPORTS JACKET: Send her up to my office.

He puts the phone down.

SUPERINTENDENT: Will you be leaving now?

MANIAC: Wouldn't dream of it... I'm not a man to abandon my friends. Specially not at times of danger!

SPORTS JACKET *and* **SUPERINTENDENT:** You're staying?

SUPERINTENDENT: Who are you going to say you are, though? If the journalist finds out who you really are, and why you're here in the first place, she's going to splash it all over the front page! Why don't you just come out with it – you're out to destroy us!

MANIAC: No, don't worry, I'm not out to destroy you at all. She won't have the first idea who I really am.

SPORTS JACKET: She won't?

MANIAC: No, of course not. I could just be someone else... It'd be child's play for me, believe me. Criminal psychopathologist... Head of Interpol... Head of forensic... Take your pick... Any time the journalist gets you in a tight corner with a particularly nasty question, you just give me a wink and I'll join in... The important thing is to keep you two in the clear.

SUPERINTENDENT: This is very good of you, your Honour...

He shakes his hand emotionally.

MANIAC: You'd better stop calling me 'your Honour'. As from this moment I am Captain Marcantonio Banzi Piccinni, from the Forensic Department... OK?

SPORTS JACKET: But there's a real Captain Banzi Piccinni... He works out of Rome...

MANIAC: Precisely. That way, if the journalist writes something we don't like, it'll be a cinch to show that she made it all up... We simply call in the real Captain Piccinni from Rome.

SPORTS JACKET: That's amazing... it's brilliant! Do you really think you can do the part of the Captain?

MANIAC: Have no fear – during the War I was an army chaplain with the bersaglieri.

He opens his bag and rummages around in it.

SUPERINTENDENT: Shush! Here she is! (*The* JOURNALIST *enters*) Ah, Miss Feletti, do come in.

JOURNALIST: Good morning. Which of you gentlemen is the Superintendent?

SUPERINTENDENT: I am. Pleased to meet you. What a shame we've only ever met on the phone...

JOURNALIST: How do you do. The officer at the front door was giving me a hard time...

SUPERINTENDENT: I'm sorry – all my fault – I forgot to tell him you were coming. May I introduce you to my colleagues here... Constable Pisani; the inspector in charge of this office...

JOURNALIST: Very pleased to meet you.

SPORTS JACKET: The pleasure is all mine... Miss.

He gives her a military handshake.

JOURNALIST: Ouch, that hurt!

SPORTS JACKET: I'm sorry...

SUPERINTENDENT: (*Pointing to the* MANIAC *who is busy fiddling around*) ...and finally Captain... Captain?!

MANIAC: Here we are... (*When he stands up, we see that he is wearing a false moustache, a black patch over one eye, and a brown leather glove on one hand. The* SUPERINTENDENT *is momentarily lost for words, so the* MANIAC *does his own introductions*) Captain Marcantonio Banzi Piccinni, of the Central Forensic Department. Please excuse the stiff handshake... Wooden, don't you know... Souvenir of the Nicaragua campaign – ex-parachutist with the Contras, working with the CIA... Make yourself at home, Miss.

SUPERINTENDENT: Would you like something to drink?

JOURNALIST: No thank you... If you don't mind, I'd like to start right away... I'm afraid I'm in a bit of a rush. Unfortunately my article has to be in tonight in time for the morning edition.

SUPERINTENDENT: Fine, as you like. We're ready, so let's get started.

JOURNALIST: I have a few questions I'd like to ask. (*She reads from her notebook*) The first is to you, Inspector, and you'll have to excuse me if it's a bit provocative... If you don't mind, I use a tape-recorder... unless you object, that is...

She takes a tape-recorder from her handbag.

SPORTS JACKET: Well, actually... we don't...

MANIAC: Absolutely no problem – go ahead... (*To the* INSPECTOR IN THE SPORTS JACKET) Rule Number Two: Never say no.

SPORTS JACKET: But supposing something slips out... If we want to deny it, she'll have the proof...

JOURNALIST: Excuse me, gents, is there a problem?

MANIAC: (*As if everything is fine*) No, no, not at all... The Inspector was just telling me what a remarkable woman you are – brave, fearless, progressive, dedicated to the cause of truth and justice... come what may!

JOURNALIST: The Inspector is too generous...

SPORTS JACKET: So, fire away.

JOURNALIST: Why is it that you're known as 'The Window-Straddler'?

SPORTS JACKET: The Window-Straddler? Me?

JOURNALIST: Yes. 'Inspector Window-Straddler'.

SPORTS JACKET: And who, might I ask, calls me that?

JOURNALIST: I have here a photocopy of a letter from a young anarchist in San Vittore prison. He was remanded in custody the same week that the anarchist fell to his death, and he says some interesting things about you, Inspector... And about this very room.

SPORTS JACKET: Oh yes? And what does he have to say?

JOURNALIST: (*Reading*) 'The Inspector on the fourth floor forced me to sit on the window-sill with my legs hanging over the edge, and then he started provoking me: "Go on, throw yourself out," and insulting me... "Why don't you jump...? Too scared, eh? Go on, get it over with! What are you waiting for?" I had to grit my teeth and hold on tight, because I really was on the point of jumping...'

MANIAC: Excellent. It reads like something out of a Hitchcock film.

JOURNALIST: Please, Captain... my question was directed to the Inspector, not to you... How do you reply to that?

She reaches the microphone in the direction of the INSPECTOR IN THE SPORTS JACKET.

MANIAC: (*Sotto voce, to the* INSPECTOR) Cool, calm and collected!

SPORTS JACKET: I have nothing to say to that... And in fact I would like to ask *you* a question: in all sincerity, do you really think that I had the railwayman sitting across the window too?

MANIAC: Sssh – don't fall for it. (*He hums to himself*) Here she goes, swinging low, bye, bye... vulture...

JOURNALIST: Am I right in thinking you're trying to disrupt the proceedings, Captain?

MANIAC: Not at all… Just humming. And if you'll allow me, I have a question for you too, Miss Feletti… What do you take us for – a TV ad for washing powder…? You're trying to suggest that we do the 'window test' with every anarchist we get our hands on?

JOURNALIST: No doubt about it, you have a wonderful way with words, Captain.

SPORTS JACKET: Thanks… You got me out of a tight spot, there…

He slaps the MANIAC *on the back.*

MANIAC: Go easy with the back-slapping, Inspector… I have a glass eye!!

He points to his black patch.

SPORTS JACKET: A glass eye?

MANIAC: And mind how you shake my hand. It's artificial.

JOURNALIST: While we're on the subject of windows, in among the papers handed over by the judge who adjourned the inquest there's no sign of the forensic report on the trajectory of the fall.

SUPERINTENDENT: What trajectory of what fall?

JOURNALIST: The trajectory of the fall of our alleged suicide.

SUPERINTENDENT: What use would that be?

JOURNALIST: It would enable us to tell whether the anarchist was alive or dead at the moment that he came out of the window. In other words, whether he came out with a bit of impetus, or whether he just slithered down the wall, as appears to have been the case… Also whether there were any broken bones in his arms and hands (which there were not – which suggests that the alleged suicide did not put his hands out in order to protect himself at the moment of impact – a gesture that, if he had been conscious, would have been normal and absolutely instinctive…)

SPORTS JACKET: Yes, but you're forgetting that we're dealing with someone who threw himself out because he *wanted* to die!

MANIAC: Doesn't mean a thing. Here, unfortunately, I have to say the lady is right... As you see, I am entirely objective. There have been many experiments done on this front: they've taken potential suicides, thrown them out of windows, and they found that right at the last moment all of them, zap... put their hands out to protect themselves!

SUPERINTENDENT: A fine support you're turning out to be... You're mad!

MANIAC: That's right. Who told you?

JOURNALIST: But the most disturbing detail, on which I would appreciate an explanation, is the fact that, again among the materials handed over by the judge who shelved the inquest, there is no sign of the cassette tape that recorded the precise time of the phone call that rang for the ambulance... a phone call which came from here, at Central Police Headquarters, and which, according to the people at the ambulance station, occurred at two minutes before midnight.

At the same time, the journalists who were present at the scene all stated that the fall happened at precisely three minutes past midnight... In other words, the ambulance was called five minutes before the anarchist went out of the window. Could any of you explain this curious discrepancy?

MANIAC: Well... we quite often call an ambulance in advance, just in case... Because one never knows, does one... And as you see, sometimes it turns out to be a good idea.

SPORTS JACKET: (*Slapping him on the back*) Well done!

MANIAC: The eye – watch out...!

SUPERINTENDENT: I don't quite see what you're accusing me of. Is it a crime all of a sudden, to plan ahead? A mere three minutes before time... Anyway, in the police we pride ourselves on keeping one step ahead!

SPORTS JACKET: And if you care to check, I'm sure you'll find that all those journalists' watches were running slow... I mean, fast...

SUPERINTENDENT: Or maybe the time-stamp clock at the ambulance station was running slow when we phoned them...

CONSTABLE: Very possible, Sir.

JOURNALIST: Sounds more like *Alice in Wonderland*!

MANIAC: What's so strange? We're not in Switzerland, you know... In Italy people set their watches as and how they feel like... fast, slow... this is a nation of artists and rebels, Miss Feletti! Individualists who set their own terms with history.

SPORTS JACKET: Well said, brilliant!

He slaps him on the back again, and we hear the chink of the glass eye falling on the floor.

MANIAC: There, you see?! What did I tell you...? You've knocked my eye out!

SPORTS JACKET: (*Going down on all fours to look for it*) Excuse me, Miss, what were you saying?

JOURNALIST: We were talking about how we're a nation of artists and rebels... and I must say, I have to agree with you: some of our judges seem to be particularly rebellious: strange how they can write off perfectly satisfactory alibi witnesses... not to mention losing vital evidence like cassette tapes and forensic reports on trajectories, and neglecting to ask themselves how come ambulances turn up five minutes before time... All mere trifles, of course! And what about the bruises on the back of the dead man's neck, for which there has not as yet been any satisfactory explanation.

SPORTS JACKET: You should be careful, Miss... Loose talk can be a dangerous thing...

JOURNALIST: Was that a threat?

MANIAC: No, no, Superintendent... I really don't think the lady is indulging in loose talk at all... I imagine she's referring to a version of the events which I have heard referred to several times... and which, strangely enough, seems to have originated here in this very building.

SUPERINTENDENT: What version would that be?

MANIAC: It is rumoured that during the anarchist's final interrogation, at just a couple of minutes to midnight one of the officers present started to get impatient, and he came over and gave him a mighty wallop on the back of the neck... Relax, Inspector... The result of this was that the anarchist was half-paralysed and started struggling for breath... So they decided to call an ambulance. In the meantime, in an attempt to revive him, they opened the window, put the anarchist in front of it, and made him lean out a bit for the cool night air to revive him...! Apparently, there was a misunderstanding between the two officers supporting him... as often happens in these cases, each of them thought the other one was holding him... 'You got him, Gianni?' 'You got him, Luigi?' And bomp, down he went...

The INSPECTOR IN THE SPORTS JACKET *comes towards the* MANIAC, *seething, but then slips on the glass eye and falls.*

JOURNALIST: That's right!

SUPERINTENDENT: Have you gone mad?

MANIAC: Yes. Sixteen times, to be precise.

SPORTS JACKET: What the hell was that?

MANIAC: My glass eye, that's what! Look, you've made it all dirty. Officer, would you mind getting me a glass of water to wash it in?

The CONSTABLE *exits.*

JOURNALIST: You must admit, that version would clear up a whole series of problems – why the ambulance was called in advance, why the body appeared to be inert when it fell... and even why the Public Prosecutor chose to use that curious phrase in his summing-up.

MANIAC: What phrase was that? Could you be more specific, my head's already aching!

JOURNALIST: The Public Prosecutor stated, in a written deposition, that the anarchist's death was an 'accidental death'. Please note. Accident, not suicide, as you have been maintaining. There's a lot of difference between an accident and a suicide. But the way the Captain here has just described it, it could very well have been an 'accident'.

The CONSTABLE *returns. He hands the glass of water to the* MANIAC, *who is so absorbed in what the* JOURNALIST *is saying that he swallows the glass eye with a gulp of water as if it was a pill.*

MANIAC: Oh God – the eye! I've swallowed my eye... Oh well, let's hope at least it gets rid of my headache...

SUPERINTENDENT: (*Whispering to the fake* CAPTAIN) What on earth are you playing at now?

SPORTS JACKET: (*Alternating with the* SUPERINTENDENT) Don't you think you've been giving her too much rope? Now she must think she's got us where she wants us.

MANIAC: Just leave it to me. (*To the* JOURNALIST) Right, Miss... I am now going to demonstrate how this last version is totally inadmissible.

JOURNALIST: Inadmissible, eh? In the same way that the judge who shelved the case dismissed the alibi statements by the old age pensioners as inadmissible?

MANIAC: This is the first I've heard of inadmissible old age pensioners.

JOURNALIST: I'm surprised you're not up to date on this! In his summing up, the judge who closed the inquest said that the three alibi witnesses offered by our anarchist friend were inadmissible. Those were the ones who said they had

spent the tragic afternoon of the bombing playing cards
with him, in a bar along the Canal.

MANIAC: So why did he say they were inadmissible?

JOURNALIST: In the judge's own words: 'The people we are
dealing with here are old, sick, and in at least one case
disabled.'

MANIAC: And he actually wrote that in his final document?

JOURNALIST: Yes.

MANIAC: Well, who's to say he's wrong? Objectively
speaking, how can anyone expect some ancient pensioner,
who's probably a war cripple into the bargain, or maybe
been invalided out of the factory – an *ex*-worker, note that,
an *ex*-worker – to have even the minimum psychological
and physical qualities required for the delicate task of
being a witness?

JOURNALIST: Why not an ex-worker? What do you mean?

MANIAC: Do you live in the real world, Miss Feletti? Instead
of jetting off to Mexico, Cambodia and Vietnam, one day
why don't you try visiting Marghera, Piombino, Rho or
Sesto San Giovanni? Do you have any idea of what
condition a worker is in, these days, by the times he gets to
his pension? (And from the latest government statistics it
appears that fewer and fewer of them actually do!) They're
squeezed dry, worn to a frazzle. Hardly an ounce of life in
them!

JOURNALIST: I think you're rather overstating your case.

MANIAC: Oh yes...? Well, in that case you should go and
look in at one of the bars where our old age pensioners go
to play cards, and you'll find them crawling up the wall,
calling each other names, and not even able to remember
who dealt the last hand: 'Oi, it was me who put down the
seven of spades.' 'No, you put it down in the last game, not
this one.' 'What do you mean, the last game, this is the first
game we've played today... You're going senile.' 'No,
you're the senile one – you seem to have forgotten,
diamonds is trumps, not hearts.' 'Oh is it – I thought it was

clubs.' 'You're out of your mind!' 'Out of my mind? Who do you think you're talking to?' 'I don't know? Do you?' 'Don't have the first idea.'

JOURNALIST: Ha, ha, you're too much. But joking apart... isn't it maybe their fault, if they end up in this pitiful state?

MANIAC: No, not at all. It's society's fault! But we're not here to sit in judgement on the world capitalist system, we're here to discuss whether witnesses are reliable or not. If a worker's a wreck because he's been over-exploited or because he's had an accident in the factory, that should not concern us; our concern is with justice and law and order.

SUPERINTENDENT: Well said, Captain!

MANIAC: If you don't have the money to buy yourself vitamins, proteins, wheatgerm, Royal jelly and calcium phosphate for your memory... well so much the worse for you, I, in my capacity as judge, must tell you no... I'm sorry, but you're out of the game, you're a second-class citizen.

JOURNALIST: Ha – you see, you see – I knew that when we got down to basics we'd get back to class prejudice... class privilege!

MANIAC: And who has ever suggested otherwise? I agree absolutely. Our society is divided into classes, and so are witnesses – there are first-class witnesses, and second-, and third-, and fourth-class. Age doesn't come into it. The point is, people go to university. They study for years. And all for what? To be treated in the same terms as some half-starved old age pensioner? You must be joking!

The MANIAC *comes out from behind the desk, and we see that he has a pirate-style wooden leg. Everyone looks at him in atonishment. The* MANIAC *continues, casually:*

Vietnam. Green Berets. Operation Cobra, rescuing prisoners behind the lines... Not a nice experience, all in the past, though, prefer not to talk about it!

The door opens. INSPECTOR BERTOZZO *looks in. He has a patch over one eye.*

INSPECTOR BERTOZZO: Excuse me, may I interrupt?

SUPERINTENDENT: Come in, feel free, Bertozzo...

INSPECTOR BERTOZZO: I just wanted to drop this off.

He is holding a metal box.

SUPERINTENDENT: What's that?

INSPECTOR BERTOZZO: It's a copy of the bomb that exploded at the bank...

JOURNALIST: Oh God...!

INSPECTOR BERTOZZO: Don't worry, Miss, there's no fuse in it.

SUPERINTENDENT: Put it down there... Now, there's a good chap... I want you to shake hands with your colleague here... Come on, you too, Inspector... Friends again!

INSPECTOR BERTOZZO: Hold on, Super – he could at least explain why he went and gave me a black eye...

The SUPERINTENDENT *elbows him in the ribs.*

SPORTS JACKET: Don't pretend you don't know. What about the raspberry?

INSPECTOR BERTOZZO: What raspberry...?

SUPERINTENDENT: That'll do, gentlemen... We have visitors...

MANIAC: Indeed we do...

INSPECTOR BERTOZZO: Superintendent, all I want to know is what on earth got into him... He comes into my office, and without so much as a by your leave... Smack!

MANIAC: He could at least have asked permission first!

INSPECTOR BERTOZZO: There, you see... But excuse me, your face is a bit familiar.

MANIAC: Must be because we're both wearing eye-patches.

EVERYBODY: (*Laughing*) Ha, ha!

INSPECTOR BERTOZZO: No, no, seriously...

MANIAC: Allow me to introduce myself. Captain Marcantonio Banzi Piccinni... From Forensic.

INSPECTOR BERTOZZO: Piccinni? No... You can't be... I know Captain Piccinni personally...

SUPERINTENDENT: (*Giving him a little kick*) Oh no you don't.

INSPECTOR BERTOZZO: Oh yes I do...!

SPORTS JACKET: Oh. No. You. Don't!

He kicks him.

INSPECTOR BERTOZZO: Look, don't you start again...

SUPERINTENDENT: Forget it...

Another kick.

INSPECTOR BERTOZZO: We were at police college together...

He is kicked by the MANIAC *too.*

MANIAC: I thought your superior just told you to forget it!

For good measure he also hits him round the back of the head.

INSPECTOR BERTOZZO: Hey, stop that!

MANIAC: (*Pointing to the* INSPECTOR IN THE SPORTS JACKET) It was him.

The SUPERINTENDENT *brings* BERTOZZO *over to the* JOURNALIST.

SUPERINTENDENT: If you'll allow me, Inspector Bertozzo, I'd like to present Miss... I'll explain after... Miss Feletti... Journalist. Know what I mean?

Another dig with the elbow.

INSPECTOR BERTOZZO: My pleasure. Inspector Bertozzo... No, I don't know what you mean.

He receives a kick from the SUPERINTENDENT, *and another from the* MANIAC. *The* MANIAC *is beginning to enjoy this; he also kicks the* SUPERINTENDENT. *At the*

same time he slaps both BERTOZZO *and the*
INSPECTOR IN THE SPORTS JACKET *on the back of
the neck.* BERTOZZO *thinks that it was the* INSPECTOR
IN THE SPORTS JACKET *who did it.*

You see what I mean, Superintendent – he's always picking
on me…!

To end with, the MANIAC *gives the* JOURNALIST
a slap on the backside, and then points to the
SUPERINTENDENT.

JOURNALIST: Superintendent, that's hardly a proper way
to…

SUPERINTENDENT: (*Thinking that she is referring to the
bickering*) You're right, I don't know what's got into them.
Bertozzo, stop that and listen to me! This lady is here for a
very important *interview*. Know what I mean?

He gives him a little kick and a knowing wink.

INSPECTOR BERTOZZO: Oh, I see…

SUPERINTENDENT: Now, Miss, if you would like to ask
Inspector Bertozzo a few questions… Among other things,
the Inspector is quite an expert on ballistics and explosives.

JOURNALIST: Oh yes – could you clarify one thing for
me…? You were saying that in that box there's a facsimile
of the bomb that went off at the bank.

INSPECTOR BERTOZZO: Well, an approximate replica,
since all trace of the original bomb was lost. If you follow
me…

JOURNALIST: But one of the bombs was retrieved, wasn't
it? Unexploded…

INSPECTOR BERTOZZO: Yes, the one from the Bank of
Commerce…

JOURNALIST: Could you explain to me why, instead of
defusing it and sending it to Forensic – which would be
normal practice, so that it could be thoroughly examined –
when they found it they took it straight out into the yard
and blew it up?

INSPECTOR BERTOZZO: I'm sorry – why do you ask?

JOURNALIST: You know perfectly well, Inspector... By destroying the bomb, they also lost the signature of the killers...

MANIAC: It's true. In fact we have a saying in Forensic: 'Tell me how you make your bombs, and I'll tell you who you are.'

INSPECTOR BERTOZZO: (*Shaking his head*) Hey, no... that's definitely not Piccinni.

The MANIAC *picks up the bomb.*

SUPERINTENDENT: Of course he isn't. Shut up!

INSPECTOR BERTOZZO: Ah, I thought he wasn't. Who is he, then?

He receives yet another kick.

MANIAC: If Inspector Bertozzo will allow me, in my capacity as head of the Forensic Department...

INSPECTOR BERTOZZO: Who are you trying to kid...? What are you up to...? Leave that box alone, it's dangerous!

MANIAC: (*He kicks him*) I am from Forensic, young man... Would you mind standing over there, please?

SUPERINTENDENT: Do you really know what you're doing?

The MANIAC *looks at him disparagingly.*

MANIAC: You see, Miss, a bomb of this sort is so complex... Look at all these wires... two detonators... the timing mechanism... the firing mechanism, all sorts of little levers... as I was saying, it's so complex that they could very well have hidden a second delayed-action time bomb inside it, and you'd never find it unless you wanted to spend all day taking it apart piece by piece... And by that time, Boom!

SUPERINTENDENT: (*To* BERTOZZO) He sounds like a real expert, doesn't he!

INSPECTOR BERTOZZO: (*Stubbornly*) Yes, but he's still

not Piccinni...

MANIAC: So that's why they decided to 'lose the bomber's signature', as you put it... They preferred to explode the bomb right there in the courtyard, rather than risk it blowing up and having an even worse massacre on their hands... Convinced?

JOURNALIST: Yes, this time you really have convinced me.

MANIAC: Amazing, I've even managed to convince myself!

SPORTS JACKET: And I'm convinced too. Well done. Good thinking.

He shakes the MANIAC's hand energetically. It comes off in his hand.

MANIAC: There – you've pulled it off. I told you it was wooden!

SPORTS JACKET: I'm sorry.

MANIAC: You'll be pulling my leg off next.

So saying he screws the hand back in place.

SUPERINTENDENT: (*To* BERTOZZO) Would you like to say something, Bertozzo, to show that our department's not asleep on the job either?

He gives him an encouraging pat on the back.

INSPECTOR BERTOZZO: Certainly. The real bomb was rather complicated. I saw it. A lot more complex than this one. Evidently put together by people with a lot of know-how... Professionals, you might say.

SUPERINTENDENT: Careful how you go, there...!

JOURNALIST: Professionals? Military personnel, perhaps?

INSPECTOR BERTOZZO: More than likely.

The other three all start kicking him.

SUPERINTENDENT: Idiot...!

INSPECTOR BERTOZZO: Ouch! Did I say something wrong?

JOURNALIST: (*As she finishes writing*) Excellent. So what did you do? Even though you were well aware that to construct – let alone plant – a bomb of such complexity, would take the skills and experience of professionals – probably military people – you decided to go chasing after this fairly pathetic group of anarchists and completely dropped all other lines of inquiry among certain parties who shall remain nameless but you know who I mean.

MANIAC: That's true, if you're going to go along with Bertozzo's version, but you can't take his opinion as gospel, because he's not really an explosives *expert*... He does it more as a sideline, a hobby!

INSPECTOR BERTOZZO: (*Insulted*) What do you mean, a hobby...?! What do *you* know about anything...? Who are you? (*Turning to the two other* POLICE OFFICERS) Who is he...? Can someone explain?

The others kick him and force him to sit down.

SUPERINTENDENT: Relax...

SPORTS JACKET: Don't worry...

JOURNALIST: Calm down, Inspector... Relax... I'm sure that everything you said was true. Just as it's true that the police and the judicial establishment have moved hell and high water to lay the blame at the door of this crazy, confused gang of pathetic dreamers, with the vaudeville dancer at their head!

SUPERINTENDENT: You're right – they did look confused – but that was only a façade they were putting up so's nobody would know what they were up to.

JOURNALIST: OK. So let's take a look behind that façade. What do we find? Out of the ten members of the group, two of them were your own people, two informers, or rather, spies and provocateurs. One was a Rome fascist, well-known to everyone except the aforementioned pathetic group of anarchists, and the other was one of your own officers, disguised as an anarchist.

MANIAC: Mind you, I know the officer in question, and I

can't imagine how he ever got away with it. He's as thick as two short planks. Ask him who Bakunin was and he'll tell you it's a Swiss cheese, the one without the holes!

INSPECTOR BERTOZZO: How come he's such a know-all? I hate people like that... But I know I know him from somewhere!

SUPERINTENDENT: I must disagree with you, Captain. The officer in question is a fine operative, very well trained!

JOURNALIST: And I suppose you have plenty more of these very well-trained operatives scattered around the Left groups?

SUPERINTENDENT: I see no reason to deny it, Miss. Yes we do.

JOURNALIST: I think you're just calling my bluff, there, Superintendent!

SUPERINTENDENT: Not at all... In fact you may be interested to know that we have one or two right here in the audience tonight, as usual... Watch this.

He claps his hands. We hear a number of voices from different parts of the auditorium.

VOICES: Sir...? Yessir...! Sir...!

The MANIAC laughs, and turns to the audience.

MANIAC: Don't worry – they're all actors. The real ones sit tight and don't say a word.

SUPERINTENDENT: You see? Our agents and informants are our strength.

SPORTS JACKET: They help us to keep an eye on things and keep one jump ahead...

MANIAC: And to plant bombs so as to have a good pretext for a police-state crackdown... (*The* POLICE OFFICERS *are startled by this*) I was just pre-empting the lady's obvious come-back.

JOURNALIST: Too easy, really. Anyway, can you explain: since you had every member of that pathetic little band of anarchists under close surveillance, how was it that that they managed to organise such a sophisticated operation without you intervening to stop them?

MANIAC: Watch out, she's coming in for the kill!

SUPERINTENDENT: The fact is, during the days in question, our undercover agent was absent from the group...

MANIAC: It's true, he even had a note from his mum (this is true, this is!).

SPORTS JACKET: Please... (*Under his breath*) Your Honour...!

JOURNALIST: But your other informer, the fascist, he was there, wasn't he...? In fact the judge in Rome considered him to have been the main organiser of the whole thing, the person who, once again in the judge's own words, had taken advantage of the naivety of those anarchists in order to involve them in a terrorist conspiracy the true criminal nature of which they did not suspect. As I say, those are the words of the judge himself.

MANIAC: A hit, a palpable hit!

SUPERINTENDENT: Well, for a start, I have to tell you that the fascist you're talking about was not one of our informers at all.

JOURNALIST: Oh no? Well in that case how come he was always popping in and out of police headquarters in Rome? And the political section in particular...

SUPERINTENDENT: I've only your word for that... This is the first *I've* heard of it.

MANIAC: (*Going to shake the* SUPERINTENDENT's *hand*) Well said! Touché!

The SUPERINTENDENT *shakes his wooden hand, and is left holding it.*

SUPERINTENDENT: Thank you... Oh dear, your hand... I'm sorry!

MANIAC: (*Indifferent*) You can keep it. I've got another one here.

He takes another hand out of his bag; this time it's a woman's hand.

SPORTS JACKET: That's a woman's!

MANIAC: No, it's unisex.

So saying, he screws it into place.

JOURNALIST: (*Taking some papers from a folder*) Ah, so this is the first you've heard of it, eh? And I suppose nobody's told you either that out of a total of 173 bomb attacks that have happened in the past year and a bit, at a rate of twelve a month, one every three days – out of 173 attacks, as I was saying (*She reads from a report*) at least 102 have been proved to have been organised by fascist organisations, aided or abetted by the police, with the explicit intention of putting the blame on Left-wing political groups.

MANIAC: (*Gesturing with an open hand under his chin*) Terrific!

INSPECTOR BERTOZZO: I'm *sure* I know him – I'm going to have that patch off!

MANIAC: (*Intervening, ironically*) What are you trying to suggest, Miss, with these blatant provocations? Are you saying that if the police, instead of wasting their time with a raggle-taggle bunch of anarchists, had concentrated on more serious possibilities – for example paramilitary and fascist organisations funded by big industrialists and run and supported by leading figures in the armed forces – then maybe we'd have got to the bottom of all this?

SUPERINTENDENT: (*To* BERTOZZO, *who is about to blow a fuse*) Don't worry... Now he's going to turn the whole argument on its head. I know how he works now. It's Jesuit dialectics!

MANIAC: If that's what you're thinking, then I have to say, yes... you're completely right... If we'd taken *that* route, we would certainly have come up with some juicy titbits. Ha, ha!

INSPECTOR BERTOZZO: So much for Jesuit dialectics!

SUPERINTENDENT: He's gone mad!

INSPECTOR BERTOZZO: (*In a flash of inspiration*) Mad! The nutter... It's him!! that's who he is!

JOURNALIST: I must say, to hear a policeman saying such things... is a bit disconcerting!

SUPERINTENDENT: Well, you should keep them to yourself and don't go spreading them around.

He leaves BERTOZZO *and goes over to the* MANIAC *and the* JOURNALIST.

INSPECTOR BERTOZZO: (*He pulls the* INSPECTOR IN THE SPORTS JACKET *aside*) I promise you, I know that man... He's not from the police at all – he's just pretending.

SPORTS JACKET: We're perfectly well aware of that. But don't let the journalist hear you.

INSPECTOR BERTOZZO: But he's a nutter... Don't you understand?

SPORTS JACKET: You're the nutter... Shut up, I can't hear what they're saying!

MANIAC: (*During the above exchanges the* MANIAC *has been in earnest conversation with the* SUPERINTENDENT *and the* JOURNALIST; *he continues out loud*) ...Of course, you're a journalist, and you could really go to town on a scandal like this... It wouldn't be very hard to discover that the main intention behind the massacre of innocent people in the bank bombing had been to bury the trade-union struggles of the Hot Autumn [6] and to create a climate of tension so that the average citizen would be so disgusted and angry at the level of political violence and subversion that they would start calling for the intervention of a strong state!

SPORTS JACKET: I don't remember where I read that – was it in *L'Unità* or *Lotta Continua*?

INSPECTOR BERTOZZO: (*He goes up behind the* MANIAC *and pulls his eye-patch off*) There, look! You see, he's got an eye, he's got an eye!

SUPERINTENDENT: Have you gone round the twist, Bertozzo? Of course he's got an eye! Why shouldn't he have?

INSPECTOR BERTOZZO: So why was he wearing an eye-patch, if he's got an eye?

SUPERINTENDENT: You've got an eye under your patch... and people don't go pulling your patch off! (*He takes him aside*) Just shut up for a minute, I'll explain after.

JOURNALIST: Oh, how marvellous, you wear an eye-patch just for fun?

MANIAC: No, it's so as to keep a low profile.

He laughs.

JOURNALIST: Ha, ha, ha... Now, I'd be interested to hear more about this scandal of yours.

MANIAC: Oh yes... A huge scandal... A lot of Right-wing politicians arrested... A trial or two... A lot of big fish compromised... Senators, members of parliament, colonels... The social democrats weeping, the *Corriere della Sera* having to sack its editor... The Left calling for the fascist parties to be banned... And then... the Chief of Police would be commended for his courageous stand... and promptly given early retirement.

SUPERINTENDENT: No, Captain... I can't accept these gratuitous innuendos...

JOURNALIST: This time I have to agree with you, Superintendent... I believe that a scandal of that scale would actually do credit to the police. It would give the average citizen the sense of living in a decent society for once, where the system of justice was a little less unjust...

MANIAC: Certainly... and as such it would have served its purpose! Are the people calling for true justice? Instead of that we'll give them a justice that is just a bit less unjust.

And if the workers start shouting 'Enough of this brutal exploitation', and start complaining that they're tired of dying in the factories, then we give them a little more protection on the job... and step up the compensation rates for their widows!

They want revolution...? We give them reforms... reforms by the bucketful... We'll drown them with reforms... or rather we'll drown them with *promises* of reforms, because we're never going to give them reforms either!!

SUPERINTENDENT: The man's completely mad!

INSPECTOR BERTOZZO: Of course he is. I've been trying to tell you that for the past hour!

MANIAC: You see, your average citizen doesn't actually *want* all the dirt to disappear. No, for him it's enough that it's uncovered, there's a nice juicy scandal, and everyone can talk about it... As far as he's concerned, that is real freedom, the best of all possible worlds... hallelujah!

INSPECTOR BERTOZZO: (*Seizing the* MANIAC'*s wooden leg and shaking it*) Hey – look! his leg... it's false, can't you see?

MANIAC: Of course it is... walnut, to be precise.

SUPERINTENDENT: It's alright, we know, we know...

INSPECTOR BERTOZZO: No, it's a *false* false leg... It's strapped to his knee!

He sets about undoing the straps.

SPORTS JACKET: Idiot... Leave him alone! I won't have you taking him apart!

MANIAC: No, let him go ahead... Thank you... I was starting to get pins and needles all up my thigh.

JOURNALIST: Do you mind?! Why do you always have to interrupt? Just because his wooden leg isn't real, you're not suggesting that he's...?

INSPECTOR BERTOZZO: No, I'm just trying to tell you... he's a faker... a 'hypocritomaniac'... He's no more a war-wounded captain from Forensic than I am...!

JOURNALIST: So who is he, then?

INSPECTOR BERTOZZO: He's just a...

The SUPERINTENDENT, *the* CONSTABLE *and the* INSPECTOR IN THE SPORTS JACKET *run over and haul him off, to shut him up.*

SUPERINTENDENT: Excuse us, Miss, he's wanted on the phone.

They move her to the front of the stage, to distract her. Then they take INSPECTOR BERTOZZO, *sit him down at the desk and force him to pick up the phone.*

SPORTS JACKET: (*Muttering to* BERTOZZO) Are you trying to destroy us? Idiot!

Downstage, the JOURNALIST *and the* MANIAC *continue their conversation, oblivious of the* POLICE OFFICERS.

SUPERINTENDENT: Don't you understand... that's got to stay secret! If the journalist finds out that they're re-opening the inquest into the anarchist, we're done for!

INSPECTOR BERTOZZO: Who's re-opening the inquest? (*Once again the phone is almost shoved down his throat*) Hello?

SPORTS JACKET: You're asking *me*?! *You're* the one who's saying he knows what it's all about... in fact you know damn-all... You're all yakety-yak... Coming in here and causing trouble...

INSPECTOR BERTOZZO: I'm not causing trouble... I just want to know...?

SUPERINTENDENT: Shush... (*He raps him over the knuckles with the phone*) Get talking on that phone, and shut up!

INSPECTOR BERTOZZO: Ouch... Hello, who's calling?

JOURNALIST: (*Continuing her conversation with the* CAPTAIN) Oh, that is terrific! Superintendent, you have no need to worry. The Captain... or rather, the ex-Captain, has told me everything.

SUPERINTENDENT: What has he told you?

JOURNALIST: Who he really is!

SPORTS JACKET *and* **SUPERINTENDENT:** He told you?

MANIAC: Yes, I couldn't carry on pretending... And anyway... she'd already tumbled me.

SUPERINTENDENT: I hope he made you promise not to put it in your paper?

JOURNALIST: Not at all. This is how I'm going to start the article. (*She reads from her notes*) 'I Met a Plain-Clothes Bishop at Police Headquarters'!

SPORTS JACKET *and* **SUPERINTENDENT:** A bishop?!

MANIAC: Yes. My apologies for not having let you in on my secret.

With a simple gesture he turns his collar round so that it becomes a dog-collar, complete with black shirt-front.

INSPECTOR BERTOZZO: (*Giving himself a smack on the forehead*) So now he's a bishop! I sincerely hope you're not going to believe him?

The INSPECTOR IN THE SPORTS JACKET *picks up a big rubber stamp and jams it in* BERTOZZO's *mouth.*

SPORTS JACKET: You're getting Very Boring!

The MANIAC *takes out a red skull-cap and places it on his head; with austere, simple gestures he unbuttons his jacket to reveal a baroque gold and silver cross; then he places on his finger a large ring with an equally large purple gem.*

MANIAC: Allow me to introduce myself: Father Augusto Bernier, Vatican *chargé d'affaires* responsible for relations with the Italian police.

He reaches out his ring for the CONSTABLE *to kiss, which he does, eagerly.*

INSPECTOR BERTOZZO: (*Coming forward, and pulling*

out his rubber-stamp dummy) Vatican *chargé d'affaires*...?

MANIAC: Ever since the assassination attempt on the Pope, the Church authorities have felt that it would be a good idea to maintain regular channels of communication...

INSPECTOR BERTOZZO: Oh no, you don't! No! This is going too far – a constabulary cardinal?!

The INSPECTOR IN THE SPORTS JACKET *jams the rubber stamp back in his mouth, and pulls him aside.*

SPORTS JACKET: We *know* he's talking bollocks, but he's doing it to save us... Understand?

INSPECTOR BERTOZZO: Save you? What is this? He's promised you eternal salvation too?!

SPORTS JACKET: Pack it in, and kiss his ring!

He forces him across to kiss the MANIAC's *ring. In the meantime, effortlessly, the* MANIAC *has succeeded in getting his hand kissed by all the other characters.*

INSPECTOR BERTOZZO: No way! Kiss his ring? You must be joking! You've *all* gone mad. He's infected you all!

The INSPECTOR IN THE SPORTS JACKET *and the* CONSTABLE *hurriedly dig out a couple of large sticking plasters and slap them over his mouth, more or less covering the bottom half of his face.*

JOURNALIST: Oh dear, what's the matter with the poor man?

MANIAC: Some kind of seizure, I should say. (*He takes out a hypodermic syringe that he has concealed in a prayer book, and prepares to give* BERTOZZO *an injection*) Hold him, a moment, this will do him good... It's a Benedictine tranquilliser.

SUPERINTENDENT: Benedictine?

MANIAC: Yes, Father Finnigan's Special. (*With cobra-like rapidity he gives* BERTOZZO *his injection; then, pulling out the needle, he says:*) there's still a bit left – would you like some too?

Without waiting for a reply, he injects the
SUPERINTENDENT, *with the agility of a banderillero at
a bullfight. The* SUPERINTENDENT *emits a stifled
groan.*

JOURNALIST: You won't believe this, your Eminence, but a
moment ago, when you were talking about the scandals,
and you said, 'that is real freedom, the best of all possible
worlds... hallelujah'... I immediately thought – I hope
you'll pardon the irreverence...

MANIAC: Go ahead, go ahead...

JOURNALIST: I immediately thought: 'Phew – what a load
of priest-talk!' I hope you're not offended.

MANIAC: Why should I be offended? It's true – it was priest
talk... but that's because I'm a priest.

INSPECTOR BERTOZZO *picks up a felt-tip pen, turns
round the portrait of the Italian president, and writes on the
back of it: 'He's mad! He's a certified schizophrenic.' Then
he holds the message up behind the* BISHOP's *back.*

Did you know that when Saint Gregory was elected Pope,
he discovered that his subordinates were up to all kinds of
skullduggery in an attempt to cover up various outrageous
scandals? He was furious, and it was then that he uttered
his famous phrase: *Nolimus aut velimus, omnibus gentibus,
justitiam et veritatem.*

JOURNALIST: I'm sorry, your Eminence... I failed Latin
three times...

MANIAC: It means: 'Whether they want it or not, I shall
impose truth and justice. I shall do what I can to make sure
that these scandals explode in the most public way
possible; and you need not fear that, in among the rot, the
power of government will be undermined. Let the scandal
come, because on the basis of that scandal a more durable
power of the state will be founded!'

JOURNALIST: Extraordinary...! Would you mind writing
that down for me...?

The MANIAC *writes the sentence – an adaptation of the words of Pope Gregory – in the* JOURNALIST'*s notebook. Meanwhile, the* INSPECTOR IN THE SPORTS JACKET *snatches the President's picture from* BERTOZZO *and begins tearing it up.*

SUPERINTENDENT: (*Going to stop him*) What have you done? You've torn up the President's portrait! You could go to prison for that! What's got into you?

SPORTS JACKET: Didn't you see what he was writing, Sir…?

He points to BERTOZZO.

SUPERINTENDENT: You've got a point, about certain people having a mania for melodramatic messages to the people… But that was no reason to go shredding up the President's portrait… Shame on you!

The JOURNALIST *stands behind the* MANIAC *as he writes, apparently pondering the meaning of Saint Gregory's words.*

JOURNALIST: So in other words he's saying that even when there aren't scandals, they need to be invented, because it's a good way of maintaining power and defusing people's anger.

MANIAC: Correct. A liberatory catharsis of tension… And you journalists are the privileged high priests of the process.

JOURNALIST: Privileged? You must be joking! Not in the eyes of our government! Every time we discover a scandal, they go potty trying to stop the truth getting out.

MANIAC: Certainly… *our* government… But *our* government is still pre-Napoleonic… pre-capitalist… You should take a look at the governments of more developed countries… Northern Europe, for example. You remember the 'Profumo' scandal in England? A minister of defence, caught up with drugs, prostitution and spying…!!! Did the state collapse? Or the stock exchange?

Not a bit of it. If anything they came out of it stronger than before. People thought: 'The rot's there, so let it float to the surface...' We're swimming about in it – even swallowing some of it – but nobody comes round telling us that everything's fine and dandy, and that's what counts!

SUPERINTENDENT: Surely not. That would be like saying that scandal is the fertiliser of social democracy!

MANIAC: Spot on! Manure! *Scandal is the fertiliser of social democracy!* In fact I'd go even further: scandal is the best antidote to the worst of poisons – namely when people come to realise what's really going on. When people begin to realise what's going on, we're done for! But look at America – a truly social-democratic society. Did they ever try to censor the true facts about the massacres carried out by the American troops in Vietnam? No they did not! It was on the front pages of all the papers – photos of women butchered, children massacred, villages destroyed. And do you remember the scandal of the nerve gas? The Americans had manufactured enough nerve gas in the US to wipe out the entire population of the world three times over. But did they try to hide the fact? Not a bit of it! In fact, when you turned on the TV, there they were. Trains. 'And where are those trains going?' 'To the seaside.' 'And what are those trains carrying?' 'Nerve gas. It's going to be dumped at sea... A few miles off the shoreline!' So that supposing there's a little earthquake one day, the containers will crack, and the nerve gas will come bubbling up to the surface, glug-glug-glug, and we'll all die. Three times over!

They've never tried to hush up these scandals. And they're right not to. That way, people can let off steam, get angry, shudder at the thought of it... 'Who do these politicians think they are?' 'Scumbag generals!' 'Murderers!' And they get more and more angry, and then, burp! A little liberatory burp to relieve their social indigestion.

JOURNALIST: But excuse me – you say America's so free, but what do you have to say about the calculated murder of

terrorists, with their families, and the burning of an entire
black area of Philadelphia?

MANIAC: I was talking of the 'right to liberatory burps', not
the 'right to life'.

INSPECTOR BERTOZZO: Get your hands up…! Backs
against the wall or I shoot!

SPORTS JACKET: Bertozzo, are you out of your mind?!

INSPECTOR BERTOZZO: Hands up, I said… And you too,
Superintendent… or I warn you, I may not be answerable
for my actions!

JOURNALIST: Oh God!

SUPERINTENDENT: Calm down, Bertozzo!

INSPECTOR BERTOZZO: Calm down yourself, Sir… you'll
see… (*He pulls several sets of handcuffs out of a drawer in
the desk, passes them to the* CONSTABLE *and tells him to
handcuff everyone*) Go on – handcuff them to the coat-rail.

*As it happens, at the back of the stage there is a raised
horizontal bar, to which all the characters are promptly
handcuffed, one handcuff round their right wrist, the other
round the bar.*

And you don't have to look at me like that. In a minute
you'll realise that this was the only way I could get a
hearing.

The CONSTABLE *is not sure whether to handcuff the*
JOURNALIST *as well.*

Yes, the lady too… And handcuff yourself as well, while
you're at it. (*Turning to the* MANIAC) Now, you, Mr
Bigmouth Bullshit, you will do me the favour of explaining
to these people who you *really* are… or, since I'm getting
very sincerely sick of the sight of you, I'll blow your damn
head off…! OK?

The POLICE OFFICERS *and the* JOURNALIST *protest
at his irreverent tone to such an august personage.*

Shut up… you!

MANIAC: I'm happy to explain, but I'm afraid that if I just tell them, straight out, just like that, they're not going to believe me.

INSPECTOR BERTOZZO: Maybe you'd like to sing it, then?

MANIAC: No, I'd just need to show them my medical card, my papers from the nuthouse, and all that...

INSPECTOR BERTOZZO: Fair enough... Where are they?

MANIAC: In that bag, there.

INSPECTOR BERTOZZO: Go get them, then. No funny business, mind, or I shoot!

From his bag the MANIAC *takes half a dozen personal documents.*

MANIAC: There...

He hands them to BERTOZZO.

INSPECTOR BERTOZZO: (*He distributes them to each of the characters, who take them with their unhandcuffed left hands*) There you are, ladies and gentlemen... Seeing is believing!

SUPERINTENDENT: Nooo! An art teacher? Indefinite sick-leave? Subject to paranoid delusions?! So he's a bloody mental case, then?

INSPECTOR BERTOZZO: (*Sighing*) Haven't I been trying to tell you that all along?

SUPERINTENDENT: (*Reading from a medical card*) It's a list of psychiatric hospitals – Imola, Voghera, Varese, Gorizia, Parma... He's done the lot of them!

MANIAC: I have indeed... the Grand Tour!

JOURNALIST: Fifteen electric shock treatments... Twenty days solitary confinement...

CONSTABLE: (*Reading from a report*) Pyromaniac. Arsonist.

JOURNALIST: Let me see? Burned down the library at Alexandria... Egypt... in the Second Century BC...?!

INSPECTOR BERTOZZO: Impossible. Give that here! (*He takes a look*) No, look, he wrote it in himself, the bit about Egypt!

SUPERINTENDENT: So he's a forger too, as well as being a hoaxer, an impostor and a quick-change artist...

The MANIAC *sits to one side, with an innocent air, and with his big bag on his knees.*

I'm going to lock you away for this, for a long time... Fraudulent impersonation!

MANIAC: (*All smiles*) Tsk, tsk!

He gestures to indicate 'not possible'.

INSPECTOR BERTOZZO: You can't, Sir. He's certified, Sir, certified mad.

JOURNALIST: What a shame. I had a really nice article all lined up... and he's gone and spoiled it!

SUPERINTENDENT: I'll spoil *him* when I get my hands on him... Bertozzo, will you please undo these handcuffs...

INSPECTOR BERTOZZO: Maybe better if I don't, Sir... You know that in Italy nutters are like the sacred cows in India... God help you if you touch so much as a hair on their heads!

SUPERINTENDENT: The bastard... Coming here... Pretending to be a judge... Pretending that he was re-opening the inquiry into the anarchist... When I think of the shock he gave me!

MANIAC: That's nothing compared to the shock I've got for you now! Take a look at this! (*From his bag he pulls the bomb that* BERTOZZO *had left on the desk*) Count to ten, and we all get blown sky-high!

INSPECTOR BERTOZZO: What are you doing...!? Put that down... Don't be stupid!

MANIAC: I'm mad, not stupid... Mind your language, Bertozzo... and drop that gun... or I stick my finger in the firing mechanism here, and poof, away we go!

JOURNALIST: Oh God! Please, Mr, er...!

SUPERINTENDENT: Don't fall for it, Bertozzo... There's no fuse in that bomb... How can it possibly explode?

SPORTS JACKET: Correct... Don't fall for it!

MANIAC: Alright, then, Bertozzo – since you're such an expert... even if you are ungrammatical... See if you can spot the firing mechanism... Look in there... See? It's a Longbar acoustic.

INSPECTOR BERTOZZO: (*He feels faint. He drops the gun and the keys to the handcuffs*) A Longbar acoustic? Where did you find that?

The MANIAC *picks up the keys and the gun.*

MANIAC: I had it in here... (*Pointing to his big bag*) I've got everything in here! I've also got a tape-recorder on which I've been recording everything you've said since I came through that door. (*He takes out a tape-recorder and shows it to them*) There you go!

SUPERINTENDENT: And what are you planning to do with it?

MANIAC: I'm going to make a hundred copies of the tape, and send them to all the papers... and to the political parties, and to the ministries... Ha, ha... it'll be a scorcher!

SUPERINTENDENT: No, you couldn't do that... You know perfectly well, everything we said was deliberately twisted and distorted by the fact that you were pretending to be a judge!

MANIAC: So? Who cares? the important thing is to have a good scandal... *Nolimus aut velimus*! So that the Italian nation can march alongside the Americans and the English, and become a modern and social-democratic society, so that finally we can say: 'It's true – we're in the shit right up to our necks, and that's precisely the reason why we walk with our heads held high!'

Postscript

In this Postscript written for the 1974 Einaudi edition of
Accidental Death of an Anarchist, *Dario Fo describes the
genesis of the play and its impact in Italy. The translation is by
Ed Emery.*

How did we hit upon the idea of staging a show based on the
theme of the State massacre? Here, we were driven once
again by force of circumstances. During the Spring of 1970 the
comrades who were coming to see our shows – workers,
students and progressives – were asking us to write a
full-length piece on the Milan bombings and the murder of
Pinelli, a piece which would discuss the political motives and
consequences of these events. The reason for their request
was the terrible shortage of information on the subject. Once
the Press had got over the initial shock, they went silent. The
newspapers of the official Left parties – with *L'Unità* at their
head – refused to take sides, and limited themselves to the odd
comment such as: 'This is a worrying episode', or 'The
circumstances surrounding both Pinelli's death and the
massacres at the banks are obscure and shrouded in mystery.'
They had decided to wait for 'light to be shed' – waiting, so as
to avoid making too much fuss.

But no. This was precisely the time to make a fuss, with
every means available: so that people who are always thinking
about other things, who don't read much and don't read well,
and even then are only interested in their own patch, could be
told how the State is capable of organising a massacre and at
the same time organise the mourning, the public outrage, the

medals for the widows and orphans, and the official funerals with carabinieri presenting arms and standing to attention.

At the begining of that Summer, Samonà-Savelli had published the book *La Strage di Stato* (published as 'Italian State Massacre', Libertaria, London, 1971): this was an extraordinarily detailed documentation, packed with material, which showed great courage and determination on the part of its authors. Then, in the Autumn, legal proceedings were started by Inspector Calabresi against the newspaper *Lotta Continua*, and its editor Pio Baldelli. It was at this point that we too realised that it was time to get something moving as soon as possible.

We in turn embarked on a research project. A group of lawyers and journalists made available to us photocopies of several articles which had been prepared by democratic and left-wing newspapers but never published. We were also lucky enough to get our hands on various documents from the court proceedings, as well as being able to read the judges' Order for the Pinelli case to be shelved (and, as we know, the important trials which, in some people's view, would have 'shed light' on the episode, were subsequently postponed and then abandoned definitively: by reason of the non-accidental death of the actor). [7]

We drew up a first draft of the play. It was, naturally, a farce, because such was the painful grotesqueness of the court proceedings and the contradictions in official statements. We were informed that we might be running the risk of legal proceedings, with trials and charges being brought against us. Nevertheless, we decided not only that it was worth the effort to try, but also that it was our duty as political militants. The important thing was to act and to act fast.

The first night of the play, in our converted warehouse theatre in via Colletta, coincided with the trial of Pio Baldelli. It was an extraordinary popular success: every evening the theatre was sold out half an hour before the performance began, and we ended up performing with people on the stage, in the wings. Despite the provocations: the usual phone calls from unnamed callers telling us that there was a bomb in the theatre; the interventions of the Flying Squad; the way the bosses' Press highlighted the incident; despite all this, we were encouraged to hold firm by the lawyer comrades in the Calabresi-Baldelli case, and performances continued, with full houses, away past mid-January.

Our difficulties began when we set off on tour. In via Colletta [8] we were on home ground. Outside Milan, the comrades who were organising things for us went out to try and hire theatres, cinemas and dance halls. There was more than one hall-owner who refused to let us use his premises, even though we were prepared to pay for any damage, since somebody had had a quiet word with him. Somebody who didn't want to lose his job as local police chief.

Often, though, apparent defeats were turned into victories. At Bologna, for example, we were denied the use of the 1,500-seat Duse Theatre. But instead we managed to get the 6,000 seats of the Sports Stadium, and the people came and packed it. It began to become clear that the police and one or two mayors more or less in league with the government, were making an effort to prevent certain things being known about... Well, certain things absolutely *had* to be known about.

But what has been the real reason for the show's success? It is not so much the way it mocks the hypocrisies, the lies that are organised so grossly and blatantly (which is putting it mildly) by the constituted organs of the State and by the functionaries who serve them (judges, police chiefs, prefects, undersecretaries and ministers); it has been above all the way it deals with social democracy and its crocodile tears, the indignation which can be relieved by a little burp in the form of scandal; scandal as a liberating catharsis of the system. A burp which liberates itself precisely through the scandal that explodes, when it is discovered that massacres, giant frauds and murders are undertaken by the organs of power, but that at the same time, from within the powers-that-be, other organs, perhaps pushed by an enraged public opinion, denounce them and unmask them. The indignation of the good democratic citizen grows and threatens to suffocate him. But he has a sense of satisfaction when he sees, in the end, these same organs of this rotten and corrupt society, pointing

the finger at this selfsame society, at its own 'unhealthy parts',
and this gives him a sense of freedom throughout his whole
being. With his spirit suitably decongested, he shouts: 'Long
live this bastard shit society, because at least it always wipes its
bum with soft, perfumed paper, and when it burps it has the
good manners to put its hand in front of its mouth!'

Accidental Death of an Anarchist has been running for two
seasons now. It has been performed something like 300 times,
and has been seen by more than 300,000 people. In the
meantime, the spiral of the strategy of tension has increased,
and has created other victims: the play has been brought up to
date, and its message has been made more explicit. With the
death of Feltrinelli, [9] a long introductory section was added,
and the title was changed to *Morte accidentale di un anarchico
e di alcuni altri sovversivi* ('Accidental death of an anarchist,
and of other subversives'). Our immediate intention was to
make it clear that the State massacre is continuing relentlessly,
and that it remains motivated by the same people. The same
people who have kept Valpreda and his comrades in prison in
the hope that they will die; the same people who have beaten
a young man in the streets of Pisa and then in prison and
finally killed him; the same ones who are behind a
revolutionary militant getting stabbed in Parma – not just an
'anti-fascist youth', as the revisionists are claiming. The same
people who are preparing for an Autumn of reaction and
violence, preceding it with blackmail against the movement,
against all those who are not willing to bow their heads.

But unluckily for them, they will have to realise that there
are a lot of us... and that this time their burp is going to stick
in their throats.

For the La Comune Theatre Collective
DARIO FO

NOTES

1. The figure of *il Matto* – the Madman, here rendered as the 'Maniac' – is a typical Fo figure – someone rejected by society who has access to the truth. A Madman appears in two episodes of *Mistero Buffo* contained in this volume. In one he gambles with death, and in the other dices with the soldiers at the foot of the cross.

2. In the Italian edition, the reference to the 'comissario Calabrese' amounts to a pun suggesting the name of Luigi Calabresi, from whose fourth-floor office railwayman the anarchist railwayman Giuseppe Pinelli fell to his death on 15 December 1969. He was to sue the Left-wing newspaper *Lotta continua* for defamation, and was subsequently assassinated. Hence the reference to the non-accidental death of the actor in the Postscript. Italian audiences would have been familiar with a newspaper photograph showing Calabresi wearing a polo neck sweater and sports jacket.

3. See note 2.

4. This song is on a old record compilation by Dischi del Sole, available in the Italian archive of Red Notes, c/o BP15, 2a St Paul's Road, London N1.

5. A famous Neapolitan actor and comedian.

6. The Hot Autumn was a large-scale movement of workers' and students' struggles which developed in late 1969, and were to spread throughout Italy during the following years.

7. See note 2.

8. Via Colletta – the warehouse in Milan occupied by the La Comune theatre collective, which was the base for their militant theatrical activities.

9. Head of the influential Left-wing publishing house of that name. Found dead in suspicious circumstances, with explosive materials near a power pylon. His death has never been explained.

Trumpets
and Raspberries

Translated by R.C. McAvoy *and* A.M. Giugni

Characters

ANTONIO BERARDI/
   GIANNI AGNELLI
LUCIA RISMONDI
ROSA MINELLI
DOCTOR/
   SECRET AGENT/
   GROUP LEADER
FIRST WARD ORDERLY/
   FIRST SECRET AGENT
SECOND WARD ORDERLY/
   SECOND SECRET AGENT
THIRD WARD ORDERLY/
   THIRD SECRET AGENT
FOURTH WARD ORDERLY/
   FOURTH SECRET AGENT
EXAMINING MAGISTRATE/
   WAITER/
   MAN WITH DISHWASHER
DUMMY
WINDOW

ACT ONE

Scene One

The stage lights come up slowly. We find ourselves in the recovery ward of a hospital. Four hospital ORDERLIES bustle about. They are wearing operating-theatre gear – green gowns, green caps, plastic gloves and clown-like antiseptic masks. As the lights come up, the WARD ORDERLIES are bringing equipment on-stage – various bits of electronic apparatus, and two office-style chairs on castors. Everything is covered with sheets of transparent cellophane, to indicate that the place is kept scrupulously germ-free.

One of the ORDERLIES arranges a very large and conspicuous bust of a man. This is mounted on a silver pedestal, and it too is wrapped in cellophane.

From the rear of the stage, enter the DOCTOR and ROSA MINELLI.

DOCTOR: This way, please, madam... we just want you to identify the patient.

ROSA: (*Almost bumping into the bust*) Oh, that's not him.

DOCTOR: This is a statue of Agnelli.[1] Our whole Recovery Ward was funded by the Agnelli Foundation.

ROSA: I thought that was the patient!

A WARD ORDERLY offers ROSA a theatre gown to put on.

Do I have to put it on?

ORDERLY: Of course, madam.

DOCTOR: Madam, if you don't feel up to it, we could postpone it till later.

ROSA: No, no... I want to see him straight away. I'm ready...

DOCTOR: Yes indeed, he looks pretty awful, even for us, and we should be used to it. He's completely disfigured, you know.

ROSA: Disfigured? (*Starting to cry*) Oh God... Poor Antonio...

The ORDERLY *slips a pair of canvas hospital overshoes onto her feet.*

What are you doing? (*Speaking normally*) Ah, it's for the polishing... Are you short-staffed? Oh all right, I don't mind. Disfigured, eh? And to think, he had such a handsome face... So open and likeable... You won't believe this, Professor, but I still loved him, even if he really didn't deserve it... when you think of the way he's treated me...

DOCTOR: She's getting overwrought. Prepare me a suppository with twenty drops of Asvanol Complex...

ROSA: Don't bother, Professor... I won't need it... I've already told you... I have no feelings for him... To me, my husband... was like a stranger... I haven't seen him for months. I can cope.

DOCTOR: I believe you... but it's just a precaution you know. I don't want to risk provoking a trauma in you, but it's for the identification... Unfortunately, the law requires it. Now come along, madam, and be strong.

At a signal from the DOCTOR, *a mobile stretcher-bed is wheeled on-stage. Lying on it is the body of* ROSA's *presumed husband,* ANTONIO. *In fact it is a* DUMMY, *which is all bandaged up and in plaster. The* WARD ORDERLIES *take the ends of the wires which hang down from an overhead frame, and connect them to the* DUMMY's *extremities. In this way, as occasion demands, he can be made to move like a large string puppet. The*

DUMMY's *entry is accompanied by a musical interlude.*
ROSA *gets up and speaks to the* DUMMY.

ROSA: Oh my God, Antonio, what have they done to you?!

She faints, and is held up by the DOCTOR *and one of the* ORDERLIES.

DOCTOR: Come on, come on... Be brave... Breathe deeply.

ROSA: His nose... He hasn't got a nose any longer...! It's all mashed to a pulp! And he already had sinusitis! And his chin... That's gone too. Let me near him!

DOCTOR: (*To the* ORDERLIES) No, keep her away!

ROSA: They've obliterated my Antonio... There's nothing left of him... apart from his ears. Antonio, Antonio! You see? He's got two ears, but he doesn't hear me!

DOCTOR: Obviously... He's in a deep coma.

ROSA: Oh, he's lost weight. It's that girl he's taken up with, the one who stole him away from me! Do you realise, she had him going out jogging?! Just imagine, a man of his age, a worker, admittedly a skilled worker... You force him to go running in a red tracksuit with 'Parmalat' written all over the back... a pom-pom hat with 'Michelin' stamped all over it, and 'Marlboro' track shoes... By the end, he looked more like a racing Ferrari...!

DOCTOR: Hurry up with that suppository... and please prepare me a syringe with Mecardizol.

ROSA: Don't bother about the hypodermic... If it's for me, at the very least I'll end up with an abcess on my backside! And then they have the nerve to talk about crime waves and terrorism... What about Agnelli? Those bastard managers at FIAT... with Agnelli at their head! They sent him to service some generator, hanging God knows how many feet up in the air, without safety gear... One careless moment and splat! A triple somersault with no safety net!

DOCTOR: No, madam, the accident didn't happen at the Circus...[2] I mean, in the factory, at FIAT.

ROSA: Oh no? And how can you be so sure... ? Were you

DOCTOR: No, but the hospital almoner's department looked into it. They made some brief inquiries. Yesterday, your husband was absent from work all afternoon.

ROSA: But where can it have happened, then?

DOCTOR: Maybe he was knocked down by a car... Some hit and run driver. In fact the person who handed him over to the Red Cross promptly – poof – disappeared!

ROSA: Poof was he aye? May God strike him down! May he give him a dose of St Vitus' Dance, and gonorrhea, so that when he gets the shakes his wotsits drop off! Oh, Antonio, if you'd only stayed with me... I bet they ran you over while you were out jogging! It's all the fault of that bitch... Don't get me wrong, Professor... She's a good-looking girl, but beauty's only skin deep and any woman of 23 can take a man's fancy... She makes me laugh! You should have seen *me* at her age! I mean, I'm boasting, but when I walked down the street, shop windows just used to shatter! What a din!

DOCTOR: I can quite well believe it. After all, you're still a beautiful woman...

ROSA: I know!

DOCTOR: It's the truth... Anyway, let's get back to your husband. Now, take a good look at his hands. Do you recognise them?

ROSA: No, not now... They look like two pieces of boiled meat... But afterwards, yes, when he gets better... because he will get better, won't he Professor... promise me that he will get better...

DOCTOR: Madam... we will do everything we can... Your husband is a very strong man...

ROSA: Ah yes, he's strong, very strong! He had such energy, such good health! He would never hold back from anything. When the *Unità* festival came round, for example...[3]

DOCTOR: So. You're communists are you?

ROSA: Oh, we've been communists for generations, from father to son... it's a custom we hand down in our family ...As I was saying, the *Unità* festival, he was always there, in charge of everything: he used to put up the stalls, sell the books, and buy them too... In his Party branch too, in the discussions, he would put forward all the arguments, and then put forward the counter-arguments, as well as the self-criticism. But don't go thinking that he was a fanatical bigot... No, far from it, he was always having arguments, particularly with the leadership... even if he had accepted the Third Road to socialism... he was also prepared for the Fourth Road ring road to socialism, and the bypass of the Fifth Road... because, as Karl Marx says, 'the roads to socialism are infinite'! Of course, she was always there behind him... the bitch, egging him on! Because she's an extremist. She doesn't even have a Party card... Nothing! Not even a Socialist Party card! She's one of those intellectuals who are always trying to teach us, the working class, everything. The kind of people who are crazy about the masses, but can't stand crowds! She isn't here, is she? She isn't hiding under the bed?

Inadvertently, ROSA *grabs hold of one of the strings and pulls on it. This results in the* DUMMY *leaping off the bed. Everyone, including the* DOCTOR, *rushes to rearrange it.*

DOCTOR: No. Madam, what are you doing! Don't touch!

ROSA: Oh my God! What have I done? Have I broken him? Hey, I'm not the only one to blame. Why do you leave the wires hanging down like that... Why don't you put up a notice: 'Don't pull on the wires!' Oh, what a fright... I can feel the tears coming on again... (*To an* ORDERLY) Excuse me, do you have a Kleenex so that I can blow my nose...

ORDERLY: Here you are, madam...

ROSA: Poor Antonio... And how's *he* going to blow his nose now that he hasn't got one?

During this exchange, the ORDERLIES *lift the* DOCTOR

up, into a horizontal position. From this curious position, he begins working on the DUMMY's face with swabs and forceps.

DOCTOR: Don't worry, madam, we'll make him another nose, and he'll be able to blow it whenever he wants.

ROSA: Professor, do you always work in such an uncomfortable position? Another nose? Will you be transplanting one from a dead person? But supposing his body rejects it, and his nose comes off into his handkerchief while he's blowing it? No, no nose! I'd rather have him like this... streamlined!

DOCTOR: No, no, no transplant! You are lucky, madam: our Institute is extremely advanced in plastic surgery operations.

The ORDERLIES now hold the DOCTOR as high as they can. He spreads out his arms, like an angel.

ORDERLY: Our Chief Surgeon is one of the best in the world!

DOCTOR: It's true.

The DOCTOR is slowly returned to the ground.

ROSA: Professor, he's looking at me! Look, there with that corner of his eye peeking out from the swelling... He's seen me, he's recognised me...! I'm sure of it... Antonio, Antonio, it's me, your Rosa... As soon as I heard what happened, I forgot everything... Here I am, and I'm not bitter... In fact, to tell you the truth, Antonio, I'm actually happy that this terrible thing has happened... No, no, I didn't mean that... What I mean is that I'm happy that I, your Rosa, can still be of use to you... I still love you, you know... I don't care if you used to go jogging with her, and eat brown rice and wheatgerm...! We'll forgive and forget, we'll get everything right just as it was before... We'll bury the past.

The DUMMY emits a groan.

No, Antonio, you misheard me. I didn't say that we'd bury *you*! Oh what a wally I am! But his jawbone here, it's all gone... there's just a big hole...

DOCTOR: The mandible is indeed in very poor shape... We're going to have to replace it with a whole prosthetic apparatus...

ROSA: Prosthetic? Whole apparatus?

DOCTOR: Precisely! We rebuild it entirely, on the basis of the original bone structure: we remove the parts which are broken, and we replace them. Incidentally, you will have to supply me with some photographs. Do you have any recent ones?

At this point, enter from backstage the actor who plays the part of ANTONIO.

ANTONIO: Excuse me... Excuse me... I'm going to have to interrupt at this point, because a misunderstanding is being created.

The ACTORS *on stage freeze.* ANTONIO *moves to the front of the stage, and addresses the audience directly. The lights go down in the operating theatre. The* ACTORS *exit.* ANTONIO *remains front-stage, and behind him, a platform is wheeled on. On it are two car seats and assorted scrap parts of motor cars. We are in a breaker's yard.*

ANTONIO: In this play, I act the part of Antonio, Rosa's husband. But I am not the doner kebab that you see here on the operating table. That's someone else. So who is it? Well, in order to explain this, I'm going to have to put things in order, and go back 24 hours, to yesterday evening. So, last night, or rather at about two o'clock this morning, I, Antonio Berardi, FIAT worker, was parked in my car in a secluded spot on the outskirts of Turin. To be precise, on the road that runs along the canal bank by Barriera di Milano. No, I was not alone. I was with a woman... and to be honest, it was not even the woman that I'm living with at the moment, Lucia, the one that Rosa calls the 'bitch'... Now, don't go getting the wrong idea... This wasn't some kind of erotic adventure... She was a colleague from work... a shop steward. We were discussing redundancies. She told me that the other day at FIAT, they sacked two workers for absenteeism – and then they discovered that they'd been dead for a month. Anyway, one thing led to another, and we made love, and afterwards I told Lucia about it... (*Calling off-stage*) Lucia, could you come in please...

Enter LUCIA. *She goes and sits down.*

...at dawn this morning, when we met in a carbreaker's yard run by a friend of mine... She didn't exactly mince her words...

LUCIA: So this is what you mean by exploring closer relations between the union leadership and the rank and file!

ANTONIO: Good God! You're a worse moraliser than my wife! You don't realise what a mess I'm in... It's a matter of life and death!

LUCIA: Life and death? I'm sorry, Antonio... Go ahead, tell me... I promise you, I won't say another word.

ANTONIO: Thank God for that.

LUCIA: Except that...

ANTONIO: Ah, Ah, Ah. Why did I get involved in all this? There I was, at peace with the world, with the shop steward... on the canal bank... having a cuddle... no mean feat in the back of a 128... when all of a sudden I see two cars tearing along, neck and neck jostling for position. I said: 'Look at those stupid lunatics, racing around at this time of night, especially on this kind of ground. They're liable to skid!' I'd hardly finished speaking, when one of the cars skidded... A terrible crash! The FIAT 132 (I knew it was a 132... It's the sort we make in our plant...) ...the 132 ended up in a mangled heap, not twenty yards away... The other one comes along, bounces off it, and ends up nose-down in the mud... I said, 'I expect they're both dead then.'

LUCIA: I can well believe it. So, what did you do?

ANTONIO: What was I supposed to do? I jumped out of my

128, just as I was, to see if I could save anyone. The car doors were jammed. I kicked them. I got them open. A cloud of smoke poured out... My God, my eyes were streaming... I was coughing... but I carried on, all the same: I dragged them out... One, two, three... They were asphyxiated. All of them, asphyxiated. I tried to pull out the fourth one. You should have seen the state of him. He was all smashed up... He was sitting next to the driver's seat. He'd smashed his face against the windscreen. Squashed flat! Flat as a 100-lire piece! All he needed was the writing round the edge: Republic of Italy...

LUCIA: Yes. All right, all right, what the hell.

ANTONIO: So, I dragged him out, dragged him out by the armpits. I was just laying him out on the grass, when suddenly Boom! The engine went up! Both of us were caught, full frontal, by the flames.

LUCIA: Oh, Christ!

ANTONIO: Well, no, not both of us... only him, actually. Because, as soon as I saw the flames, instinctively I pulled up our squashed friend and put him in front of me. You know how it is, it's instinct... One doesn't think... A spur of the moment thing!

LUCIA: So.

ANTONIO: So now he's all on fire, so I started pulling all his clothes off: his jacket, his shirt, his trousers... But he still carried on burning, because he was covered in oil which had caught fire. So I took off my jacket and wrapped it round him... to put out the flames.

LUCIA: Well, I must say, you're a dirty old man, but you've got a big heart.

ANTONIO: Yes, I've got a tiny brain and all! Because, if I'd minded my own business...

LUCIA: Speaking of your own business, what about your colleague, the shop-floor delegate... Did she delegate everything to you? Did she jut sit there and watch?

ANTONIO: No, she didn't. As soon as she saw the flames, she grabbed up her stuff, just as she was, stark naked, and ran off down the road, in her high-heel shoes... tac-tac-tac... flobber, flobber, flobber, stark naked!

LUCIA: So, she was naked, eh? And you too?

ANTONIO: No! I had my jacket on...! No trousers, but a jacket, yes... Do you mind! Let's have a bit of decency...!

LUCIA: Just a moment, Antonio, do you have any idea of who it was that you pulled out of the burning car?

ANTONIO: No. Why, do you?

LUCIA: I've a suspicion. But hasn't it even occurred to you that it wasn't just an ordinary road accident, but that it might have been... I don't know... an attempted kidnap?

ANTONIO: What do you take me for, an idiot? Obviously it occurred to me. But only afterwards! When they began shooting at me with guns!

LUCIA: Shooting at you? But who? When?

ANTONIO: For heaven's sake, listen, will you let me tell the story as it happened...

LUCIA: But...

ANTONIO: Oi! Don't keep interrupting!

LUCIA: I won't say another word.

ANTONIO: So. When I dragged Squashy out of the car, he was all on fire. I wrapped him in my jacket. I noticed that the people whom I'd dragged out who I thought were all suffocated, were starting to cough; they were coming round. So, I shouted over to them: 'Oi, stop all that coughing, and come over here, help me take your friend, your colleague, to hospital, because he's dying here.' They completely ignored me... They were going round on all fours... Just like constipated sheep. At that point, what was I supposed to do? Wait for a vet? I picked up Features and took him over to my car, the 128. I put him inside. I pulled on my trousers. I started the engine, and at that moment: Bang! Bang! Who was that? It was our suffocated friends. They were coughing and shooting at the same time. Bastards! Good God, I'd saved their lives, and, by way of thanks, they start popping off at me!

LUCIA: What did you do?

ANTONIO: I shone my headlights in their eyes, and tried to run them over... Whoosh! They leapt out of the way... like frogs. I swerved round the other car, and you'd have thought they were dead... But no: Bang! Bang! It was like Starsky and Hutch. Like Sam Peckinpah come back to life, and it wasn't in slow motion either. I was lucky to get away with my goolies.

LUCIA: Goodness, it's sending shivers down my spine... What kind of world are we living in?!

ANTONIO: Yes, you said it! But it's not over yet... I drove into town, and got as far as Porta Susa, where there's a Red Cross ambulance parked by the roundabout.

LUCIA: That's right, that's where they park.

ANTONIO: Exactly... And I called to the stretcher bearers to come over. They turn up and start giving it a bit of that: 'Dear, oh dear, oh dear, look at the state of this one. Who did this, then, eh? What is it – factory-fresh or home-made?' I saw right away that they thought that it was me who had done it. 'Look,' I said, 'Let's just get him down to the hospital, to casualty. There'll be a policeman there. I can explain everything to him.' 'OK.' They loaded Features into the ambulance... and told me to follow them in the car. As soon as we got to the first crossroads, whoosh, I scarpered

LUCIA: But you're crazy! Why did you go and do a thing like that?

ANTONIO: Because I was afraid. All of a sudden I imagined myself in the police station, with the police interrogating me. I mean, who was ever going to believe me? Who was ever going to believe that I was on the canal bank by accident, and that I was with a girl whose name I can't even remember... At the very least they would have arrested me, beat shit out of me...

LUCIA: You're right, it's enough to make anyone lose their head. More to the point, though, Antonio, do you know who it was that you saved?

ANTONIO: No, why? Do you?

LUCIA: Yes. It was Agnelli.

ANTONIO: Agnelli? Don't talk rubbish: Agnelli!

LUCIA: I'm not talking rubbish. They said so this morning, on television. A news flash: 'The kidnapping took place at about two o'clock this morning in Barriera di Milano.' So he *must* be your squashed friend.

ANTONIO: Agnelli?!I saved Agnelli? I took him in my arms, I wrapped him in my jacket... Me! If my workmates get to hear about this at Mirafiori,[4] they'll line me up and run me over with tractors...! They'll bang me up against a wall and... splosh! splosh! splosh!... they'll gob me to death...! Just think... with all this bronchitis that's going around! But why didn't you tell me, instead of letting me ramble on like a fool...

LUCIA: I wanted to be sure. I didn't interrupt you so as not to influence you. But what a mess! Do you realise the trouble that you've got yourself into? This'll teach you to go out whoring with female shop stewards!

ANTONIO: Obviously, it's my just reward, isn't it? 'Anyone who goes whoring with female shop stewards is punished by God, who makes him save Agnelli's life!' Get on with your story! What else did the telly have to say!

LUCIA: Well, first of all they gave the news that Agnelli had been kidnapped, and then they said that, according to statements by some of his bodyguards, the kidnappers drove up alongside the car in which Agnelli was travelling, and fired a bazooka through the rear window.

ANTONIO: A bazooka. They used a bazooka?! Obviously. Nowadays they only use bazookas... it's safer... more convenient. 'Excuse me mate. Have you got a light?' Bang!

LUCIA: The window shattered, and the shell went off inside the car, giving off a cloud of poison gas which paralysed his bodyguards.

ANTONIO: Ah, so that smoke was gas?! It's true, they were really coughing badly.

LUCIA: Then they said that when the bodyguards came to, they woke up just in time to see one of the terrorists' accomplices, 'who had clearly been parked on the embankment for some time'.

ANTONIO: Accomplice, eh! For some time! Like any self-respecting accomplice, I was parked on the embankment... 'Oi! Terrorists! I know I'm your accomplice, but do me a favour! Get a move on! I'm a bit parky because I've got no trousers on! So as to be less conspicuous.'

LUCIA: Antonio, they said that Agnelli was unconscious, and that you loaded him into a red FIAT 128 and drove off.

ANTONIO: So... I'm done for, now... I'm an accomplice! Or rather, the main organiser of the kidnap... What an idiot! You go and play the Good Samaritan, you go and save the life of bosses who gamble with your life like they were playing gin rummy. The bastards!

LUCIA: Antonio, calm down. Agreed, they're bastards, but there's no point in getting all dramatic about it. You'll see. As soon as Agnelli regains consciousness in the hospital, he'll explain that he is Gianni Agnelli, and he'll tell how you saved his life, and everything will be fine and dandy.

ANTONIO: Well that is very likely, isn't it! 'Hello. I am Gianni Agnelli... I demand to see, immediately, the trouserless engineering worker who saved my life... Where is he, I feel that I love him! I shall marry him... We'll be married... In white!' Leave it out... with the knocking that he took, it'll be a miracle if he even remembers his name when he wakes up... 'Who are you?' 'Ga, Ga, Ga, Ga!'

LUCIA: Is he really in such a state?

ANTONIO: No – *I'm* the one in the state! The ambulance men got a good full-frontal of me, from three yards away! My picture's going to be in all the papers today... My identikit! And underneath there'll be a caption: 'Head of the terrorist organisation in Lombardy, Piedmont, and Canton Ticino!'

LUCIA: You're exaggerating, as usual. For a start, there's no identikit in the papers.

She pulls a newspaper out of her handbag and gives it to ANTONIO.

ANTONIO: Which newspaper is that?

LUCIA: A special edition. I bought it an hour ago.

ANTONIO: Jesus – they're really quick! (*He reads*) '*Fury as Tearaway Terrorists Nab FIAT Supremo.* Fifty-three groups claim responsibility... *Barriera Bombing. It's the Mafia Again.* President Reagan demands televised debate with Frank Sinatra... *Bishop of Durham Speaks Out.* See page ten... *Andreotti Lashes the Bazooka Bandits.* Andreotti claimed that the state will not give in to blackmail, and asked to be made managing director of two banks. He also asked for Life Senatorships for everybody involved in the P2 Freemason Scandal... *Pontiff Pips Premier.* His Holiness the Pope pipped the Prime Minister to the post and offered himself as hostage in Agnelli's place; together with thirteen cardinals, ten of whom are black... *Play Terrorist Bingo and Win a Panda*'

LUCIA: There, you see? It's the usual mad house... But there's not a word about you, and about Agnelli in hospital. Listen, Antonio. Tomorrow you should go into work at FIAT, as if nothing had happened.

ANTONIO: You're crazy... I'm going to go down there, and say, 'Here I am'... Here I am!

LUCIA: Where?

ANTONIO: Down here... (*He points to the newspaper*) '*Factory Worker in Frazzle Mystery.* Forty-year-old Antonio Berardi, skilled worker at the FIAT-Mirafiori plant, was admitted to hospital by persons unknown earlier this morning. His face was seriously disfigured by burns. His wife, Rosa Minelli, has been traced, thanks to documents which the victim had in his jacket...' I left everything in my jacket! I left my driving licence, my Party card... my Union card... (*He stops short, and bursts out laughing*) Ha, ha, ha!

LUCA: What's so funny?

ANTONIO: Agnelli, a member of the union now! If he dies now, they'll give him a funeral with red flags! 'Rosa Minelli has been invited to attend the hospital in order to identify her husband...'

LUCIA: Hey, Antonio, Rosa's bound to identify Agnelli as you.

ANTONIO: Look, you're going to have to stop seeing my wife as some kind of mental defective. This is a trap, and I'm not falling for it.

LUCIA: What do you mean, a trap?

ANTONIO: They've written that on purpose... so that I go to the hospital, like some prize twat: 'Hello, Rosa, look, don't identify me as me, because here I am, large as life, and this fellow is somebody else.' Bang! Immediate arrest of halfwit terrorist. Why don't *you* go and take a look.

LUCIA: You're right. I'll go to the hospital and see what's going on...

ANTONIO: (*Now turns directly to the audience*) Now we can get back to the operating theatre, and pick up where we left off...

Re-enter the DOCTOR, ROSA *and the* WARD ORDERLIES. *Exeunt* ANTONIO *and* LUCIA.

DOCTOR: Incidentally, madam, you will have to bring me some photographs. Do you have any recent ones?

ROSA: No, Professor, I'm sorry, but since my husband left me, I haven't really been bothered with having photographs taken. I still work as a hairdresser in town...

But I've let myself go a bit, you know.

DOCTOR: But no, you misunderstand… Not photographs of you… photographs of your husband…

ROSA: Ah, yes, how stupid of me. I do have some – very fine ones. (*She pulls out from her handbag two large photographs of* ANTONIO, *and hands them to the* DOCTOR) Quite by chance, I happen to always carry them with me. They were taken by a friend of his who knows that I still love him… They are recent… I hope you don't mind if they're cut a little bit short on this side… (*She points to one side of the photo*) but, you see, the bitch was with him in the photo, and I can't really be expected to carry the bitch round with me in my handbag all day… from morning till night, looking at her smiling all over her face as she clings to my husband. I cut her out and hung her on the wall… with two pins in her eyes, so as… people tell me that it really does work, you know… An Indian custom… Or maybe African… Since you're a doctor, you wouldn't happen to know if she's likely to… go blind? (*Showing him the photographs*) Will they do? Look what a nice face!

DOCTOR: Yes, good, they are fairly clear… We are lucky. These will help us a lot in the projections.

ROSA: Projections?

DOCTOR: Yes. First you project the image of the patient's face, from the photograph, and then you reconstruct it around a wax skull.

ROSA: A wax skull?

DOCTOR: Exactly. First we reconstruct the bone structure, and then the whole thing is covered with skin.

ROSA: With skin? With artificial skin? Like leatherette?

DOCTOR: No, not artificial skin, real skin! His skin! We take it from here… from the buttocks…

ROSA: From his bum? You're going to put bits of bum on his face…?! Oh, Antonio, my poor Antonio, what a terrible situation…!

ROSA *suddenly moves away from the patient, and inadvertently leans on a lever. This releases the central operating theatre lamp, which crashes down onto the* DUMMY. *General pandemonium ensues.*

DOCTOR: No! Not the lever!

A musical interlude follows. As the lamp falls, enter the POLICE INSPECTOR. *He approaches the* DOCTOR.

INSPECTOR: A moment... Allow me... Are these recent photographs?

ROSA: Yes... Is he a surgeon?

INSPECTOR: No, I am the police inspector.

ROSA: Ah, police? And are you here to find out who did this streamlining job on my husband?

INSPECTOR: I might be.

ROSA: Well there's no point in asking him. Go and ask those bastards at FIAT. Go and ask Agnelli.

INSPECTOR: Now, madam, there's no need to bring Mr Agnelli into all this, particularly at a time like this. Who knows where the poor man is at this moment?

ROSA: Antonio, I promise you that if they ever find him, I'll go looking for him, and I'll mash his face up just like yours!

DOCTOR: Madam, is all this really necessary? I've already told you he doesn't understand...

ROSA: Oh yes he does! There's a glint in his eye...

Enter an ORDERLY *with a sheet of paper in his hand. He goes over to the* DOCTOR..

ORDERLY: Excuse me, Professor, there's somebody here. Says they're a relative of the patient, Antonio Berardi, and asks if it's possible to see him.

ROSA: Let's have a look... Who is this relative?

ORDERLY: I don't know. Here's the details.

ROSA: Can I see them, eh...?

DOCTOR: No, madam, please. I am the doctor here, until

proven otherwise, and it's me who decides who is to be let in. Lucia Rismondi.

ROSA: *It's the bitch!* She has the nerve to pass herself off as a relation, just because she was sleeping with my husband! The whore!

DOCTOR: Madam, calm down!

ROSA: Calm down? Why should I calm down? I'm furious! Humiliating me like this! Here I am, heartbroken, with my husband looking like a Michelin Man... all wrapped up like a packet of fish fingers, and *she* comes here just to spite me.

DOCTOR: Madam, will you stop that! I can't stand scenes! I warn you that if you don't start behaving very civilly indeed, I shall have you shown out of here, and I shall not let you come back to visit your husband for at least a month. Clear?

ROSA: (*Looking at the* DOCTOR *in amazement*) Just who you think you are talking to me in that arrogant tone? Use it on some patient in a coma. Not on me. I'm involved in politics, me! I've opened birth control clinics. I'm not some timid woman who lets herself be put down by people who shout! No, sir! I am the patient's wife! I can come in when I want! That's the law! My husband, after all, is in a coma! And if you have something to say about it I'll stage such a sit-in, right here and now.

INSPECTOR: Madam, listen, I am conducting investigations precisely in order to discover what has happened to your husband. It's possible that this woman might be able to give us some useful information.

ROSA: But she doesn't know anything, because she never saw anything! Anyway, she's also about to go blind, with the pins! Isn't she, Doctor?

DOCTOR: Get out! Get out!

ROSA: (*She moves off, reluctantly, but after a few steps, she faints*) Oh, God, I feel ill... Oh, my head...

DOCTOR: (*Lifting* ROSA *up*) Madam, please don't start

play-acting... (*They help her to sit down*) Would you pass me the smelling salts. Come on... Come on... Take a deep breath.

He forces ROSA *to smell the salts.*

ROSA: Cough, cough! Cough... I'm suffocating... Professor, you're mad! What is this vile stuff you're making me breathe...? Cough... There, now I really do feel ill!

DOCTOR: No, you're not ill... Come on, be good, get out of here...

ROSA: Let me get my breath. (*She breathes, very ostentatiously*) I'd like to make a self-criticism.

DOCTOR: Oh my God.

ROSA: You're right, I've behaved really badly... I've been selfish. When all's said and done, that poor girl has the right to see my husband too. If she's fallen in love, it's hardly her fault... She's so young and pretty too... She's educated. She's got a degree! She's a doctor! She could have taken up with a professor like yourself, or, if the worst came to the worst, with an Inspector, like yourself... But no... She decided to choose my husband... a man old enough to be her father... I mean any wife should feel proud, don't you think? I'm really happy... Please, Inspector, don't send me away. I would really like to meet her...

INSPECTOR: OK... OK. As long as you stay there and keep your mouth shut.

DOCTOR: Alright, Inspector, shall we ask her in?

He signals to the ORDERLIES *to put a screen in front of the bed, so that* LUCIA *does not see the patient at once.*

INSPECTOR: All right. Get her in here!

DOCTOR: Show her this way please.

Enter LUCIA. *There is a moment of embarrassment and tension.*

LUCIA: Mrs Berardi... Please excuse me if I... Perhaps I shouldn't have... I know...

ROSA: Oh you were right. I'm very pleased to meet you. I'm sure he will be pleased to see you as well, although I don't suppose he will recognise you!

She embraces her formally.

LUCIA: Hasn't he regained consciousness yet?

ROSA: Yes he has... he definitely recognised me. Of course it might be more difficult with you, though, because he hasn't known you very long...

LUCIA: Are you sure that it really is him?

INSPECTOR: A moment, excuse me... Miss, would you please mind stepping over to the bed...

ROSA: Wait a moment, Inspector.

LUCIA: Inspector?

ROSA: Yes, he's here for the investigation... Don't let him rush you. Be brave... He's got nothing left... Only two ears...

LUCIA: (*Going up to the bed, and barely glancing at the* DUMMY) Oh my God, it's really horrible! It's him... It's him... (*She clings to* ROSA)

DOCTOR: Are you sure? By what do you recognise him?

ROSA: From his hands, no...?

INSPECTOR: Come along, don't lead her on!

ROSA: Who's leading her on!

LUCIA: By his ears.

INSPECTOR: By his ears?

LUCIA: Yes, because I have studied those ears inch by inch...

DOCTOR: You've studied his ears?

ROSA: What an intellectual!

LUCIA: Yes, you see... I practise acupuncture... and I've even been to China on a training course... And since Antonio suffered from sinusitis...

ROSA: Yes, yes, sinusitis… it's true… he had it really badly!

LUCIA: To cure him, I used to stick needles in his ears…

> ROSA *mimes sticking needles in her ears and at the same time starts running on the spot.*

> That's how I recognise him. As you may know, Professor, every ear has its own particular physiognomy…In fact, if you take a wax mould of the auditory pavilion, you get a shape which looks like a little foetus, which is none other than a miniature portrait of how we were in our mothers' wombs.

INSPECTOR: Like seeing a snapshot of yourself as a baby!

ROSA: A foetus in your ear!! I'll have to tell them that at the clinic!

DOCTOR: It's true! Our police forensic departments no longer use the usual fingerprint system, but take wax moulds of the auditory chambers of their suspects!

INSPECTOR: You mean every time you're arrested, wallop, a dollop of hot wax in your earhole! Incredible! You scientists are amazing! Well, that wraps it up: it's him, Antonio Berardi. Doctor, I would like to thank you for your collaboration.

LUCIA *and* **ROSA:** Don't mention it…

INSPECTOR: Let's go and have a drink.

ROSA: Well, Antonio, you've been positively identified as my very own Antonio Berardi. She's a bit of a know-it-all, isn't she Antonio… *Doctor, Doctor,* he's trying to say something…

> ROSA *suddenly turns away from the patient. Somehow she contrives to lose her balance. She supports herself by grabbing one of the wires hanging down. The* DUMMY *flies up in the air, amid scenes of general pandemonium.*

> *Blackout*
> *Musical interlude*

Scene Two

When the lights come up again, we find ourselves in the same scene as before. The bed with the dummy on has disappeared. On stage are ROSA *and the* DOCTOR.

DOCTOR: Madam, this may seem a bit presumptuous, but you're going to have to give us credit for the miraculous things that we've managed to achieve. You will see... a masterpiece!

The DOUBLE *is wheeled on-stage in a wheelchair pushed by three* WARD ORDERLIES. *His face is swathed in bandages. Everyone bustles around him, busily removing the bandages, to reveal his face.*

The DOUBLE's *face is encased in a kind of mask of elastic tapes. Small rings are fixed to various positions of the tapes – one on his chin, one on his nose, one on each cheek, and one on his forehead. Wires or cords are connected to each ring, and they pass through pulleys in an overhead metal or wooden frame. The other ends come down to stage level. Each* ORDERLY *holds one or two of these wires.*

As the action unfolds, ROSA *says:*

ROSA: Oh, the suspense is killing me! It reminds me of a film I saw when I was a girl: 'The Living Mummy!' where they unbandaged someone just like this.. There he is... Look... It's him... It's him...!

DOCTOR: But what are you saying, madam, he's perfect!

ROSA: Oooh. Well done... You've caught him really well... Mind you, all those stitches all over his face...

DOCTOR: Yes, but they can't be helped... In a few days they will disappear, though, some of them will dissolve... and with the others, you just pull one end, and out they come.

ROSA: But if you pull on one end of the thread, won't he come undone, and won't his face fall all over the floor?

DOCTOR: Nein, nein.

ROSA: I'm sorry. You can tell, I'm so happy I'm beginning to talk rubbish again. Oh, Antonio, if you could only see yourself... You're almost better than before! Antonio, how do you feel? Tell me!

The DOUBLE *doesn't move.*

DOCTOR: Gently, madam, gently... He has to get used to speaking again... We must proceed gradually... You should remember that we have rebuilt his entire jawbone and palate.

ROSA: Ah yes, I suppose now he's just running in.

DOCTOR: So leave it to me. Mr Berardi, try opening your mouth, slowly, let's see if you can do it...

The DOUBLE *does as he says.*

Well done...

The DOUBLE'*s attempts to speak are assisted by the* WARD ORDERLIES, *and by the* DOCTOR. *They pull on the various wires, and through mime amplify his facial movements. This gives the impression that every movement of his mouth is brought about by operating the 'machine'.*

ROSA: It's opening, it's opening!

DOCTOR: And now, try with me, repeat after me: Ahaaa...

DOUBLE: Ahaaa...

The DOCTOR *and the* ORDERLIES *continue their mime action.*

ROSA: He said Ahaaa!

DOCTOR: Please keep quiet, madam. Once again: Ahaaa... Oooh...

ROSA: Come on, Antonio, say Oooh, as the doctor tells you!

DOUBLE: Oooh...

DOCTOR: No, no, first Ahaaa, then Oooh! Pay attention to me, not to your wife! Once again: Ahaaa... Oooh...

DOUBLE: Ahaaa... Oooh... Eheee...

ROSA: He said 'E'... all by himself! How intelligent!

DOCTOR: No, not at all! He mustn't do that! Mr Berardi, you must make only the sounds that I ask you to make!

ROSA: Alright, but if he decides he wants to go 'Eheee', don't you think that it's a bit much to stop him?

DOCTOR: Madam, you should realise that the sound 'Eheee' requires the jawbone to extend to its maximum limit, with the risk that it might come out of its mastoid socket.

ROSA: So does that mean that my Antonio, when he talks, will never be able to say 'e's'? Here, so you won't be able to say wheatgerm, then, will you?

DOCTOR: No, no, he *will* be able to say 'e's' too, but later! First he must make the intermediate sounds, like: Braaa, Brooo, Bray.

DOUBLE: Braaa... Brooo... Bray...

Repeated several times, evolving into Satchmo impersonation.

DOCTOR: There, that's just perfect! And now, say: gastric... gastropod...

DOUBLE: Gaaastric, gaasopo...

DOCTOR: No, articulate it properly: gas-tero-pod...

DOUBLE: Troppo...Gastopo... Braaa, Brooo, Bray!

DOCTOR: Silence! And now say: astronaut, concupiscence, manumission.

ROSA: But Professor, have you gone mad? What are these words that you're making him say? He's never going to say words like that... He's a worker... Make him say the words that he's going to use every day: wage packet, lay-offs, redundancies... Astronaut? Why, we don't even know one!

DOCTOR: Listen, I'm the one who knows how to teach! Come along, Mr Berardi: astronaut, manumission, concupiscence.

DOUBLE: Conc... Concup... Concup... Piss off!

DOCTOR: What???!

ROSA: See, now you've upset him!

The DOUBLE *gets up and goes to walk out towards the exit.* ROSA *tries to stop him.*

I'll stop him. I'm his wife. Antonio, you can't go out...

She approaches her husband, who is walking like Frankenstein. She tries to stop him.

Antonio, stop! But look how he's walking! You must have made a mistake somewhere! Antonio, you're not a robot!

DOUBLE: Don't *you* start too, madam!

ROSA: Professor, did you hear? He called me madam. He's pretending he doesn't recognise me. But Antonio, dear, I'm Rosa, I'm your wife!

DOUBLE: What do you mean, wife... wife, indeed? F... F... F... Forget it!

He goes out, dragging the wires behind him. The WARD ORDERLIES *follow him, trying to untangle the wires.*

ROSA: Did you hear that?! Where's he going, Professor? Stop him!

DOCTOR: No, let him move about a bit, let him take a little walk. Anyway, where's he going to go? He'll go to his room. And you, madam, don't go feeling all hurt. You must understand, after all these months of tension, with one operation after another... it's natural that he's on edge. Instead, you should think about the happy outcome of this whole experiment... treatment.

ROSA: What happy outcome? I've been visiting him for months and months, and he's never even looked at me.

Then, finally, he speaks! All that comes out is Braaa, Brooo, Bray... and then he says: 'What do you mean, wife...?'!

Enter the POLICE INSPECTOR.

INSPECTOR: Excuse me, Professor, did you give the prisoner... sorry, the patient permission to leave?

DOCTOR: Ja, just to go back to his room.

INSPECTOR: But he's not going back to his room. He's taken the lift down to the ground floor, to the way out.

DOCTOR: My God. Stop that man.

INSPECTOR: Already done. I've despatched two officers to persuade him to rejoin us. Only our vigilance prevented him from doing a runner.

ROSA: Doing a runner? Have you seen him walk?

INSPECTOR: Exactly... Listen, madam, would you mind stepping outside for a moment? I have something private to say to the Professor.

ROSA: Yes, yes, I'm going. People are always throwing me out. I'll go and find Antonio... I'll give him a bit of my speech therapy... I'll teach him to say: I love you, Rosa... I'm leaving the bitch... I'm coming back to you...' You can stick your astronaut up your manumission.

ROSA *exits.*

INSPECTOR: So, Professor, everything's sweet?

DOCTOR: Yes. We're progressing well. We're building up a basic vocabulary for him. In a couple of days he'll be speaking almost as well as you.

INSPECTOR: Magic. I'd like to start straight away putting a few simple questions to him...

DOCTOR: Yes, but only under my control.

INSPECTOR: Yes, yes, you can stay... In fact, you can give us a hand. Would you mind if I invite the Examining Magistrate in...? (*Without waiting for an answer, he calls offstage*) Your Honour, step this way.

Enter the EXAMINING MAGISTRATE.

Professor... No, you can make your own introductions.
I'm very bad at names.

Enter a POLICEMAN *with a portable typewriter.*

This is my assistant... You know, to take down his
statement.

DOCTOR: What statement? Leaving aside the fact that I still
do not know what you suspect him of...

EXAMINING MAGISTRATE: Well, for start, we have
discovered that the red FIAT 128 registered in Berardi's
name is the same car that the terrorists...

The INSPECTOR, *standing behind the* DOCTOR, *signals
abruptly to the* EXAMINING MAGISTRATE *to keep
quiet.*

Now then, what were you saying about the patient?

DOCTOR: But you surely can't think that the patient is
ready... We must proceed gradually. It will be very
difficult to get him to answer questions logically. Almost
certainly, the trauma which caused his coma has flattened
all his mnemonic-responsive anafracts.

INSPECTOR: Mnemonic-responsive anafracts? What does
that mean?

The DOCTOR *goes and stands behind the* POLICEMAN,
*who is sitting on a wheeled office chair, and has put his
typewriter on one of the pieces of theatre equipment (an
encephalogram recorder) which is also on wheels. The*
DOCTOR, *carried away with his explanation, grasps the*
POLICEMAN's *head, and describes what's in it. Then he
pushes the wheeled* POLICEMAN, *together with his
typewriter, to centre-stage.*

DOCTOR: You see, in the central-posterior part of the brain,
known as the mnemechaea, there is a space which we
might call the memory warehouse. In this warehouse there
are thousands of relays, which, when activated, switch on a
number of tapes, on which are stored memories, words,

sensations, in short, everything that has happened in our lives...

INSPECTOR: So, the trauma will have wiped all his tapes?

The INSPECTOR *too manhandles the junior* POLICEMAN's *head.*

DOCTOR: No, not all of them, but most of them... It may be that only one tiny, maybe insignificant, detail will pop up. Everything else will have been erased.

INSPECTOR: What if he just makes out that he can't remember, in order to avoid telling the truth?

The DOCTOR *and the* INSPECTOR *in turn grapple with the* POLICEMAN's *head, gesticulating. By now the* POLICEMAN *is thoroughly terrified.*

DOCTOR: No, impossible! In this first phase – which we call the phase of innocence – the patient is not capable of practising deception... because the fiction mechanism, which is the most exposed and ephemeral part of the brain, is always the first to be destroyed by any violent trauma.

EXAMINING MAGISTRATE: In short, (*He also tries to get his hands on the* POLICEMAN's *head, but the* POLICEMAN *ducks out of the way to prevent him*) they are no longer capable of pretending or lying. And does this happen in every case?

DOCTOR: Yes. Every case, but not in the case of politicians... For them, traumas have no effect.

INSPECTOR: Here he is... Hand built by robots.

Enter the DOUBLE, *walking like a wobbly flamingo. They sit him down (centre-stage) on the wheeled office chair. When the* DOUBLE *enters, the* POLICEMAN *on wheels moves, together with his equipment, to the* DOUBLE's *left-hand side.*

DOCTOR: Here you are, Mr Berardi, sit down here and relax... These gentlemen would like to ask you a few questions... Please, you mustn't force him. Let him freewheel...

The DOUBLE *jerks his head, like a suspicious flamingo.*
He fixes on the POLICEMAN, *eyeing him mischievously.*
The gag is repeated ad libitum.

INSPECTOR: Of course. Freewheel... Tell us, where were you going to in such a hurry...

DOCTOR: Try and answer, there's a good chap.

DOUBLE: Gasteronomical... gastero... Could you repeat the question, please...

INSPECTOR: Where were you running off to?

DOUBLE: Ruuunning ooofff... but I didn't waant to run off... I ooonly waaanted to gooo...

EXAMINING MAGISTRATE: Go where?

DOUBLE: To Head Quarters...

INSPECTOR: What Head Quarters?

DOUBLE: To the Heead Quaarters... which... after... over... theere! (*With a series of gestures, he describes stairs, lifts, doorbells, automatically-opening doors*) Fruuut... Tracht... Driing... Whoosh... Ching!

DOCTOR: No, don't strain yourself, calm down, relax...

EXAMINING MAGISTRATE: Yes, yes, relax, calm down. We only want to have a little chat... among friends...

INSPECTOR: And so as to help you... so that you can practise speaking.

DOUBLE: Speeaking, among frieeends...? Are these your frieeends, Professor? (*He fixes a beady eye on the* POLICEMAN *like a pointer eyeing its prey*) What's he writing?

INSPECTOR: He's taking notes of what you say... so that we can monitor your progress.

DOUBLE: Ah, yes? And theeen you'll leet me reeead whaaat I said... and what he has written?

INSPECTOR: Certainly, and sign it...

DOUBLE: Sign? Why sign?

INSPECTOR: No reason.

DOUBLE: No, you're lying. Liar!

INSPECTOR: Cut that out.

DOUBLE: Liar!!

INSPECTOR: Let's start from what you remember... For example, what's your name?

DOUBLE: Well, everyone calls me Antonio... even the Professor... and that horrible woman... who's driving me mad... Antoniooo, Antonioooo... Antoniooooo...!

EXAMINING MAGISTRATE: Your wife?

DOUBLE: My wife? Yes, she says she is my wife. But I don't remeember her... becaause... Whoosh... Clang... Vroom... (*He starts waving his arms in vague and meaningless gestures*) Toniinoooo... Bruuuuu! Antoninoooo! Antonino-o-o-o...

DOCTOR: Now then, now then, calm down, we won't talk about your wife any more...

EXAMINING MAGISTRATE: We won't talk about your wife any more.

INSPECTOR: We won't talk about her any more.

DOUBLE: We won't talk about my wife any more? Promise?

INPECTOR: What do you mean, promise?

DOUBLE: Promise!

EXAMINING MAGISTRATE *and* **DOCTOR:** Promise!

INSPECTOR: Promise.

DOUBLE: Dib, dib, dib.

INSPECTOR: Look... Now... What about the accident?

DOUBLE: (*He explodes like a madman, terrorised*) Ahaaa... Vrooom... Chugga-chugga... Bang... Kerrash... Biff... Oooooh.

DOCTOR: No, look, you're doing this all wrong. You have to deal more tactfully, give him more leeway...

EXAMINING MAGISTRATE: You're right. Listen, Mr Berardi, do you remember any particular details of your childhood?

DOUBLE: My childhood! Yes... When I was a child... I liked motor cars, when I was a child...

EXAMINING MAGISTRATE: But all little boys like motor cars...

DOUBLE: But I liked them mooore! I lived in a greeeat big maaansion...

DOCTOR: In childhood memories, everything is always big.

DOUBLE: Yes. And when you're big it can be fucking enormous if you play your cards right. I remember when I was fourteen I was given a cowboy outfit.

EXAMINING MAGISTRATE: Cowboy outfit?

DOUBLE: Yes, and I've been running it ever since. Does that mean anything to you?

POLICEMAN: (*With typewriter*) ...Cowboy outfit.

INSPECTOR: Scrub that out. Cowboy outfit.

EXAMINING MAGISTRATE: What do you remember about your mother and your father?

DOUBLE: My mother... I don't remember... No... Nothing... Mummy, no... At this moment, have no recollection of mother...

EXAMINING MAGISTRATE: You don't remember?

DOUBLE: I'm trying to remember... my mummy...

INSPECTOR: But don't strain yourself...

DOUBLE: Wait a minute, I want to remember...

EXAMINING MAGISTRATE: But you don't have to...

DOUBLE: I want to remember! I loved my mummy. I don't remember my mummy... I haven't got a mummy! (*He cries, heartbroken*) I've looked everywhre in my memory, but I haven't got a mummy!

He rests his head on the INSPECTOR'*s shoulder.*

INSPECTOR: What are you doing?

DOUBLE: Won't you give me a little cuddly-wuddly... ?

INSPECTOR: Cuddly-wuddly!

DOUBLE: Just a little one...

INSPECTOR: Please, pull yourself together!

DOUBLE: Please. Peezy, weezy, weezy.

INSPECTOR: Get off me. Stuff your mummy.

DOUBLE: He said he wants to stuff my mummy!
You'd better start praying that my memory doesn't come back, because if my memory does come back and I remember who I am and who I was... then... Whiish, roar, roar! (*He becomes like King Kong*) I do remember my father, though... He always used to take me to see the cars...

INSPECTOR: Did he work at FIAT too?

DOUBLE: Eh? Work?

He slyly rests his head on the INSPECTOR'*s shoulder.*

INSPECTOR: Pull yourself together...!

DOUBLE: Oh look – I can laugh! Ah, it does me good to talk. I feel as if I'm getting better already.

EXAMINING MAGISTRATE: Well done, carry on.

DOUBLE: Gasteropod, astronaut... concupiscent... astronaut...

POLICEMAN: How do you spell gasteropod?

The POLICEMAN *types frantically.*

INSPECTOR: But what are you typing there?

The POLICEMAN *breaks off momentarily, and then starts again.*

EXAMINING MAGISTRATE: Listen, would you feel up to

telling us about the accident? Without straining yourself, though.

DOUBLE: Ah... vrrr... beeee.... ooonly little bits... I remember...! I was in a car... and there was another car... two cars...

INSPECTOR: There were two cars...

DOUBLE: There was a race...

EXAMINING MAGISTRATE: A chase... And you...?

DOUBLE: I was in the car...

EXAMINING MAGISTRATE: Behind.

DOUBLE: Behind...

EXAMINING MAGISTRATE AND INSPECTOR: The car behind. Well done!

DOUBLE: No, no... That's wrong...

INSPECTOR: What do you mean, no?

DOUBLE: I made a mistake!

INSPECTOR: The first answer is always the one that counts!

DOUBLE: Liar...

INSPECTOR: Don't let's start all that again!

DOUBLE: Liar, liar... etc.

DOCTOR: Now look, you really shouldn't put words in his mouth... (*He grabs the wheeled chair and pushes it up-stage*) I told you! Let him freewheel...

INSPECTOR: Very well, we'll let him freewheel...

He grabs the chair and hurtles it towards the audience.

DOUBLE: Yes... We're going... going fast... faster and faster... Bing, bang, bong... Crash... Smack... then... I can't remember... any more...

INSPECTOR: Try. There was a crash, a smash. What then? Blood, mangled bodies, headless torsos, smoke...

DOUBLE: Ah, yes... flames... I'm on fire... HEEELP!

INSPECTOR: What's the matter with you, calm down!

DOCTOR: I told you not to push him too far!

The DOUBLE's *jaw becomes dislocated.*

DOCTOR: Oh I see what's happened. Let go. Let go.

DOUBLE: Thank you very much.

DOCTOR: You're most welcome.

INSPECTOR: Not a lot to go on there Your Honour?

EXAMINING MAGISTRATE: Indeed. We're going to have to try something else.

DOUBLE: Then I remember a voice shouting out: 'Agnelli... They're carrying away Agnelli!'

INSPCTOR: Brilliant! Write that down!

DOUBLE: Why brilliant? What does that mean? Would you care to explain to me who this Agnelli might be...? Because every now and then I have that name on my mind...

EXAMINING MAGISTRATE: I should think so too!

DOUBLE: What?

INSPECTOR: Never mind. Now, what does the name FIAT mean to you...?

DOUBLE: FIAT? Well, it's something almost... how can I say: like family... FIAT.

EXAMINING MAGISTRATE: Your family?

DOUBLE: Like something that belongs to me.

DOCTOR: It's incredible how attached these FIAT workers are to their company!

EXAMINING MAGISTRATE: And now, could you tell us a bit about your work...?

DOUBLE: Work?

EXAMINING MAGISTRATE: What work did you do at FIAT?

DOUBLE: Work?

INSPECTOR: Yes, work.

DOUBLE: At FIAT...? Work?

EXAMINING MAGISTRATE: Work...

INSPECTOR: Work!

EXAMINING MAGISTRATE: Working... Labouring...

DOUBLE: Labouring... Work... Labour...

EXAMINING MAGISTRATE: At FIAT...

DOUBLE: Work... Labour?

INSPECTOR: Yes!

DOUBLE: These words have no meaning for me...

EXAMINING MAGISTRATE: (*He dictates to the* POLICEMAN *with the typewriter*) Filthy little skiver.

INSPECTOR: And what about profit, production...? Do they mean anything to you?

DOUBLE: Oh yes... A lot... And restructuring... net profit... holding company... mobility of labour... summary sackings! Ha, Ha!

INSPECTOR: And the word terrorism...? What does that mean to you?

DOUBLE: It means: radical and accelerated development of the armed struggle with consequences which may be positive or negative depending on the general situation of conflictuality between the various combined interests.

INSPECTOR: Magic!

DOCTOR: Magic!

EXAMINING MAGISTRATE: Magic!

The EXAMINING MAGISTRATE *and the* INSPECTOR *are pleased. They laugh.*

DOUBLE: Have I said the right thing?

INSPECTOR: Exactly the right thing!

DOUBLE: I don't understand what it is I've said. I would like to know what it is that I've said.

INSPECTOR: Let's proceed. Let's see if you remember any contacts, for example, with foreign groups...

DOUBLE: Yes, indeed... foreign groups... I remember...

INSPECTOR: Russians?

DOUBLE: Russians... Oh yes... Russians... Many contacts...

EXAMINING MAGISTRATE: Very good...

DOUBLE: Was it magic? Are you pleased?

EXAMINING MAGISTRATE: Yes, very pleased. And with Libyans?

DOUBLE: Libyans? Libya... Ah yes... I remember... I paid a special visit to Libya. Armed men in uniform coming to meet me.

EXAMINING MAGISTRATE: And did you talk about clandestine activities?

DOUBLE: Yes: very clandestine! Traffic...

EXAMINING MAGISTRATE: Traffic? Traffic of arms?

DOUBLE: Yes, arms too... all kinds of arms... heavy and light...

INSPECTOR: Were you aware of why and for what purpose those arms were to be used?

DOUBLE: Water.

INSPECTOR: What?

DOUBLE: Mineral water. Not carbonated.

EXAMINING MAGISTRATE: What's he saying?

DOCTOR: It's simple. He's saying he's thirsty...

INSPECTOR: Wait a moment, answer my question.

DOUBLE: No, I'm thirsty... non-carbonated mineral water, cool but not iced!

DOCTOR: Wait a minute, I'll see to it. I've got a fridge here.

EXAMINING MAGISTRATE: Alright... get him his bloody water...

DOUBLE: I hope it's not carbonated, because if I burp I'll blow the nose off!

INSPECTOR: I'll have a glass of that as well...

DOUBLE: Oh, the funnel... Doctor, do you have the funnel?

DOCTOR: Yes... yes...

He pulls a funnel out of the fridge, and hands it to the DOUBLE.

EXAMINING MAGISTRATE: A funnel? What's that for?

DOUBLE: In order to drink... Otherwise I spill it all over the place... Wait while I get the tube... (*He takes the funnel and sticks it into his neck, on the right hand side*) Doctor, could you help me to screw the funnel in? Ah, no, thanks, look, I've done it myself... (*The* DOCTOR *pretends to pour water into a glass*) Your health! Gentlemen. (*He pours the water contained in the glass into the funnel*) Brrr... It's cold.

INSPECTOR: Excuse me, where exactly have you poured it?

DOUBLE: Ah, directly into my oesophagus...

DOCTOR: Yes, for a few more months yet he won't be able to swallow either food or liquids by mouth.

EXAMINING MAGISTRATE: So his food has to go through the funnel too?

DOCTOR: Yes, only food that has been mashed and puréed... Everything by neck.

DOUBLE: They purée everything for me, my starter, main course, dessert and coffee. No... not the coffee. I have special suppositories for the coffee.

INSPECTOR: Listen, would you mind if we get back to our little chat?

DOUBLE: Yes, let's begin again... You were asking me if... I remember traffic of arms... and who were they aimed for. Vaguely... I remember the word... Wing, plot, right.

EXAMINING MAGISTRATE *and* **INSPECTOR:** Wing, plot, right?

DOUBLE: Wing.

EXAMINING MAGISTRATE: Plot.

INSPECTOR: Right.

EXAMINING MAGISTRATE: Wing.

DOUBLE: Plot. Right Wing Plot. That's right. And the word... 'destabilise'... But I didn't agree... but there was somebody... police, I think...

EXAMINING MAGISTRATE: Police? Which police?

DOUBLE: Well, I don't remember... Maybe ours...

EXAMINING MAGISTRATE: Italian police? Special Branch? Secret services?

DOUBLE: Very secret... Special services... One time they were on the point of exposing them... I knew about it... I was scared they'd implicate me too... Ah, now I remember the trial... Generals, ministers... then everything was exposed... and then covered up again! Whitewash.

INSPECTOR: Whitewash?

POLICEMAN: Generals... ministers... I didn't quite catch that. What was it he said before 'whitewash'...?

INSPECTOR: Don't write that down you pillock. Rub it out. Rub it all out!

EXAMINING MAGISTRATE: No, not everything. Only from 'police' onwards...

DOUBLE: Ah, now, that period I remember really well, really clearly... All the big-nobs, all their names... There was even an admiral involved... a judge... a minister...

EXAMINING MAGISTRATE: Will you stop remembering.

INSPECTOR: Do something.

DOUBLE: If I make a little effort, it'll all come back to me. I could name all five hundred of them... Now, I'll start in alphabetical order, from 'A'... The first is Andreot...[5]

the first is...

As the DOUBLE *is speaking, the* EXAMINING MAGISTRATE *and the* INSPECTOR *try to interrupt him. He carries on regardless. The* INSPECTOR *signals to the* DOCTOR, *who immediately gives the* DOUBLE *an injection in the arm.*

DOUBLE: ...Andreot... Andreottolo... (*He loses his powers of speech, and breaks down*) Oh... oh... oh...

DOCTOR: There you are, Inspector. For ten minutes now he won't be able to either speak or hear.

INSPECTOR: Thank God for that! I don't think we need to hear any more, he's a terrorist... Damned himself out of his own mouth... Can't tell a lie.

EXAMINING MAGISTRATE: In fact, it's almost criminal to take advantage of his honesty.

INSPECTOR: Your Honour, don't forget that these are people who shoot you in the back!

EXAMINING MAGISTRATE: Correct. We must never forget it! As we suspected, he was part of the gang who kidnapped Agnelli. He was done over in the rumble. Thinking he was about to snuff it, his colleagues got shot of him, bringing him here.

INSPECTOR: We're going to have to put the word about that he's turned into a poor babbling idiot, because if they suspect that we're getting him to talk, the terrorists in his group are liable to come here and do him in. Or the fellows from the secret services...

DOUBLE: I remember that...

EXAMINING MAGISTRATE *and* **INSPECTOR:** Shut! Up!

The DOCTOR *rushes up and gives another injection.*

DOUBLE: Ah... oh... never mind!

He goes all floppy again.

EXAMINING MAGISTRATE: It couldn't be better if we'd arrested him red-handed... Let's whisk him away without letting anybody know, and lock him in a total isolation cell, or even better, in a container, like the Anti-Terrorist Squad do with theirs.

INSPECTOR: Yes, the Anti-Terrorist Squad!

DOCTOR: Yes, go ahead. That'll just finish him off! He will become completely deranged, just like the Prime Minister.

DOUBLE: (*Coming round, mischievously*) Now I'll tell you all the names... that I've remembered...

INSPECTOR *and* **EXAMINING MAGISTRATE:** That's enough!

The action is repeated. The DOCTOR *gives him another injection. And again the* DOUBLE *goes all floppy.*

DOUBLE: What a hit!

DOCTOR: Listen to me – if you want him to carry on talking, leave him alone for a while. Don't show your faces for at least ten days.

INSPECTOR: But you must be joking, ten days? We can't... We're holding the key to picking up a whole gang of terrorists, finding Agnelli – maybe even alive – and you...

DOCTOR: Alright, I understand... Let's make it five days...

EXAMINING MAGISTRATE: No, no, two, three at most...

DOCTOR: Alright, as you think best... But then if his brain blows out, the responsibility will be yours, alright!?

INSPECTOR: Two days, and then we'll be back to interrogate him. We'll keep ten of our men here in the hospital, disguised as nurses and doctors...

EXAMINING MAGISTRATE: Yes. Just so as to keep an eye on him and protect him.

DOCTOR: Ten? Don't you think that's a bit many?

EXAMINING MAGISTRATE: No, this is the best breakthrough that we've had to date. This fellow really is a Grade A supergrass!

INSPECTOR: He talks so much that it's a pleasure to listen to

him. He's worth more than Peci, Sandolo, Fioroni and
Barbone [6] put together... He's a repentant terrorist and
doesn't realise it!

DOUBLE: (*He leaps to his feet like an uncoiled spring, and
heads directly for the* EXAMINING MAGISTRATE *and
the* INSPECTOR) Now I remember the name of that
Minister...

EXAMINING MAGISTRATE *and* **INSPECTOR:** Shut! Up!!

DOUBLE: (*He pretends to go away, but suddenly turns round
again*) I'll tell you...

EXAMINING MAGISTRATE *and* **INSPECTOR:** Shut! Up!

DOUBLE: You shut up!

Blackout
Musical Interlude

ACT TWO

Scene One

We are in a big room in ROSA's *house. There is a door in each of the three walls: the right-hand door gives onto the hallway landing, the centre door leads into the bedroom, and the left-hand door leads to the kitchen.*

Set: There's a table in the middle of the room. On it stands a plastic head with a wig on it. To the left stands a sideboard. Up-stage left there is a television set. Up-stage right, next to a chest of drawers, stands a free-standing coat rack.

Up against the wall on the right stands a heavy wooden armchair, with arms and castors.

Front-stage, leaning up against the right-hand wall, is a small trolley. On it stands a papier mâché bust representing a two-headed mythical Greco-Roman character. There is also a standard lamp, from which hangs a clarinet.

As the lights come up, ROSA *and* LUCIA *enter from outside.* ROSA *has a shopping-bag, with her shopping. Front-stage centre we see a window. As* ROSA *says her first lines, she goes and flings the window open. Then, as she moves off to continue her dialogue with* LUCIA, *the window moves across the front of the stage and disappears into the wings stage right.*

ROSA: Oh, Lucia, I *am* sorry. How long have you been waiting here for me?

LUCIA: Oh, about half an hour...

ROSA: Oh, good heavens... If I'd known, I'd have hurried up. Excuse the mess... I was combing a customer's wig.

ROSA *shifts the wig, and puts it on the chest of drawers at the back of the stage.*

LUCIA: Oh, don't worry... In fact, I'm the one who should apologise for turning up just like this. The fact is, I was very worried. I don't know what's going on with Antonio. The hospital won't let me in. They say that he's in a terribly volatile psychological state, with one crisis after another...

ROSA: It's true, unfortunately... (*She goes over to the window and flings it open*) A breath of fresh air! They only let me in to see him for five minutes, and no sooner had I gone up to him than he started shouting: 'Go away! Go away! I don't want that pest of a woman anywhere near me! Go away! Go away!'

The WINDOW *exits, stage right.*

LUCIA: How dreadful! But what are the doctors saying? Are they doing anything for him?

ROSA: Well, they're doing what they can. They had the idea of driving Antonio out to the FIAT-Mirafiori plant and taking him to his old work section to try and budge something in his memory. When he went into the factory, he seemed quite at home. He was going round the various sections, cool as a cucumber, almost as if he owned the place. But when they put him in front of the assembly line, and stuck a welding gun into his hand, and told him: 'Come on, Antonio, weld... You've been doing it for so many years...', it was as if his brain exploded: his eyes bulging in his head, he began shouting like a madman: 'No! I'm not doing shitty work like this!

LUCIA *barely succeeds in holding back a stifled laugh.*

'Take me away from this infernal machinery!'

LUCIA: (*Trying not to burst out laughing*) Ha, ha... ha, ha...

ROSA: I mean, it's not funny, is it... What's the matter with you? Why are you laughing?

LUCIA: Excuse me… It's just a nervous reaction… To think of a man like Agnelli, I mean Antonio… reduced…

ROSA: Ah yes, it's enough to drive you mad! Ah yes, I forgot to tell you. Last Thursday they brought him home for a couple of hours.

LUCIA: Thursday? So you've seen him quite recently?

ROSA: No, I was not there. They asked me to go out, because if Antonio sees me, he has another attack. Just imagine it. They bring my husband home, and I have to go out, as if I had scabies!

LUCIA: And did you manage to find out how he reacted here?

ROSA: Yes. Indifferent. They told me that he went round the house, but didn't remember a thing… He didn't even remember his little statue over there, with the two faces, of Plutarch and Suetonius…[7] (*She goes over to the papier mâché bust, which has a movable head. She takes it and turns it, revealing the second face*) …He was crazy about it! When he married me, he brought it as his dowry.

LUCIA: Ah, yes… he told me about it… he really had a thing about ancient history.

ROSA: Precisely… And he didn't even glance at his books… And there was I, keeping them all properly for him, all in order… I said to myself, one of these days he's going to be coming back… He's going to get tired of the Bitch… I mean, of Lucia… Well, you know, these things can happen… a man leaves his wife, takes up with another woman, then he gets tired of the other woman, and goes back to his wife… That's life. I even saw it once, in a film. A very good film! Ooh… it *was* a good film! I saw it seven times! Afterwards, she, the girlfriend, became seriously ill, and died in excruciating pain…

LUCIA *looks at her*.

Come on, I'm only joking… It's true, she did die a horrible death… But I'm joking, Lucia, I like you… You've helped me through this tragedy, you've given me a hand… Of course, at first I had it in for you… In fact I put curses on you... Incidentally, how's your eyesight, Lucia?

LUCIA: Excellent!

ROSA: Ah, I'm glad! So it was rubbish what they told me...
Just as well it was lies... because otherwise, by now you'd
be going round with a guide dog... and a white stick... Oh
Lucia, what terrible times these are... Antonio has erased
everything... Suetonius, the furniture... the table... me!

LUCIA: Cheer up, Rosa, you'll see... Antonio will get
better...

ROSA: No, Antonio won't get better... he'll never get
better... I'm going to hang myself... Would you like a
coffee?

LUCIA: Thank you, but only if you're making one for
yourself...

ROSA: Yes, it's alright, I'll make a coffee. I'll hang myself
another day. (*Looking in her shopping bag*) Where's the
coffee? It's gone! I might have known it... I've only just
bought it... and I forgot it at the grocer's. I'll go down and
get it. This terrible business with Antonio is making me
behave really strangely!

ROSA *exits.* LUCIA *is alone. She looks around her. A
moment or two passes. The telephone rings.* LUCIA *stands
there, uncertain. Then she lifts the handset.*

LUCIA: Hello, who's that? No, she has gone out... I am a
friend of hers... Ah, Professor, it's you... Yes, Lucia, that's
right, the teacher. How clever of you to recognise me at
once... How's it going? What? Who? He's escaped...? But
how did he manage that, with so many policemen
around...? Incredible...! From the laundry... and the
coat... his coat? I am sorry... No, he hasn't come here, I
assure you, I would tell you, Doctor... Don't worry, if he
turns up, I shall telephone you... Alright, yes, yes, without
anyone noticing... Goodbye, Professor.

She puts down the phone. Behind her, enter ANTONIO –
the real ANTONIO. *He is wearing a leather coat which is
coming apart at the seams. He looks pretty rough.*

ANTONIO: Oh, Lucia, thank goodness I've found you!

LUCIA: Antonio... What the hell are you doing here, have you gone mad? What's come over you?

ANTONIO: And where was I supposed to stick myself? I've been round to your house, but everything was locked up.

LUCIA: Good God, why aren't you in that basement? It's such a safe spot...

ANTONIO: Yes, safe as a grave... My grave! No, enough, I can't take any more... For heaven's sake, I want to see people, talk... You come and see me every once in a blue moon...

He takes off his coat, and hangs it on the coat rack.

LUCIA: But try to understand, I can't... the police are breathing down my neck everywhere I go... I was scared of leading them to you, and you getting arrested.

ANTONIO: No way am I going back in there, I don't want to go mad!

LUCIA: Alright – but you can't stay here. It's dangerous!

ANTONIO: Why dangerous? Who's going to imagine that I'd come and hide here? I haven't been to Rosa's house in more than a year...

LUCIA: Yes, but all the same, you can't stay... Your wife will be back in a minute.

ANTONIO: Well, maybe it's better that way. I shall tell her the whole truth. It's time to put an end to all this! It's a rotten trick that we're playing on the poor woman! And I'm paying the price too... You have no idea what it's like, night after night, huddling up every night like an animal, first with those wrecked cars, and now among all the cockroaches. Yesterday, I was so desperate, that I caught twenty of them, and put them in a circle, and with me sitting in the middle, we played at being the Commission of Inquiry into the Brescia massacre.[8] I'm going mad, I tell you.

LUCIA: I know, I know it's not very funny, but be patient, don't give in... particularly not now... Just another few days, and...

ANTONIO: Lucia, Lucia, it's been months that you've been telling me to be patient: 'Let things calm down, and then we can run off with no problems... Your wife won't cause us any more bother, because she'll have a husband, even if he is a bit of a mixed-up mess. Then, in a few more weeks, people will stop talking about Agnelli..' No. Every day – it never stops, newspapers, television, the radio... everywhere I go, I see that face. It's beginning to haunt me! On television they're even making a multi-part serial about him – the Agnelli Story.

LUCIA: Alright, it's a bit of a mess. But what do you think you'll achieve by coming and telling your wife the whole truth and explaining to her that there are two Antonios? Just when she's convinced herself that the idiot Agnelli is in fact her Antonio, i.e. you... In another few days, Agnelli will be better, and they'll send him here, and they'll both of them live happily ever after!

ANTONIO: Agnelli, going to bed with my wife?!

LUCIA: Well? What? Don't tell me that you're jealous?

ANTONIO: No! Of course I'm not jealous. But the idea gets up my nose! He's screwed me all my life! He pulled the plug on me when he made me redundant. Then I save his life, and now he's going to be screwing my wife!

LUCIA: Antonio, don't be vulgar!

ANTONIO: What do you mean, vulgar! The fact is, he's a bastard! Now they'll grant him a permanent disability pension... They'll send him home to live a life of ease... in my house... and what'll he do? He'll end up with my redundancy money, my life insurance money, my pension and my clarinet no doubt. No, I'm sorry, but I'm going to explain everything.

LUCIA: Oh brilliant! That way, you'll go straight to prison for at least four years – just on suspicion alone! Do you really think that Rosa will be able to keep her trap shut, even for two minutes?

ANTONIO: Just leave my wife out of this will you.

Enter ROSA, *with her shopping bag.*

ROSA: Here I am...

ROSA *sees* ANTONIO. *She stops in her tracks, speechless.* LUCIA *continues, pretending not to have seen her come in.*

LUCIA: Antonio... what do you mean you don't recognise me any longer?! Look at me... It's me... Lucia!

ROSA: Have they sent him home...?

LUCIA: Surely, at least you recognise her, your wife?

ROSA *makes as if to approach* ANTONIO.

No, Rosa, stay there, don't come too close to him...

ROSA: Don't worry... I won't come too close... You've healed up really well... Your scars don't even show...

LUCIA *pushes* ANTONIO *over towards* ROSA.

LUCIA: Go on, Antonio.

She kicks him furtively on the shins.

ROSA: Why did you kick our Antonio?!

LUCIA: Ah, well, you can't always afford half-measures with psychologically unstable people... they'll never get well! Our professor at the university always used to say: 'A punch and a kick brings a man back to his senses!' Come on, Antonio! (*She gives him another kick*) Look, see, it works! Well done... Embrace her! (ANTONIO *embraces* ROSA.) Oh God. It did work.

ROSA: He's embracing me... Oh Lord, I'm getting all emotional! I feel weak at the knees... Can I embrace him too?

LUCIA: Yes, Rosa... certainly...

ROSA: Are you sure? With both arms?

LUCIA: Yes, certainly...

ROSA *timidly embraces* ANTONIO. *He stands stock-still, embarrassed, but at the same time moved by the situation.*

ROSA: Hello… how are you feeling Antonio? Do you recognise me…? Who am I…? Who am I…?

ANTONIO: You are Rosa, you are my wife…

ROSA: His voice has come back to normal and he recognises me! Now then. Concentrate. Now who is she? Come on!

She kicks his leg, hard.

ANTONIO: Stop it! Let's not carry on with this charade! Listen, it's time you knew what's really going on.

LUCIA: Stop it, Antonio, don't be stupid!

ROSA: Give him another kick to calm him down!

She gives him another kick. LUCIA *does likewise.*

ANTONIO: Ouch… stop it!

ROSA: We're only doing it for your own good: a punch and a kick brings a man back to his senses.

ANTONIO: I want to tell you what happened.

LUCIA: Stop it… shut up a minute… (*The* WINDOW *enters, from stage right. It stops centre-stage.* LUCIA *goes over to it and looks down onto the road*) There's no time to lose, Antonio. You're going to have to scram.

ANTONIO: Why? What's going on?

LUCIA: I might be mistaken, but there's something strange going on down in the street. I bet it's those people from the hospital, coming to get you…

She goes to the coat rack, and takes down ANTONIO*'s jacket.*

ROSA: Ah, so they didn't let him out, then?

LUCIA: No, he escaped. A short while before he arrived, the Doctor telephoned to know whether, by chance, he had come to hide here, in your house…

ANTONIO: It's not true, it's a pack of lies, don't believe her. She's just saying that because…

LUCIA: I promise you, listen... let's get out of here... let's go to my house, while we've still got time...

She gives him his jacket.

ANTONIO: No, I'm staying here, till I finish telling Rosa everything.

He puts his jacket on the table.

ROSA: Sit down! Bitch! With that excuse about how the people are coming to take him away... you were just trying to steal my husband again!

The door bursts open. Enter two POLICEMEN, followed by the INSPECTOR; the DOCTOR is also with them. The WINDOW exits, stage right.

INSPECTOR: Here he is! What did I tell you, Professor. I was sure that we'd find him at his wife's house.

LUCIA: I suppose you're happy now! And I'm a liar!?

ROSA: Oh, please, don't hurt him, don't frighten him, he's sick...

INSPECTOR: Who wants to frighten him? We're among friends, isn't that right, Antonio?

DOCTOR: You had us worried, you know... How are you? Your pulse rate is a bit high. What you need is a sedative...

INSPECTOR: I don't know about sedatives...! This one's playing the fool, and making us waste a lot of time! I know what our little Antonio could do with, really!

ANTONIO: But who are you... I don't even know you!

ROSA: You see? Carrying on like that, you've made him lose his memory again... To think, up to a moment ago, he recognised everybody. It was a pleasure to see...

POLICEMAN: Inspector, what shall we do, shall we put handcuffs on him?

INSPECTOR: No, it's not necessary...

DOCTOR: Give me a hand.

He goes to the table, and pulls out of his bag the necessaries for performing an injection.

ANTONIO: Inspector, eh? Listen, I would like to tell you something... Listen, because I am going to tell you...

LUCIA: Antonio, are you mad?

ANTONIO: Shut up, you! Inspector, listen to me.

ANTONIO *speaks excitedly with the* INSPECTOR. *He has his back to the* DOCTOR. *The* DOCTOR *comes creeping up on him, in order to give him an injection. But* ANTONIO *and the* INSPECTOR *suddenly contrive to switch positions, and the* INSPECTOR *ends up getting the needle in his own backside.*

INSPECTOR: Aagh!

DOCTOR: Oh, excuse me. It's a sedative...

ANTONIO: Inspector, listen to me...

INSPECTOR: You are nothing but a troublemaker...! Now he's telling me again that he is Agnelli!

ROSA: Agnelli?

DOCTOR: (*Preparing a second injection*) Yes. Ever since he made that unfortunate visit to FIAT, he's got it into his head that he is Mr Agnelli!

ROSA: Oh, that's all we need!

DOCTOR: It's nothing to be alarmed at – it's the classic split personality phenomenon. Now, come along, take your trousers down...

ANTONIO: My trousers?

DOCTOR: It's for the sedative... (*He is about to perform the injection, but continues talking with* ROSA) In these past few months, when he's been confined to his bed, all in plaster, as if he was in a trap... he's been chewing over his hatred towards the person who, in his opinion, is responsible for his tragedy... in other words, Agnelli. (*Turning to one of the* POLICEMEN) Oh forget it! Just lift up his jacket... (*To* ROSA) ...and he has ended up identifying with him.

ANTONIO *once again succeeds in transposing the* INSPECTOR, *who receives yet another injection in the backside.* .

INSPECTOR: Aaaargh!

DOCTOR: Oh, don't be such a cry baby, it's only a little prick.

At this point, the ACTORS *pretend to make a slip-up on stage. The* DOCTOR *pretends to trip, and loses his hypodermic syringe. The* ACTRESS *playing* ROSA *looks disconcerted as she picks up the syringe. The* ACTORS *burst out laughing. The* ACTOR *playing the* DOCTOR *feigns embarrassment and consternation. The* ACTOR *playing the part of* ANTONIO *speaks.*

ACTOR PLAYING THE PART OF ANTONIO: Well, there you are, it could have happened to anybody... particularly to real doctors! But anyway, it's my fault, because I spun him round too fast. It's my fault. Doctors, as we know, are never responsible, either in civil or in criminal law. OK, let's start again where we left off...

DOCTOR: (*He makes as if to start again, but breaks into confused laughter*) Hold his jacket up...

ANTONIO: Don't be embarrassed, Professor...

DOCTOR: You, hold his jacket up... and he has ended up identifying with him.

ROSA: Oh heavens, he's identified with him, with Agnelli, and he's getting a split personality... Like Dr Jekyll, who at the start was... and then became... and so, when he doesn't recognise me, it's because he's convinced that he is Agnelli.

DOCTOR: Ten out of ten!

The DOCTOR *prepares a third injection.* ANTONIO *is in deep converation with the* INSPECTOR, *who by now is reeling from the injections.*

INSPECTOR: Excuse me, Doctor, come over here a moment. Now he's saying that he was the one who saved Agnelli. I don't know about split personalities, this one's just trying to make idiots out of all of us!

ANTONIO *takes advantage of a momentary lack of attention by the guards. He makes a dash for the door. He goes out, and locks it behind him, as he runs off. In order to escape, he has to shift one of the* POLICEMEN. *The* POLICEMAN *ends up getting the injection that was meant for* ANTONIO.

POLICEMAN: Aaaargh! He's escaped!

INSPECTOR: Don't stand there like a dummy! Get after him, quick!

POLICEMAN: He's locked us in... The key was on the outside!

INSPECTOR: Well then, shoot the lock off!

ROSA: No, please, don't shoot the door down... I've got another key. Wait a minute, I'll find it...

INSPECTOR: No, there's no time... Fire! Fire! Fire!

The POLICEMEN *fire* – BANG BANG. *From outside the door, we hear a stifled scream. A musical interlude follows, during which everyone freezes for a moment.*

ROSA: Antonio! Antonio was behind that door! You've killed him...!

The door swings open. After a moment, enter the EXAMINING MAGISTRATE.

EXAMINING MAGISTRATE: My leg... There's a hole in my leg... Why did you shoot me?

INSPECTOR: Your Honour! What on earth were you doing behind the door?

EXAMINING MAGISTRATE: I was knocking... But do you always shoot people when they knock at the door?

He falls to the floor.

INSPECTOR: Hurry up, Doctor... he's fainted... And you, could you help too?

DOCTOR: Don't worry. Amputation is my favourite.

INSPECTOR: Look, if anybody lets slip a word about this incident, I'll kill them! If it ends up in the newsapers – 'Magistrate Kneecapped by the Police...' – I'll top myself!

Exit the POLICEMEN, *the* INSPECTOR, *the* DOCTOR *and* LUCIA, *carrying the* EXAMINING MAGISTRATE. ROSA *remains on stage. She is dazed and bemused by what has happened. She closes the door, and looks at the wrecked lock.*

ROSA: Madness! Nobody's going to believe me if I tell them! Did you see that? Nasty habit they've got, of pulling out their guns at the slightest provocation...

The WINDOW *whizzes onstage.* ROSA *looks through it.*

Poor Antonio... Let's hope they're not going to shoot him too... Oh, God, there he is... That's him, hiding behind the bus... No, he's gone... Maybe it wasn't him... (*She goes to the table, where* ANTONIO's *car coat is still lying*) Oh I hope they don't take him back to that hospital because then he really will go barmy, sharing a split personality with Dr Jekyll, who's half beast and half Agnelli... Well it's the same thing really... Hey, but here's his coat... He went off without a coat... he's bound to catch cold...

ROSA *takes* ANTONIO's *coat and goes to hang it on the coat rack. The door opens. Enter the* DOUBLE. *He is wearing an overcoat. His head is wrapped in a long scarf. As the* DOUBLE *enters, the* WINDOW *leaves the stage.*

DOUBLE: Excuse me.

ROSA: Antonio! You've given them the slip... it's you... you got away... you made it!

DOUBLE: Maaay... I... cooome... iiin...? Is aaaaanyone in?

ROSA: Yes, no one's in... they've all gone off to take a gentleman to hospital, because he knocked at the door and they shot him in the leg... so as to open the door... and then he turned out to be an Examining Magistrate.

DOUBLE: Iiiii've... goooot... awaaaay!

ROSA: Yes, I know!

DOUBLE: Thaaat... creeetin of an Inspeeector... is convinced that I kiiidnapped myself... an autoterrorist!

ROSA: Calm down, Antonio, slow down and get your breath back... All that running that you've been doing, your scars are beginning to show again... They've all swollen up with the fright... Look how you're sweating... Are you thirsty, would you like something to drink?

DOUBLE: Yes, please, a little non-carbonated mineral water... because otherwise I'll burp, and I'll blow my nose off...
The DOUBLE *takes off his coat, and goes over to the coat rack.*

ROSA: OK, I'll bring it at once. (*She notices the overcoat*) But what are you doing with a coat on?

DOUBLE: It's cold!

ROSA: Did you have two overcoats?

DOUBLE: No, this one's a long jacket...

ROSA: This doubling-up of yours is beginning to be obsessive...

DOUBLE: Listen, madam, I have to tell you something... which obviously you are not aware of...

ROSA: But now you're calling me madam...?!

DOUBLE: Madam, I do not know you... I am not your husband...

ROSA: Yes, dear, calm down... sit down... Now you just drink your non-carbonated mineral water, and try not to talk nonsense...

ROSA *goes into the kitchen, and after a moment returns with a bottle and a glass.*

DOUBLE: But madam, I am not talking nonsense at all! I have never been so lucid and self-aware!

From the plastic bag that he has with him, the DOUBLE *pulls out a funnel.*

ROSA: Jesus Christ! Well, why don't you show it, and stop calling me madam!

DOUBLE: Alright, I'll stop calling you madam. Would you be so kind as to help me to screw the funnel into the tube… (*He fiddles with the funnel*) No… it's alright, I've done it.

ROSA: The funnel? What for?

DOUBLE: So as to drink.

ROSA: You drink through your neck?

DOUBLE: Yes… I can't yet drink through my throat… until the scar tissues heal up completely on my glottis and epiglottis… Ah… it's cold! Just pour it straight out of the bottle, it's more convenient.

ROSA does as he says.

ROSA: Oh Lord, what am I seeing – my husband, with a funnel stuck in him. You look like a bloody beer barrel!

DOUBLE: And now, will you please sit down, because I want to tell you my story… the real story!

ROSA: Alright – tell me.

DOUBLE: After the accident, for months it was as if I had disappeared…

ROSA: Yes, I know…

DOUBLE: Then, that day when they took me to the assembly line at the Mirafiori plant, it was as if a bomb had exploded in my brain: 50,000 electric shock treatments all in one go! All of a sudden, I remembered who I was. That I was Agnelli, and that I didn't want anything to do with the shit and the mess and the grime. And now there I was, I… Agnelli, hooked up with a welding gun which was spitting blinding sparks all over the place, and I started trembling as if I had a 220 volt plug up my arse…

ROSA: Calm down, Antonio…

DOUBLE: I am not Antonio! I am not some stupid worker who starts trembling! I am above everything, I am! They think that I have been kidnapped… but no, I have only

been swapped! And look at me now, with this loony
puppet's face! The face of one of my lineworkers... what a
humiliating joke...

ROSA: Listen, Dr Jekyll... will you stop that? I've had it up to
here, with all these personality changes! Either you calm
down, or I'll break your leg!

She kicks him.

DOUBLE: Aaargh! Are you mad?!

We hear the sound of a police siren. Enter the WINDOW,
from stage right. ROSA *looks out through the window.*

Is that the police?! Are they arriving?

ROSA: No, it's not them. They're not stopping. But at the
same time, it's not a very clever idea for you to wait here
until they *do* turn up and arrest you... Let's go up in the
loft... Take your scarf, for your scars... I've got it all fixed
up, you see. You can even sleep there; I set it all up so as to
rent it to a student. Come on, come on, I'll show you up
there. I've had a water tap put in, too. (*They exit. We hear*
ROSA's *voice disappearing off upstairs*) Remember to
watch out for the steps, they're a bit steep. Nobody knows
that this room is here, because I've not yet reported it to
the authorities. There you are, come in. Look, I've had
electric light put in too.

Then the hall door opens, and ANTONIO *the worker
enters.*

ANTONIO: Rosa! Are you there, Rosa? Anyone in? Well,
thank goodness, they've all gone away, and let's hope that
they all leave me in peace. Look how I'm sweating! I'm
soaked! (*He removes his jacket and shirt, and throws them
on the floor in the middle of the room*) I wonder if Rosa's
got a clean jumper for me to change into.

He exits via the centre door. Enter ROSA. *She stands by the
door for a moment, speaking to the* DOUBLE *upstairs.*

ROSA: Now you stay there and behave. Don't make any
noise. I'll bring you some food in a moment... (*She goes*

towards the kitchen) Goodness, I'm all emotions...! I'd never have expected to get so emotional, having my husband back home! I'm all worked up. I'm really all worked up...! (*She sees his clothes thrown in the middle of the floor*) That shows how worked up I am! I didn't even notice that he'd taken his clothes off... (*She picks up his clothes*) ...and he's dumped them all here on the floor, just as he always used to... Oh, how pleased I am to have him back... how happy I am to have his nice dirty shirts to wash... and iron... and to cook for him, slaving like a skivvy... that's living for you!

ROSA *exits into the kitchen. She is radiant with happiness.* ANTONIO *re-enters. He has put on a clean jumper. He is drying his head and arms with a towel.*

ANTONIO: Rosa, are you back... are you back?

ROSA: Why are you back here? Is something wrong? Why have you come back?

ANTONIO: Ah, why, shouldn't I have come back? I suppose you'd rather I let myself be locked up like a poor sod, for the rest of my life?

ROSA: But what do you mean, 'the rest of your life...'? Just a day or two, until things sort themselves out.

ANTONIO: No. If I go inside, I'll never come out again. I could be inside for twelve years...

ROSA: Don't say silly things... You don't think I'll be keeping you up there for twelve years...

ANTONIO: Up where? What do you mean, up there? Rosa, what are you raving on about?

ROSA: (*Thinking that her husband does not remember having been upstairs*) Look, nothing is going right around here... I am beginning to lose patience. Look, if you don't get yourself sorted out, I... I am going to pour twelve pints of bromide down the hole in your neck! (*She takes the funnel and points it meaningfully at* ANTONIO) You're driving everybody nuts! First things are black, then they're white, then you change your mind, and you don't even remember!!! Come on, up into the loft, do as I say!

ANTONIO: In the loft? Why in the loft?

ROSA: Because it's a safe hiding place!

ANTONIO: No, it's not safe at all. The loft has no way out, it's a trap. If you don't mind, I would prefer to stay over there; in the other room. (*He points towards the bedroom*) Because that leads onto the terrace, and so, if they come looking for me, I'll be able to get away over the roofs...

ROSA: You'll fall and end up in bits... and then we'll start all over again: Bruuu... braaa... bray... astronaut! astronaut! But do what you want!

ANTONIO: Rosa, who's this astronaut?

ROSA: Stop it! Do what you like. It's impossible to reason with you. I'm going to get you something to eat.

ROSA goes into the kitchen.

ANTONIO: At last you've said something intelligent. I'm starving!

He notices that there are two coats hanging on the coat rack: the one belonging to him, and the other to the DOUBLE. ROSA re-enters, bringing bread, glasses, a bottle of wine, plates, cutlery and serviettes. She goes to the table and starts to lay it.

ROSA: You're very lucky, you know. Today I prepared the stew for the whole week, with a pig's trotter...

ANTONIO: (*Lifting off the DOUBLE's overcoat*) Whose is it?

ROSA: The pig's trotter? It's ours... we'll eat it!

ANTONIO: (*He goes over to ROSA with the two coats*) I'm talking about the coat. Whose is it?

ROSA: It's yours. Whose do you expect it to be?

ANTONIO: My one is that one – so whose one is this one? The astronaut's?

ROSA: It's yours!

ANTONIO: Rosa, who is this astronaut who leaves coats all over the place?

ROSA: You can pack that in! It's yours. You had two of them, one on top of the other! Two overcoats! You were going round with two overcoats!

ANTONIO: Me? I had two overcoats, one on top of the other!? I was going round with two overcoats... one on top of the other!!

ROSA: Yes, you!

ROSA picks up a chair, and is about to throw it at him. ANTONIO addresses her extremely calmly, as if trying to deal with a raving loony.

ANTONIO: Of course. (*He points to his leather car coat*) And I suppose this was my waistcoat!

ROSA: (*Going back to the table*) So, shall I heat it up?

ANTONIO: What? The coat?

ROSA: No, the stew! You know very well I meant the stew. How are you going to eat this stew...?

ANTONIO looks at her in increasing amazement. Then thinking that ROSA has gone completely round the twist, he moves slowly to the door to make a getaway.

ROSA: No, seriously, how do you do it? How do you swallow? Do you suck it down through the funnel? Or through the tube in your neck? And how are we going to get it down... There's no way it'll go through... even if I push it, because even if I cut the meat up into little bits, it's still going to be too big... and since it mustn't touch your glottis, or your epiglottis... which, incidentally, are two words that I have never heard of... then how are you going to eat? Will you be sucking it down, or not? But then, it won't go through the tube in your neck... it won't go through!

Only now does she notice that ANTONIO is about to leave the room.

ANTONIO: Yes, carry on... you're quite right... Carry on just like that. Perfect! When it doesn't pass via the glottis... the tube is the best way... suck it through the funnel... the funnel is designed especially for sucking... and as for me, my glottis... you know... and then also my epiglottis...

ROSA: Where are you going? This is no laughing matter... Come over here...

ANTONIO: Yes, yes... Hang on a minute. I'm going out for a moment to get my third overcoat, which I left downstairs... I had three coats, you know!

ROSA: Careful... somebody's coming... Quick, go into the bedroom...

ANTONIO *scrambles into the bedroom.*

I'll lock you in... I'll give it two turns of the key. (*She does as she says*) ...and you stay quiet...

ANTONIO: Yes... Who is it?

ROSA: For God's sake shut up. (*She goes to the door and peeps out*) Yes? Oh it's you... and you. (*She shuts the door again, runs to the centre door, and without re-opening it, shouts*) Don't worry, it wasn't anyone... it's next-door... I don't like him at all, a right Peeping Tom...! The minute he hears a noise, he comes out nosy parkering... I can't stand the man... I'm... I'm going to report him... I'll report him for 'unnatural curiosity'!

ROSA *goes out into the kitchen. No sooner has she gone than the* DOUBLE *appears round the front door.*

DOUBLE: Rosa, can I come in? Am I bothering you?

ROSA: Be patient for a moment! I'm dishing out the stew. I'll be there to open the door in a moment.

DOUBLE: Oh, there's no need to bother, I'll let myself in.

ROSA *enters, with a saucepan brimful of stew. She stares at him, dumbfounded.*

ROSA: But how did you get in?

DOUBLE: Through the door, why?

ROSA: But it was locked!

DOUBLE: No, it wasn't locked!

ROSA: How stupid of me, obviously, as I was turning the key a moment ago...

We hear the wail of a siren. The WINDOW *whizzes on-stage.* ROSA *rushes over and looks down into the street.*

There they are again... Oh no, it's an ambulance, it's not stopping...

Exit the WINDOW.

DOUBLE: The police!

ROSA: Yes, but they're not stopping... Oh, what a life this is! Sweet, I would like so much for the two of us, me and you, to sit here, nice and comfortable, and eat, but it's too dangerous. Listen, let's take the plates and the cutlery, and go into the room...

DOUBLE: Oh no, please, I can't stand it. When I'm in there, I get ghastly nightmares, like in the hospital, I want to be sick... I can't hold my food down...

ROSA: Alright, let's take a chance...

The DOUBLE *sits at the table.*

...but at the slightest suspicious noise, you'll have to disappear. Here you are, help yourself. (*She passes him the stewpot, and then goes over to the sideboard, where she takes two jars and brings them over to the* DOUBLE) Look, I've bought you some Cremona mustard too, and there's some green sauce...

DOUBLE: But Rosa, this is boiled beef...

ROSA: Yes?

DOUBLE *and* **ROSA:** Yes?

DOUBLE: And boiled sausage... and even a boiled pig's foot...

ROSA: Yes...?!!!

DOUBLE: Everything boiled...

ROSA *is about to lose her grip on herself.*

ROSA: Yes? So? Is something wrong? Changed your mind yet again?

DOUBLE: No, I really like stew... it's just that you've forgotten that my tube is very thin, and the food won't go through the funnel... particularly a sausage that size...

ROSA: We've been through this before, haven't we? I could mince it... But even then it's too big to go through that little hole!

DOUBLE: It won't go through the hole in my neck, but it will go through my nose!

ROSA: You eat stew through your nose?!

DOUBLE: Yes. In hospital they even made me suck spaghetti up through my nose... the bolognese sauce made a terrible mess... Now I'll show you a little gadget that I've brought with me from the hospital... (*From his plastic bag, he pulls out a kind of mask*) There, you see, these tubes go up into the nostrils. Here you connect the output socket from a meat mincer. I had a really good one in hospital, electric... But I forgot it in the rush.

ROSA: Oh, how stupid of me, I've got a mincing machine too, but it's one of those old ones, with the handle that you turn.

She goes over to the sideboard to get it.

DOUBLE: Let's have a look. The important thing is that the back end has to be the same diameter. Perfect! Size 12!

ROSA: Incredible! Antonio... even the colour matches!!

DOUBLE: Now I'll show you how it works. There, you see, first you put on the mask like this. Then you put the tubes up your nostrils, and then put the meat grinder here, on your head... (*He suddenly takes the mask off again*) Oh goodness, look...

ROSA: What's up, Antonio?

DOUBLE: The meat grinder grinding on my head, I feel as if my brain's being ground up... Have you got any cords?

ROSA: Cords?

DOUBLE: Yes cords. To tie me down.

ROSA: Tie you down?

DOUBLE: Yes. Otherwise I won't be able to resist the instinct to pull the tubes out of my nose.

ROSA: Well, we could try it with these straps. They're the straps I use for my suitcases...

She pulls some straps out of a drawer.

DOUBLE: Perfect! And this armchair with the arms is tailor-made. (*He arranges a couple of straps on each arm of the armchair*) And with this one, you can tie my neck back against the upright part, like this!

ROSA: Oh, it's horrible – you look as if you're in an electric chair!

DOUBLE: You said it! I *am* in the electric chair. Rosa, you're going to have to be strong. Please, Rosa, don't be swayed if, at the beginning, I plead with you to set me free. You must be strong, you must make me eat at any cost!

ROSA: Yes, indeed, at any cost! I shall be very strict. I shall make you eat everything! (*The phone rings*) Oh God, the phone... I can't answer... I'm crying... (*She answers the phone in a perfectly normal voice*) Hello, yes Professor, it's me. No, I've not seen Antonio. No, no, I assure you, he hasn't been here. I would tell you, Professor. I wouldn't say a word to the Inspector – he's so uncouth – but I would tell *you*! Please, let me know if anything happens. I'm in agony here! Goodbye.

She puts the phone down again.

DOUBLE: What did he say?

The DOUBLE *has arranged the straps around the arms of the armchair.*

ROSA: It was the Professor... If you ask me, he wasn't taken in. They'll be here any minute. Quick, let's take everything upstairs, into the other room...

DOUBLE: No, for heaven's sake, don't you understand – I

can't wait any longer – I'm dying of hunger! Rosa, you've got to grind some stew up my nose, or I shall go mad!

ROSA: I'll grind for you in a couple of minutes… Go on up, I'll join you. Take the bottle of wine, and the glasses.

DOUBLE: Bread, I want bread…

He makes a dive for the bread basket.

ROSA: Leave the bread alone…

DOUBLE: But without bread I won't be able to eat the stew…

ROSA: I've got grated breadcrumbs… Go on up… I'll bring the rest up, including the electric chair. (*She runs into the kitchen*) Hurry up!

DOUBLE: Alright. I'll wait for you. But you get a move on.

The DOUBLE *exits via the door leading to the hall landing.* ROSA *calls out from the kitchen:*

ROSA: Just a moment, I'll turn off the gas. I've got some fruit down here. Afterwards I'll make you a fruit salad. (*She re-enters, goes over to the table, and puts the plates, cutlery and the stewpot etc. onto the archair*) Imagine, what a shame, having to mince up such a good bit of beef, as if it was meat for meatballs…

ANTONIO *the worker calls from the bedroom.*

ANTONIO: Rosa, can we get a move on – I'm still here, waiting!

ROSA: Don't be so impatient! What am I supposed to do? Sprout wings? I'm loading up the electric chair!

ANTONIO: Loading what? Rosa, what nonsense are you talking now?

ROSA: Hurry up and give me a hand… I can't manage it… it's too heavy…

ANTONIO: Alright. Just come and unlock the door…

ROSA: It's open! Push it and see.

ANTONIO: Don't talk rubbish, Rosa… It's locked, solid!

ROSA *looks at the door, speechless. Then she goes to the bedroom door and turns the key. Re-enter* ANTONIO.

Oh, at last!

ROSA *looks at him, bewildered.*

ROSA: Antonio, please you're going to have to explain to me how you managed to go into the bedroom, lock yourself in, and still leave the key on the outside of the door...!

ANTONIO: What did I do?

ROSA: You locked yourself in the bedroom, with two turns of the key!

ANTONIO: I did? It was you, you who locked me in with two turns of the key.

ROSA: Yes, but that was before. But then you got out!

ANTONIO: I got out?

ROSA: Yes!

ANTONIO: How?

ROSA: Through the door! How else?

ANTONIO: I came out by the door?

ROSA: Yeees!!!

ANTONIO: When?

ROSA: Before!

ANTONIO: Don't talk rubbish!

ROSA *picks up a chair and makes as if to throw it at him.*

ROSA: You *did* come out! You did come out!

ANTONIO: It's true! I was trying to keep it a secret from you, but obviously I failed. (*He mimes everything that follows*) I got out by using an old trick that we use at the Mirafiori factory. The foremen lock us in, so we get out by sticking our hands under the door... Of course, at first we stick them, i.e. our hands, under a stamping press... so as to squash them flat a bit... Then we stick our hands under the door, and push them through as far as the elbow... Then we give a little twist, so as to get the knobbly bits through more easily... until we get our arms through as well, right up to the shoulder. Then we grab the key. But the key is too thick, it won't go under the door! So, we stick our heads under the door, and push... and push... and... whoopsi! That's how we get out. Are you happy now? They call me the Scarlet Pimpernel!

ROSA *listens to him in blank amazement. As* ANTONIO *finishes speaking, she removes her scarf from round her neck, and wraps it round her head.*

Alright? Rosa, Rosa, what are you doing, Rosa?

ROSA: I've got a headache!

ANTONIO: Well maybe if we sit down to eat, maybe it'll go... (*Without answering,* ROSA *goes over to the electric chair. She looks at* ANTONIO, *meaningfully.* ANTONIO *does not understand*) Now you're talking.

ROSA: (*Persuasively, talking as if to a mad person*) The electric chair... come on... let's go into the bedroom, and I'll grind for you... I shall be ruthless... down to the last particle of meat...

ANTONIO: Stooooop it! You're driving me mad! It's a trick, to drive me out of my mind! Stooop it!

ROSA: I shall do my duty! In spite of everything that's happened! Antonio, let's go in there!

ANTONIO: In where?

ROSA: Into the bedroom...!

ANTONIO: To do what?

ROSA: To eat!

ANTONIO: Noooo!!! For months I've been eating like a wretch. Now, just once, I want to eat here, sitting down like a good Christian... A Christian, and a Marxist! Sitting down! A Marxist Christian, sitting down ...and slightly puzzled... because of what's happened in Poland! (*During this speech,* ROSA *slips slowly to the floor. She curls up in a heap, with her head resting on the floor, and stays there,* *silent, as if crushed*) What's up now? What are you doing, Rosa…? Rosa, I know where you've been all this time… You've become a hippy, haven't you? Were you in a commune? And who was your guru? The astronaut?!

ROSA: Antonio, I am very confused…! Antonio, we must go in there, into the other room…

ANTONIO: What, like that? Crawling along the floor?

ROSA: …because if the police arrive… (*The* WINDOW *zooms in.* ROSA *shouts at it*) …I said 'if' the police arrive!

The WINDOW *takes fright, and rushes back into the wings.*

ANTONIO: Who cares! Lock the door, and put the door chain on! (*He sits down at the table*) You know that door chain I had put in specially. And if the police want to get past that, they'll have to batter the door down.

ROSA *picks herself up off the floor, and goes to lock the door with the door chain.*

And while they're battering the door down, I'll be eating this wonderful stew! (*He clears the armchair off, putting the various objects on the table. He sits down, holding the stewpot*) I've said it before and I'll say it again, Rosa, that nobody in the whole world makes stew the way that you do…

ROSA: Yes, I know you've said it before.

ANTONIO: I could eat this with my eyeballs!

ROSA: And instead you're going to have to eat it with your nose!

She goes up to ANTONIO *and straps his hands to the arms of the armchair.*

ANTONIO: Rosa? Rosa! What are you doing? Why are you strapping me down?

ROSA: To make you eat, right?

ANTONIO: Rosa, please, afterwards we'll have time to talk, and you can tell me about all the customs in your commune. Not now, though…

ROSA: Stop it! Let's start with a nice bit of broth... just to whet your appetite... But... Antonio, how are you going to eat it?

ANTONIO: I won't eat it, I'll drink it...

ROSA: But do you want it down your neck, or are you going to suck it up through your nose...? How would you prefer it? It would be better through your neck. (*She picks up the funnel*) Let's hope I manage to find the hole...!

She sticks the funnel down his neck.

ANTONIO: You've punched a hole in my shoulderblade! Please... untie me...

ROSA ignores his pleas. She puts a strap round his neck, pulling his head back against the upright of the armchair.

Rosa, please... Rosa, it's true, I've been a louse... Rosa, I've treated you badly, I've been like a son of a bitch... I've not respected you... But you must be generous... and forgive me. I'll come back to you, Rosa! Please, let me go!

ROSA: My sweet, my sweet...

ANTONIO: Forgive me, Rosa. I love you, Rosa!

ROSA: How long have I waited to hear you say those words!

ANTONIO: Rosa...

ROSA: I love you too...!

She picks up the mask from the table, and fits it on his head. She pushes the tubes up his nose. As ANTONIO speaks, ROSA adjusts the mask to get a tight fit.

ANTONIO: Rosa, Rosa... my nostrils are all blocked up... I've got something up my nose... Rosa, I feel like an elephant... Why do you go to see those kinds of films... You know that they only give you ideas!

ROSA: Ssssh – keep quiet...!

ANTONIO: That's enough, now, Rosa... Let me go... Help! Help!!

ROSA: Antonio, don't shout like that...

ANTONIO: Heeelp!!

ROSA: Antonio, don't shout! Don't you realise that you're torturing me!

She completes the operation of fitting the machine.

ANTONIO: No, you're torturing me! Help… help…!

ANTONIO's shout transforms into the trumpeting of an elephant.

ROSA: Antonio, stop it… Antonio… Stop pretending to be an elephant… What will the neighbours say? …Stop it!

ANTONIO carries on howling.

Shut up! (ROSA *no longer knows what to do to shut him up; in desperation she shoves a serviette into his mouth*) Stop it! You must eat. Keep quiet!

ANTONIO continues howling, but slowly his howls are transformed into the sound of a steamboat siren.

Antonio, stop that! The neighbours will hear… Stop it! I won't have you being a steamboat! Oh my God, he's turned puce… Oh, how stupid of me, I've blocked up all his holes… So how's he going to breathe…? What shall I put in place of the serviette…? Ah yes, your favourite clarinet…

The clarinet is hanging from a standard lamp. ROSA picks up the whole caboodle, and puts it in front of ANTONIO.

We'll leave it hanging from the lamp, so that you can breathe, and play at the same time, if you want!

She takes the serviette out of his mouth, and inserts the clarinet's mouthpiece. ANTONIO moves the fingers of his right hand up and down the keys of the clarinet, which gives out a blues sequence of high and low notes, commenting grotesquely on the situation.

Now I can give you your broth… (*She pours the broth down the funnel*) Don't worry, it's not hot… I've put some grated cheese in, and a couple of drops of lemon to knock out the grease… There, that's goood… swallow it down, it'll do

you good... but... but... what's this – you're doing a wee??
Oh no... it's the soup running out of your trousers... I must
have missed the hole with the tube! Oh well, too bad. Let's
get on to the stew. Let's start with this nice bit of rump...

ROSA *takes some pieces of meat, and puts them into the
meat grinder. The clarinet's wailing transforms into a
desperate rock rhythm. ROSA, unperturbed, continues
grinding, turning the handle of the mincer. There is a loud
knocking at the door. From outside the door, the
INSPECTOR shouts:*

INSPECTOR: Open up! Police! Open up, or we'll knock the
door down!

ROSA: There they are! I told you that they'd be back... Keep
quiet, don't budge.

ANTONIO *lets out a groan, through the clarinet.*

Keep quiet!

*With a big crash, the door bursts open, under the weight of
the two POLICEMEN. ROSA continues turning the
handle of the mincer, unperturbed. ANTONIO plays the
clarinet with increasing desperation. The INSPECTOR and
the POLICEMEN stare at the scene in amazement.*

INSPECTOR: But what on earth are you doing?

ROSA: I'm feeding my husband.

INSPECTOR: With a clarinet in his mouth?

ROSA: Yes, it's the only way he'll eat! Would you mind giving
me a hand? Carry on grinding up his meat... I'll go and
prepare him a nice fruit salad... But don't let yourself feel
sorry for him, if he asks you to unstrap him... He must eat:
it's a matter of life and death!

ROSA *goes into the kitchen. One of the POLICEMEN
removes the clarinet from ANTONIO's mouth.*

ANTONIO: Help... I've got a bit of boiled sausage up my
nose... Have you got a nose-pick?

INSPECTOR: What are you babbling about?

ANTONIO: Help! Set me free! That woman's a horror! Take me away from here...

INSPECTOR: Take you away where? To prison, perhaps?

ANTONIO: To the zoo, if you like... Just get me away from here. That woman is mad! She's killing me, sausage by sausage!

INSPECTOR: Alright... we'll set you free, if you do us a little favour. You're going to tell us a few details about the Agnelli kidnap. You were there, weren't you, that evening, on the embankment?

ANTONIO: Yes, certainly I was there, on the embankment...

INSPECTOR: Very good!

ANTONIO: But I had nothing to do with the kidnap. In fact, it was me who saved Agnelli...

INSPECTOR: Give the handle a little twirl!

The POLICEMAN *does as he says.*

ANTONIO: No, no! Stop it! Yes, it's true... I confess! I am the head of the armed gang that kidnapped Agnelli! (*The* POLICEMAN *stops turning the handle*) I'll tell all... I'll spill the beans... Just set me free!

INSPECTOR: What a wonderful little machine! We ought to have a little gadget like this down at the nick!

The POLICEMEN *set* ANTONIO *free.* ROSA *enters, carrying a soup tureen.*

ROSA: I've made some fruit salad for you.

ANTONIO *leaps from his seat and runs to seek protection among the* POLICEMEN.

ANTONIO: No, no, not the fruit salad, get me out of here!

ROSA: But why did you set him free?

INSPECTOR: Don't worry, madam... we're just taking him down to HQ with us for a while... He's got a few little things to get off his chest... Now you just sit down there, eat your fruit salad, and keep your mouth shut! Let's go, let's go

ANTONIO *exits, with the* POLICEMEN.

ROSA: Oh, Antonio! Inspector, where are you taking him? Wait, his tubes... and the meat grinder...

INSPECTOR: No thank you. We use less sophisticated methods down at the station.

The INSPECTOR *exits.* ROSA *is beside herself.*

ROSA: Oh God. Poor Antonio, what a terrible thing to happen! But why on earth are they taking him to the police station...?

Enter the WINDOW. ROSA *looks out of it.*

Poor Antonio... There he is... they're loading him into the wagon... Antonio... Antoniooo...

The DOUBLE *enters again, via the door, which is still wide open.*

DOUBLE: Yes?

ROSA: He answered me! Antonioooo!

DOUBLE: I'm here... No need to shout! Since you took so long coming up, I came down. Now, please, hurry up with that food... I'm dying of hunger...

ROSA: Oh God... one Antonio here, and another Antonio there... Two Antonios...!! Your personality's completely split in two!

ROSA *crashes to the floor. The* DOUBLE *wanders over to the window and looks out.*

DOUBLE: Ah yes... One Antonio here, one Antonio there... If I can find a third one... I'll be God!

Blackout
Musical interlude

Scene Two

We are still in ROSA's *house. As the lights come up, there is nobody on stage. The bedroom door opens. A character appears, wearing a leather jacket full of pockets and zips. He wears a commando-style woollen beret, with motor cycle dark glasses, a knife down his boot, and a big pistol in his holster.*

He sneaks along the wall, and looks under the table. He peers into the other rooms. In his hand he has a walkie-talkie, which is making noises: squeaks and whistles. He goes to the window and pulls something off. Then he goes to the coat rack and pulls off a little gadget. He goes to the hall door, opens it and signals to someone to come in.

Another character, almost identical, enters, walking on tiptoe, und followed shortly after by two others, carrying false drawers and shelves in order to disguise the sideboard in which their group leader will be hidden, with his head inside a false soup tureen.

All this is done ballet-style, to the accompaniment of waltz music. The second AGENT, *assisted by his colleague, pulls the drawers out of the sideboard. The* GROUP LEADER *pulls out a small radio with a long aerial, and talks into it:*

GROUP LEADER: Hurry up with the furniture. Hello, hello, 008½ Fellini calling HQ, do you read me? Yes, we are setting up our observation post... The woman is still upstairs, talking excitedly with a man in the loft... No, it's not her husband. He keeps calling her madam. I don't know who it is... I am waiting for them to come down...

The two AGENTS *have removed the sideboard. They bring on-stage another sideboard, which has been constructed as a kind of stocks, with a big hole, through which the* GROUP LEADER *will put his head. On either side there are smaller holes for his hands to go through.*

GROUP LEADER: Yes, I've already searched the place, I've located the hidden microphones. No, not our stuff. Must be the f...ing anti-terrorist mob... Yes, already dealt with... (*As he continues his report, he is fitted into the sideboard. In a squatting position. His head is now disguised with a soup tureen, arranged like an armoured helmet*) Watch out – they're coming down... I'm in position. Over and out!

The sideboard is returned to its original position. One AGENT *climbs into the television. The others exit. At the end of this action, enter* ROSA *and* AGNELLI.

ROSA: Ladies and gentlemen. Three days have passed since the last scene. Well if he can do it so can I. Here, do you know who he is? It's only Gianni Agnelli, living in Rosa's house. I mean, I don't mind looking after your own, but this is ridiculous. I mean he is useless around the house; he can't even change a plug. He thinks that manual labour is a Spanish waiter. And there's my Antonio in prison being kicked about by the police. They think he's a terrorist, and Agnelli won't do anything about it. He's got something cooking in that tiny brain of his and he won't tell me what it is. Anyway, back to the play... (*She continues acting, addressing* AGNELLI) In prison, getting kicked about, and it's all your fault!

ROSA *goes over to the sideboard. She opens one of the drawers, and then closes it, worried.*

DOUBLE: All my fault?

ROSA: Where's my cigarettes...!

She opens another drawer, into which the GROUP LEADER *swiftly slips a packet of cigarettes.*

DOUBLE: Calm down, please... before you say it's 'all my fault'...!

ROSA: Ah, here they are…

ROSA *takes the packet, takes out a cigarette and puts the packet back in the drawer. She turns to look at* AGNELLI *for a moment, and the drawer shuts of its own accord, pulled in by the* GROUP LEADER.

DOUBLE: I would like to know, my dear Mrs Rosa, (*He lights* ROSA*'s cigarette with a match*) if this so very generous Antonio of yours moved so much as a finger when I was down there at the hospital, having my face rebuilt to look like his. Did he ever move so much as a finger? No, sir! He didn't give a damn! (*He lifts the lid off the soup tureen, and throws in the match. He puts the lid down again, but not before seeing the head of the* GROUP LEADER) I'm not feeling well today…! And then they say that we employers are cynical! What's this if it's not cynicism? (*He sees the television*) But excuse me, speaking of strange things… Is it normal to find a television stuck between the kitchen and the dining-room? Following you around! What channel are we…?

ROSA: Good God, what a fuss-pot you are! I must have moved it to clean up, and forgotten to put it back. Anyway, if you don't like your present face, you can always have it rebuilt just as it was before… with the money you've got…

DOUBLE: Yes, have my face rebuilt! But first of all, I would have to have all my features dismantled, back to basics… (*The chest of drawers moves*) Excuse me, is it normal in this house for drawers to move of their own accord? What is this, the commode's revenge? As I was saying… in order to rebuild my face, they're going to have to dismantle my present features, and peel me like an apple, from my chin to my forehead. And then, once they've rebuilt my skull, what are they going to cover it with, what kind of skin… since they've already stripped my backside as bare as a baboon's bum!

Enter a MAN IN OVERALLS, *pushing a dishwashing machine.*

MAN: Excuse me, don't mind me, does Mrs Berardi live here?

ROSA: Yes, that's me – If you don't mind my saying so, do you always come into people's houses without even knocking first?

MAN: What difference does it make? Even if I had knocked, you wouldn't have suddenly turned into someone else, would you?

ROSA: What a comedian!

MAN: Who's that gentleman? Your husband?

AGNELLI *disappears off into the bedroom.*

ROSA: That's my business… And what's this white thing? Your wife?

MAN: No, it's a dishwasher, for you.

ROSA: For me? A dishwasher? You're mad. I never ordered a dishwasher.

MAN: Obviously, they've given you a present!

ROSA: Me?! Who did? You can take it away with you!

MAN: All I know is that it's for you, and I'm not taking it back. Goodbye!

He exits.

ROSA: Look, you're not going to force it on me…

DOUBLE: (*From within*) What's going on now?

ROSA: They've forced a dishwasher on me!

The DOUBLE sticks his head round the door.

DOUBLE: And what's strange about that? For 80 years, we've been forcing our cars on the whole of Italy, and nobody's ever said a word.

They both exit, into the bedroom.

Musical interlude

The lid of the dishwasher opens, and another AGENT sticks his head out. The MAN IN OVERALLS comes back through the hall door, and dismantles the papier-mâché bust

of Plutarch/Suetonius. He takes the bust over to the
AGENT *whose head is sticking out of the dishwasher. He*
puts the bust over his head. The AGENT *freezes, like a*
statue.

The GROUP LEADER, *in the sideboard, takes the lid off his*
soup tureen, and looks over at the dishwasher, with the bust on
top. Then he puts the tureen lid back on his head.

At that moment the television comes on: inside we see the face
of the AGENT *whom we already know. He too eyes up what's*
going on in the room. Then he switches off, and disappears into
darkness. Enter LUCIA.

LUCIA: Rosa, Rosa, are you in?

ROSA *enters.*

ROSA: What's up?

LUCIA: Extraordinary news...!

ROSA: Of Antonio?

The DOUBLE *also enters.*

LUCIA: No, not exactly, but indirectly. Good morning, Mr
Agnelli, how are you?

The furniture is suddenly startled by the word 'Agnelli'.

DOUBLE: No! Don't call me Agnelli! I've already told you,
never! Just Mr Gianni!

ROSA: So, what's this extraordinary news, then?

LUCIA: It was on the radio, less than half an hour ago... and
on television... Didn't you hear?

ROSA: On television?

She goes over to the TV set and switches it on. On the screen
we see the SECRET AGENT, *who mimes a TV announcer.*
He opens and shuts his mouth like a fish, but we hear no
voice.

DOUBLE: No, we haven't heard anything.

ROSA: The sound never works on this damn thing!

She bangs the TV on the side. It goes dead.

DOUBLE: So anyway, what is the extraordinary news?

LUCIA: It said that Prime Minister Spadolini has received a letter from Agnelli.

ROSA: Don't be silly...

LUCIA: Yes, and another letter has been received by Minister of the Interior Rognoni...

ROSA: Well, obviously, they must be fake letters! Where's he supposed to have written them from?

LUCIA: From the Red Brigades hideout where he's being held prisoner.

ROSA: But he's here...

DOUBLE: Yes, those letters are authentic. I wrote them!

All the bits of furniture shuffle forward a few inches to where the three are sitting round the table, centre-stage.

ROSA *and* **LUCIA:** You? When?

DOUBLE: Three days ago. I wrote them, and then I went down to post them.

He goes over to the telephone, and picks up a book.

ROSA: But why? And what did you write in those letters?

DOUBLE: Just a moment, and you can read for yourselves... There you are. Pages one and two.

He hands them the book.

LUCIA: But this is a collection of Aldo Moro's letters during the kidnap...

ROSA: Yes, it's one of my books.

DOUBLE: Precisely. In fact I found it in the other room there... The idea came to me as I was thumbing through it. I copied out the letters... with a few minor alterations. Here, look, I copied word for word the letter addressed to Cossiga,[9] but instead of addressing it to Cossiga, I addressed it to Spadolini... Then I took the one to Rognoni... Rognoni was already Rognoni in Moro's[10] time... then he was Rognoni in Forlani's time... and

Rognoni is still Rognoni now... Rognoni is always Rognoni! However, first of all, I made copies of my letters. Here they are. Obviously, I signed them, with my name.

The dishwasher moves closer to the DOUBLE, *so as to get a closer look at the signature. The other pieces of furniture also shuffle up. They form a little circle around* AGNELLI.

DOUBLE: I don't feel very well today...

LUCIA: Rosa, what's the matter with that dishwasher... It seems to be moving of its own accord!

ROSA: It must be the vibrations from the motor...

LUCIA: But it's not switched on...

ROSA: Well switch it on, then... Maybe it'll stop.

She wheels the dishwasher back to its place. The other bits of furniture also move back into position.

LUCIA: What are you saying? It stops when you switch it on?

ROSA: But why did you send those copied letters? They'll realise immediately that they're the same as the Moro letters.

DOUBLE: Yes, of course they will... All of them, the politicians, the ministers, the journalists... But they'll pretend they haven't noticed. In fact I made one big change. I came straight to the point: I demanded an immediate exchange with political prisoners... in exchange for my life, 32 prisoners, all of them prisoners serving life sentences.

ROSA: And my Antonio?

DOUBLE: No, your husband isn't serving a life sentence... at least, not yet. And anyway, if we were to ask for him as well, it would imply that Antonio is an authentic terrorist. Let's not forget that everyone will be 100% convinced that I wrote these letters from the Red Brigades hideout where I'm being held prisoner.

ROSA: You did well not to mention Antonio... But why are you sending letters...? You're not a prisoner. What satisfaction are you hoping to get out of this?

DOUBLE: Well, I want to find out what the government and the state think of me, what value I have, for them… I want to see whether the government, and the parties, will have the nerve to sacrifice me as they sacrificed Aldo Moro. I want to see whether, in my case too, they will reject any exchange even with a prisoner who was seriously ill… In order for me to be released, I'm asking for 32 to be set free… 32 political prisoners, all healthy in mind and limb! I've checked them one by one. And I want to see if they're going to order a blackout with the newspapers, like they did during the D'Urso kidnapping…[11] I'll go out and buy all the newspapers! Including *Peanuts* and *Teenage Romance*.

LUCIA: Excuse me, My Gianni, do you mind if I say something? This presumptuousness on your part is pretty disgusting. Just who do you think you are?

DOUBLE: I am Gianni Agnelli!! Two hundred and seventy five factories in Europe alone…! Of which four are in Poland… In Poland… with those troublesome workers…! But I sorted them out straight away! I put one of my trusted foremen in charge… a certain Mr Jaruzelski…

LUCIA: So, you're hoping to take advantage of the protection offered by your prestige and your power. You have copied Moro's letters, but it's not going to do any good.. Tomorrow, the journalists and the politicians in their turn will simply copy out the same replies that they gave at the time of Moro, when *he* asked them.

DOUBLE: That remains to be seen!

ROSA: She's absolutely right. I can see the headlines already: 'The State Must Make a Show of Strength By Sacrificing One of its Most Outstanding Citizens'…

DOUBLE: Who wrote that?

ROSA: Leo Valiani,[12] life senator, in *Corriere della Sera*… writing about Moro. From that day onwards, they now call him 'death senator'!

DOUBLE: Anyway, in the event that they do perform as you suggest, I already have my reply ready. My last will and testament!

He pulls a sheet of paper out of his pocket.

ROSA: Your will?

DOUBLE: Yes, exactly: my will. I shall read it to you. 'Dear friends, gentlemen of the government, with my death, you are all sacked! At my funeral I want nobody to be present, no government representatives, nobody from the State. I want no priest, and nobody from my family, in particular my rather stupid younger brother. I wish to be cremated. My ashes are to be taken in a helicopter, which will fly over Turin, scattering them in handfuls over the Rivalta, Spa Stura and Mirafiori factories... So that the workers, when they breathe, will cough, and will remember me. I may not remain in their hearts... but I shall remain in their lungs. For ever!'

ROSA and LUCIA spit in unison.

Enter the POLICE INSPECTOR, with his customary insolence, accompanied by a POLICEMAN.

Meanwhile, the AGENT who hid under the table, extends the table-top by a couple of feet, leaving a gap in the middle. Through this gap, the AGENT sticks his head. He takes the wig off the wig-stand on the table, and puts it on his own head, thereby turning himself into a wigstand.

INSPECTOR: Good afternoon. Not disturbing you, am I?

ROSA: No! I'm very happy to see you, Inspector, so that, at last, I can see my husband and find out how he is!

INSPECTOR: Unfortunately, your Antonio isn't too well. He's feeling a bit swollen... Partly because he keeps tripping up, and having bad falls...

ROSA: Onto your fists, eh?

LUCIA: Shut up, Rosa, don't fall for it.

INSPECTOR: And partly because he keeps drinking like a fish.

ROSA: But how can that be? He's almost teetotal!

INSPECTOR: True enugh. It was only water he was drinking, with a bit of salt.

ROSA: Water and salt?

INSPECTOR: Yes, by the gallon, down a rubber tube. You should see what a guzzleguts he is!

ROSA: You rotten, horrible, stinking, pigging bastards. Torturing…

INSPECTOR: Now, language! (*He goes to lean on the table, but it suddenly shifts out of the way, moved by the* AGENT *underneath*) What's going on?

LUCIA: Don't pay any attention, Inspector. You must understand…

INSPECTOR: Indeed I do understand. I am very understanding, as you can see from the fact that I've taken the trouble to bring your fellow up here. Get a move on, there! (*To* ROSA) Your fellow, so that you can persuade him to tell the truth! (*He bangs his fist down twice on the table, as if to underline what he is saying. The third time, the table suddenly shifts out of the way*) What's going on here?

ROSA: I don't know, Inspector. This has been going on all day, with the furniture moving round of its own accord… It must be the vibrations from the subway…

INSPECTOR: Anyway, up until now… your husband has spun us a load of cock and bull. He even went so far as to say that you, Mrs Minelli, are the person responsible for logistical operations in the Red Brigades, and that you have got Mr Agnelli hidden here…

The DOUBLE *pokes his head out of the fridge.*

DOUBLE: Please, don't give me away!

INSPECTOR: Oi, you! Will you get a move on?

ROSA: My Antonio said that? About me?

LUCIA: Obviously, since they'd filled him with water, they could make him say anything they wanted!

INSPECTOR: (*Looking out of the door*) Will you get your finger out?!

POLICEMAN: We're not going to make it, Inspector. He keeps falling down, and taking us with him!

INSPECTOR: Well haul him up with a rope, then. Wait – I'll come down. You, come with me.

The INSPECTOR *and the* POLICEMAN *leave the stage.*

ROSA: They're killing him!

The DOUBLE *pokes his head out again.*

DOUBLE: Listen – our only way out is not to contradict him. In fact, give him as much leeway as possible. You must tell him the biggest load of nonsense you can think of... Fill him up with ridiculous stories. Otherwise he'll drown you like he did with Antonio. He's a raving loony!

ROSA: What do you mean? Tell him that, yes, I really am in charge of logistics for the Red Brigades?

DOUBLE: You must give him fibs, stories... you must give me time... We're going to spring a trap that I've set up, which will save all of us...

ROSA: But I'm incapable of telling lies...

DOUBLE: Pretend that you're a journalist from the *Sun*. Be inventive – make it all up! Look out, they're coming back.

The DOUBLE *gets back into the fridge. Enter the* INSPECTOR, *with the* POLICEMEN.

INSPECTOR: One more flight, and your husband will be here.

ROSA: Yes, and I could spit in his eye! I knew that cretin wasn't to be trusted. He's sung like a canary!

INSPECTOR: What... he's sung, has he?! So there was some truth in what the cretin said!

ROSA: Yes, too right! I'm going to talk. Talk, talk! I'll talk... and soon I'm going to repent, too. Up until yesterday, I knew where Agnelli was.

INSPECTOR: Oh yes? Where?

ROSA: In an airship, a balloon, you know, the one that advertises condoms and contraceptives over the city.

INSPECTOR: What? A contraceptive dirigible?! See here, Mrs Berardi, look me in the eye.

ROSA: Which one?

INSPECTOR: Don't try to make a fool of me, because there's a water pipe ready for you as well!

Out of the fridge, a shoe is passed to LUCIA, *who then hands it on to* ROSA.

ROSA: Nobody's fooling here. Just for a start, here's the first evidence.

She puts the shoe on the table.

INSPECTOR: What's that?

ROSA: Can't you see? It's a shoe. Agnelli's shoe.

INSPECTOR: Still fooling about, eh?

He takes the shoe and examines it closely.

ROSA: Not at all: size forty-four and three quarters, hand-made, by Lenzuer Brothers, London...

LUCIA: They're specially made for him!

ROSA: If you don't believe it, phone the Agnelli family and ask if it matches.

INSPECTOR: I don't need to. (*He instructs the* POLICEMAN) Call HQ.

The POLICEMAN *goes over to the telephone, and lifts the receiver.*

No, not on the telephone, on the radio. They've got all his details there. Check with the clothing department.

The POLICEMAN *switches on a portable radio. Suddenly we see aerials sprouting from all the bits of furniture. Enter* ANTONIO, *accompanied by another* POLICEMAN. *His belly is swollen. As soon as he enters, he sprays water everywhere – even from his ears, if possible.*

POLICEMAN: Hello, HQ...?

ROSA: There's the stool pigeon! We'll fix you, you rat!

LUCIA: Please, don't be so severe!

ANTONIO: But Rosa... Glug, glug...

He begins to gargle.

ROSA: Shut up, slobberer! You've ruined everything, damn traitor!

INSPECTOR: Good God! And to think that I took her for a fool.

ANTONIO: Rosa, I'm sorry, but they filled me with... oooooh... water

With the sponge trick, he fills his mouth with water, and squirts it in the POLICEMAN's *face.*

INSPECTOR: Take him into the toilet! Otherwise he'll drown us all!

POLICEMAN: Inspector, HQ tell me that the make, the type and the size match... Agnelli was the only person to wear that kind of shoe in Italy. Him and the Pope.

INSPECTOR: Good God! (*He grabs the shoe*) Let's have a photo immediately...

ROSA: Oh yes, all of us together, round the shoe!

They form up in a 'family photograph' group, around the shoe. One of the POLICEMEN *pulls out a flash camera. The* SECRET AGENTS *also jump out of their bits of furniture, and blast off with their flash cameras.*

INSPECTOR: What is this? A day outing to Clacton?

ROSA: So, now will you believe that we're not talking nonsense?

INSPECTOR: Yes, true, it is evidence... but fairly, how can I say, relative.

LUCIA: What do you mean, relative?

INSPECTOR: Well, one of Agnelli's shoes does not prove that you have got Agnelli himself.

ROSA: What about two shoes?

She takes the other shoe, which the DOUBLE has passed to LUCIA, and bangs it down on the table. Once again, the SECRET AGENTS loose off with their flash cameras.

INSPECTOR: Well, yes, two shoes...

ROSA: And that's not the end of it...

She pulls a sheet of paper out of one of the shoes.

INSPECTOR: Three shoes?

ROSA: No, the original carbon copies of the letters to Spadolini and Rognoni, written in Agnelli's own hand.

She hands the sheet to the INSPECTOR.

INSPECTOR: The copies? Are you sure? Watch out, because if this is a joke, it could cost you dearly.

All the furniture comes shuffling up to the INSPECTOR and ROSA.

ROSA: It could cost you even dearer, my dear Inspector, if you don't hurry up and carry out the necessary handwriting examination.

INSPECTOR: Get a move on, run down to HQ.

POLICEMAN: Yes, I'm running.... (*He bumps into the coat rack*) Oh, excuse me!

AGENT: Don't mention it.

POLICEMAN: Wait a minute, Inspector, I've got the evening edition of two newspapers: this one's got the letter sent to Spadolini. It's an enlarged reprint.

The INSPECTOR compares the copy with the newspaper.

INSPECTOR: Well, yes, the handwriting is very clear, and it looks pretty much the same...

In order to get a better view, the furniture begins to take things to excess, climbing up on the table, leaning up against the group of POLICEMEN, forming a kind of pyramid.

But don't keep pushing!

POLICEMAN: It's not me, Inspector, it's the table, the hat stand, the TV and the sideboard!

The pieces of furniture slowly disentangle themselves from the pile, and go back to their original positions.

INSPECTOR: That ruddy subway really is playing up!

The WINDOW *whizzes out from the wings, and stops in front of the group standing centre-stage.*

INSPECTOR: I need a magnifying glass…

ROSA: I've got one in the drawer… (*She goes over to the sideboard, and goes to open a drawer. A hand comes out of the tureen and hands her a magnifying glass*) Ah, no, it was in the tureen! (*She hands the glass to the* INSPECTOR) There you are, it's got a little light built in, too.

The SECRET AGENT *standing behind the coat rack shines a big torch on the newspaper.*

INSPECTOR: Good Lord, what a powerful light! (*He examines the letter and the newspaper closely*) It looks like a pretty good forgery to me.

LUCIA: What do you mean a forgery? Who could have done it? Nobody has ever seen a single line written by Agnelli up until now. And this newspaper only came out an hour ago!

POLICEMAN: It looks pretty authentic to me too.

ROSA: Right, that'll do!

She snatches the sheet of paper from the POLICEMAN *and runs off. She gives the paper to* LUCIA. *Everyone chases after* ROSA, *who disappears behind the coat rack.*

All the pieces of furniture start a merry-go-round. Lights flash on and off. The music gets louder. Shouting and laughter, as at a funfair.

INSPECTOR: Stop it! My head's spinning…! (*Suddenly everything returns to normal, and the furniture returns to its initial position*) You're nicked. Talk! Where have you stashed Mr Agnelli?

ROSA: I will only talk if I'm free, and only if I have Crown witness immunity, repentant terrorist, special category, supergrass status.

LUCIA: That's right, without immunity, you won't talk!

INSPECTOR: You'll talk or I'll blow your brains out!

ROSA: Alright, I'll talk... But only in front of an Examining Magistrate.

INSPECTOR: He's coming. I've sent for him. You know the Examining Magistrate I mean – the one who was here last time.

ROSA: Ah yes, that poor fellow whose leg you shot.

INSPECTOR: Sssh! Please!

ROSA: Alright, let's wait.

INSPECTOR: No, here nobody is waiting, understand! Because I'll kill you!

The INSPECTOR pulls out a pistol, and points it at ROSA, who hides behind the table. Everybody dives for cover. The SECRET AGENTS also disappear into their respective pieces of furniture, like snails into their shells.

ROSA: Inspector, don't shoot... I'm not a car at a roadblock! Don't shoot. Alright, I'll talk...

INSPECTOR: Oh, so you've finally come to your senses. Listen here, from now on, I'm not going to ask you questions... You're going to talk loud and long, and God help anyone who interrupts! (*Turning to the two POLICEMEN*) Incidentally, is our swollen friend still in the toilet?

POLICEMAN: Yes, sir, I locked him in...

INSPECTOR: Well done. Go and take a look at him.

Exit the POLICEMAN. He returns after a moment.

Alright, get on with it. Be precise, and keep to the point: when did you first decide to kidnap Agnelli? (*To the two POLICEMEN*) You write, and you record.

The DOUBLE begins to feed ROSA ideas from the fridge.

ROSA: The idea of kidnapping Agnelli developed at about the time when we were preparing the via Fani operation...[13]

The furniture shuffles slowly closer, so as to hear ROSA'*s story.*

INSPECTOR: I want details, names, dates, addresses, everything!

ROSA: The story begins in early January... 1978... I was in Milan. It was a lovely day. A pale sun shone weakly through the mist that hung over the city...

INSPECTOR: Never mind the hazy sun and the mist... This is a verbal, not fucking Shakespeare...

ROSA: (*To the* DOUBLE) See, you're making a fool of me! Alright, no poetry. The strategic meeting to discuss kidnapping Agnelli took place in a... cinema!

This last phrase came out of its own accord. Spontaneously, with no prompting from the DOUBLE. *The* INSPECTOR *is bewildered. He slowly comes over to her. The* DOUBLE *retreats into the fridge.*

INSPECTOR: In a cinema?! A strategic meeting in a cinema?

ROSA *looks towards the fridge, seeking help. She pushes her seat towards it, in an attempt to get closer. Then she gives up, and carries on, regardless. With vigour.*

ROSA: Yes! The Astoria... a nice little cinema, near my house... So we have our meetings there, because of my feet... And... when they called the meeting, I was in Piazza del Duomo, with my girlfriend Caterina...

INSPECTOR: Who is Caterina?

ROSA: He's a priest...

INSPECTOR: A priest? There's a priest involved too?

LUCIA, *worried by the enormity of it all, starts signalling desperately to stop it.* ROSA, *unperturbed, warms to her theme.*

ROSA: Yes... Don Anselmo... a worker priest from

Canegrate.[14] He's infiltrated the church establishment.

INSPECTOR: And he dresses up as a woman?

ROSA: Yes. He looks great in drag. He's really elegant, with high heels, lovely perfume, and long, wavy hair.

INSPECTOR: Does he wear a wig?

ROSA: No wig. Just his own natural hair. It's very long... and when he goes back to being a priest, he gathers it in a bun, like so, and tucks it under his hat.

INSPECTOR: And his titties...? Presumably they're his own as well, presumably they're also *au naturel*?

ROSA: No, he always keeps two lightweight hand grenades in his bra: for tactical use! We call him Brother Boob Bomb.

INSPECTOR: But this is out of this world! Listen, you're not making all this up...?

ROSA: Well, all you have to do is phone the Vatican, ask for Don Anselmo... and when a woman's voice answers... Bob's your uncle!

POLICEMAN: Hello... is that the Archbishop's office?

ROSA: Oh come on, Inspector. You know very well, repentant terrorists never lie! Alright, so there we were, in the Astoria... They were showing a porn film... the story of a sex-mad police inspector, who falls in love with a transvestite, and who, in the end, turns homosexual himself... He ends up soliciting in the park... gets caught in a police round-up. They take him down to the police station, where he's beaten up by the police chief... a known sadist, who beats him almost to death. The sex-mad transvestite inspector is about to breathe his last, when the police chief is suddenly seized with passion and and shouts: 'Don't breathe your last... I love you!!' They marry, and live happily ever after. Nice story, eh?

INSPECTOR: Hmm... Continue, please!

ROSA: Yes, let's continue. So there we are, watching the film, when the doors of the cinema swing open, and who should come in but the lawyer for... Mr Big!

INSPECTOR: No!!

LUCIA: Rosa, no!

INSPECTOR: Mr Big! So he really does exist, then! Who is he?

ROSA: My friend Lucia is right, at this point I don't think I can continue... From now on, we're dealing with names, places and people who are too important... I can't go on.

INSPECTOR: Stop fooling about eh?

ROSA: No, Inspector, I am not starting tricks. Even the President of the Republic, Pertini, on 31st December 1981, when he made his New Year speech to the people of Italy, made a clear reference to terrorism and its bases... which, he said, were not in Italy, but abroad, in Europe as a whole...

INSPECTOR: Ah, yes... when he spoke about international connections...

ROSA: Yes, international. So, if the President of the Italian Republic, with all the protection that he has, and the knowledge that he has... limits himself only to a passing reference... and does not name names... he, who could... he, who knows... and you, a humble Inspector... please don't get me wrong... want to play at Don Quixote... want to risk your own life by knowing too much! Do you actually want to die? Well, if you want to die, then why should I stop you, Inspector? After everything that you've done to my family... to my husband... No, I shall tell you the names. (*To one of the* POLICEMEN) Are you ready to record this, for the 'last' time (*To the other* POLICEMAN) Are you ready to write this down for the 'last' time? (*To the* INSPECTOR) Are you ready to listen, for the 'last' time?

LUCIA: Rosa, if you're going to talk, then I'm going...I don't fancy dying.

LUCIA *exits*.

FIRST POLICEMAN: Excuse me, Inspector, I've got to go too...

INSPECTOR: Go where?

FIRST POLICEMAN: My shift's over, and also my wife is ill. I have to take her to the hospital...

SECOND POLICEMAN: I've got to go too, Inspector... I've got an abcess come up on a tooth, and I've got to go and have my gum lanced...

INSPECTOR: You're a bunch of rotten cowards! The abcess is not on your gums... it's up your arses!

Exit the two POLICEMEN, *followed by all the furniture.*

ROSA: Inspector.. my furniture... It's moving of its own accord! Stop it... (*Shouting after the fleeing furniture*) Come back...! Come back!

INSPECTOR: (*His hand goes to his heart*) Oh God, I feel ill... my heart...

He slumps down in a chair.

ROSA: Are you feeling ill? You see what happens when you try to find out too much? (*She runs to the hall door and shouts*) Lucia... Officers... Hurry up... the Inspector is ill!

Re-enter LUCIA, *followed by the* POLICEMEN.

LUCIA: What's happening?

Enter a POLICEMAN *with newspapers.*

POLICEMAN: Look, Guv, I've got the special editions. What's in them is unbelievable!

Slowly all the pieces of furniture come back on-stage, and line up behind the actors. The fridge opens, and out pops the DOUBLE.

DOUBLE: Pass me one too. (*The* POLICEMAN *passes him a newspaper*) Thank you.

POLICEMAN: Hey, but that's the prisoner, what's he doing in there?

DOUBLE: Just keeping cool... Listen, the whole Cabinet has met and issued a communiqué. Here it is, under the headline: 'Kidnap Chaos. Cabinet Caves In. Yes. In the

Moro Case, the State answered: No Exchange. This Time it Must Answer: Yes'.

ALL IN UNISON: No!

DOUBLE: No, yes. 'The prisoners asked for in exchange will be set free today.'

ALL IN UNISON: Oh no!

DOUBLE: (*Still reading*) Yes. 'We are aware that, after the 32 prisoners have been released, Agnelli's jailers might demand the release of an unlimited number of further prisoners. In order to prevent this...'

ALL IN UNISON: Well?

DOUBLE: 'The Cabinet, with the approval of the various organs of state, has decided to free all political prisoners already serving sentences.'

ALL IN UNISON: No!

DOUBLE: Yes! 'And also all prisoners awaiting trial'.

ALL IN UNISON: Evviva!

ROSA: Evviva! So my Antonio is free!!

LUCIA: Yes, everyone's free!

INSPECTOR: No, impossible, have they all gone mad?!

DOUBLE: Sorry, Inspector. 'All anti-terrorist proceedings have been dropped as well.' You can retire peacefully.

INSPECTOR: All the work that I've done, my hard work, flushed down the pan! It's disgusting! Bastard politicians!

The furniture standing behind the actors also begins to get agitated.

ROSA: Bastard politicians is right. They let Moro be killed like a lamb led to the slaughter; everyone agreed that he should be sacrificed. Be firm! And now, with Agnelli, they've done a somersault... The loathsome pigs!

LUCIA: Yes, all of them with their trousers down, giving in like crazy!

They all look at each other in amazement.

DOUBLE: You don't understand? Tell me, have you never read Karl Marx? Ah yes, of course… These days only we captains of industry study *Das Kapital*.. Especially where it says: 'The only true power is financial-economic power, in other words, holding companies, markets, banks, commodities… In other words, Capital.'

One of the POLICEMEN *leaves the stage by the centre door.*

And then he adds a sentence, which children should memorise and sing in the playground: 'The sacred laws of this state… the economic state… are written on watermarked paper money. So government, state and institutions are nothing other than supporting services, for the real power, which is economic power.' Supporting services… you see? So, Aldo Moro was sacrificed in order to save the respectability of the aforementioned financial state, not for the supporting services, for which nobody gives a damn! (*He moves upstage, and starts climbing up the pieces of furniture, which have been arranged like the steps of a temple*) Get it into your heads: I am the state! The capital which I represent is the state! It is my dignity that you must save, even at the cost of your own lives! How could they think of sacrificing me, in order to save the state? For I am the state!

INSPECTOR: What's he saying now? Who's he talking about? Has he gone silly in the head again? Who do you think you've turned into this time?

DOUBLE: (*Reaching the top of the pile of furniture*) I am Gianni Agnelli! And don't be fooled by my face, it's because of plastic surgery…

INSPECTOR: Listen, I'll give you plastic surgery if you don't stop…

ROSA: Calm down, Inspector, he really is Agnelli.

The POLICEMAN *enters.*

POLICEMAN: Inspector, in the toilet there's another Antonio, the spitting image of this one…

ROSA: Yes, only that one is my Antonio, and this one is Agnelli.

The SECRET AGENTS *emerge from their various pieces of furniture. In chorus:*

AGENTS: Yes, Inspector, we can assure you, we have been listening in on their conversations for quite some while.

INSPECTOR: (*Pointing to the* AGENTS) Just a minute: SISMI, SISDE, Interpol, SAS, DHSS...

GROUP LEADER: It seems that this gentleman really is Mr Agnelli, and that, by mistake, his face has been rebuilt in the image of Antonio Berardi, one of his workers. It was he who wrote the letters to the government, and posted them from this house, pretending that he was held prisoner by terrorists; it was he who organised this whole bloody shambles...

As if hypnotised, the INSPECTOR *slowly climbs up the pile of furniture, approaching* AGNELLI, *who reaches out a hand, and with his forefinger touches the forefinger of the* INSPECTOR. *This is an obvious and grotesque allusion to Michelangelo's famous 'Creation' painting in the Sistine Chapel.*

DOUBLE: I created you. Go forth!

The INSPECTOR *comes down again, bewildered.*

INSPECTOR: You're having me on! You're taking the piss?! I don't care if you are the upper reaches of the state! (*He pulls a gun out of his pocket*) I'll shoot this state in the bollocks!

CHORUS: No, stop it, you're mad! Think of what you're doing! Stop him!

Everyone tries to stop him. They manage to get hold of him. At that moment, enter the EXAMINING MAGISTRATE, *on crutches.*

EXAMINING MAGISTRATE: What's up? What's going on?

A shot is fired from the INSPECTOR's *gun. BANG! The* EXAMINING MAGISTRATE *is hit in the leg.*

Aaaargh! They've kneecapped my other kneecap! This is getting to be a habit!

He falls flat on his face.

Musical interlude

Blackout

NOTES

1.   Agnelli, head of the FIAT Motor Corporation, Chairman of Confindustria, the equivalent of the CBI. International financier. A powerful political force in Italy aiming at a 'strong state'.

2.   A famous old-established Italian circus.

3.   The Communist Party daily newspaper.

4.   One of the main FIAT plants in Turin.

5.   Christian Democrat politician; has held many offices, including that of Prime Minister.

6.   Members of terrorist groups who became 'supergrasses'.

7.   Greek and Roman historians.

8.   A right-wing bombing in Brescia in Northern Italy, which caused a number of deaths.

9.   Christian Democrat politician, Prime Minister at the time of the kidnapping of Moro, the Christian Democrat chairman who was one of the chief architects of the 'historic compromise' with the Communist Party, which thus for the first time since the war was part of the Italian government.

10. Christian Democrat politicians who held various posts in successive coalitions; they formed part of what Pasolini, the writer and film-maker, called 'the Palace' – the centre of political power in Italy.

11. An examining magistrate who was kidnapped but freed after negotiation with the terrorists.

12. Senator for life, who had a distinguished Resistance record; advocated the use of the death penalty for terrorism.

13. Scene of a right-wing terrorist attack.

14. An industrial area of Milan.

The Virtuous Burglar

A One-Act Farce

Translated by Joseph Farrell

Characters

BURGLAR
BURGLAR'S WIFE
MAN
WOMAN
ANNA
ANTONIO
SECOND BURGLAR

A BURGLAR, *having forced open a window, is climbing into a third floor apartment in a well-to-do block of flats. On one side stands a classical shaded lamp. He looks around carefully. From the dark, we see furniture, rugs, old valuable paintings emerge. The* BURGLAR *closes the shutters, then switches on the light.*

Just when he is about to pull open a drawer, the telephone rings. His first panic-stricken impulse is to make off as quickly as possible but then, realising that no one in the house comes to answer it and that he has nothing to fear, he returns to where he was. He would like to ignore the ringing of the phone but cannot. He makes his way stealthily over to the phone and leaps at it. He grabs the receiver and, almost as if he wished to suffocate it, presses it against his chest, covering it with his jacket. As though to make the act seem more criminal, an increasingly feeble and suffocated sound begins to emerge from the receiver:

BURGLAR'S WIFE: Hello. Hello. Would you kindly answer… Who's speaking?

The BURGLAR *can finally let out a sigh of relief. The voice has stopped. The* BURGLAR *takes the receiver from under his jacket, raises it cautiously and puts it to his ear. Then he shakes it several times and hears a kind of groan.*

BURGLAR: Oh! At last.

BURGLAR'S WIFE: Ooooh! At last… who's speaking?

BURGLAR: (*Surprised once again*) Maria. Is that you?

BURGLAR'S WIFE: Yes, it's me. Why didn't you reply?

At this point, lit up by one of the footlights, the figure of the woman who is speaking on the phone appears on the side of the stage which has so far remained in darkness.

BURGLAR: You're crazy! Are you even phoning me at work now? Suppose there had been someone in the house. You're a great help you are.

BURGLAR'S WIFE: But you told me yourself that the owners were at their country cottage... anyway, I'm sorry, but I just couldn't stand it any more... I was worried about you... I didn't feel well... even a few moments ago, when I was ringing up, I could hardly breathe.

BURGLAR: Oh well, I'm sorry too, I didn't mean it, it never occurred to me that it might be you...

BURGLAR'S WIFE: And just what do you mean by that?

BURGLAR: Nothing, nothing... but let me get on... I've already wasted enough time.

BURGLAR'S WIFE: Ah, I'm wasting your time now! Thank you very much. Here I am in agony, nearly sick with worry... I don't know what to do with myself...

BURGLAR: What are you doing?

BURGLAR'S WIFE: I'm going through absolute hell, all because of you... and you treat me like this... charming, just charming that is... but don't worry... from now on I'm not interested... from now on don't even bother telling me where you're going, because as far as I am concerned...

BURGLAR: My dear, try and be reasonable... Can't you get it into your sweet head that I am not here for fun... just this once, couldn't you let me get on with my burgling in peace?

BURGLAR'S WIFE: There you go. You're at it again. Playing the martyr. There are plenty of people who burgle, shoplift, even go in for armed robbery without all this fuss. Just as well you stick to petty crime, otherwise God knows what sort of state I'd be in.

BURGLAR: (*Who has heard a strange noise behind him, instinctively putting his hand over the mouthpiece*) Quiet!

Fortunately it was only the sound of the grandfather clock about to strike. It strikes midnight.

BURGLAR'S WIFE: What's that?

BURGLAR: (*Recovering from his fright*) It's only the grandfather clock, thank goodness.

BURGLAR'S WIFE: What a clear sound it has! – It must be quite old. Is it very heavy?

BURGLAR: (*Absent-mindedly*) …Might be quite… (*Suddenly realizing his wife's intentions*) Come on… You're not really expecting me to bring it home… sometimes I wonder…

BURGLAR'S WIFE: Oh no, don't you bother your little head about me… How could you imagine that I'd ask anything like that… a nice thought from you! …You giving a little present to me! …The very idea!

BURGLAR: You're mad, that's what you are… If I try to carry off that box, you tell me where to put the silverware and anything else I find.

BURGLAR'S WIFE: In the box…

BURGLAR: (*Sarcastically*) You wouldn't like me to bring home a fridge? There's a nice big one through there, with a freezer department.

BURGLAR'S WIFE: Don't raise your voice, please. You're not at home now.

BURGLAR: Sorry. I got carried away.

BURGLAR'S WIFE: Besides, you might be overheard, and you'd look singularly ill-mannered.

BURGLAR: I've already said I'm sorry.

BURGLAR'S WIFE: And anyway, I didn't say I wanted a fridge, never mind one with a freezer compartment, I wouldn't know where to put it. But I would like a little something… it's the thought that counts. I'll leave it to you. It's you that's giving the present, after all.

BURGLAR: How am I supposed to know what you would

like. I've got other things on my mind right now.

BURGLAR'S WIFE: If that's all it is, I could come along and choose it myself.

BURGLAR: That's all I'd need!

BURGLAR'S WIFE: I'd love to see what a real luxury flat is like. I'd make them die with envy at the coffee morning.

BURGLAR: It's me that'll die from something or other, not the women at the coffee morning... I'm here to burgle this house, can you not understand that? Cheerio, see you later.

BURGLAR'S WIFE: What's the rush? Is it too much for you to be nice to me once in a while? I am your wife after all. You even married me in church, not in a registry, like some whore, so you can't get out of it.

BURGLAR: (*Annoyed*) I've already said goodbye.

BURGLAR'S WIFE: Just a little kiss.

BURGLAR: Oh all right.

He purses his lips in a comic way and emits a loud kissing sound.

BURGLAR'S WIFE: Do you love me?

BURGLAR: Yes I love you.

BURGLAR'S WIFE: Very much?

BURGLAR: (*At the end of his tether*) Very, very much. But now will you put down the phone?

BURGLAR'S WIFE: You first.

BURGLAR: All right... me first.

He is about to put the phone down when he hears his wife's voice assailing him loudly for the last time.

BURGLAR'S WIFE: Don't forget the present!

The BURGLAR replaces the phone, staring at it all the while with hatred. At that moment the figure of the woman disappears in the dark. Finally alone, the BURGLAR begins to look around the apartment in search of his booty.

He opens a drawer. He has clearly found the right one. He pulls a bag out of his jacket pocket and is about to start filling it when the sound of someone fumbling with the door lock makes him start. Voices are heard just offstage.

WOMAN'S VOICE: There's a light in the living room. My God, I'm so frightened. Let's get out of here.

MAN'S VOICE: Calm down. I must have left it on myself. Who else do you imagine it might have been?

WOMAN'S VOICE: Suppose your wife has come back?

Meantime the BURGLAR, *in a state of terror, has attempted to climb out of the window but has lost too much time, so has no option but to dive inside the grandfather clock.*

MAN: (*Entering cautiously*) What do you mean... my wife? What could have brought her back to town? (*Peering into every corner*) She wouldn't come even if she knew they were stripping the place. Well, are you satisfied? There's no one here.

WOMAN: (*Still cautious and suspicious*) I feel so guilty. (*As the* MAN *helps her off with her fur coat*) I wonder what you really think of me. Maybe I was wrong to give in to you so soon. I'm sure your wife resisted for much longer than me.

MAN: What's my wife got to do with it? She was always full of complexes, she had so many petty bourgeois prejudices... She wouldn't do it, just so she could get married in white.

WOMAN: (*Petulantly*) Yes, petty bourgeois, full of prejudices, but you married her just the same. I'd like to see if you would do the same for me.

MAN: (*Caressing her and trying to push her towards the centre-stage settee*) My dear... I assure you that if my wife didn't have so many old-fashioned ideas and if your husband were not so hostile... come closer to me.

The WOMAN *has sat down and the* MAN *moves closer to her.*

WOMAN: (*Freeing herself from his embrace*) There, you have ruined everything. (*The* MAN *loses his balance and knocks* *against the back of the settee, which gives way. He ends up lying full length against the cushions*) Why did you have to remind me that I have a husband? What am I supposed to do now? You've brought back all my remorse, my guilt complex, my...

MAN: I'm sorry, I really didn't mean to. (*He gets up and replaces the settee back*) Maybe if we could talk about something else, just have a little chat, perhaps you'd manage to forget once again and we could go in there.

WOMAN: In where?

MAN: (*Awkwardly*) My bedroom.

WOMAN: Perhaps that is the best idea. Let's try.

MAN: (*Hopefully*) Try and go into my bedroom?

WOMAN: No. Try and chat a little.

MAN: Couldn't we go in there and chat?

WOMAN: Please, don't rush me. Let's just have a conversation, let's talk about when you were a child. I'm very fond of children.

MAN: (*Resigned*) Okay. If you don't mind, I'll begin from when I was five, because I don't remember anything before that.

WOMAN: Five! Pity, I prefer little children, they are more innocent, there's no harm in them... But if it's the best you can do...

MAN: Here we go. I remember that at five years old I was still a child, but I used to be taken for a six year old... (*Bursting out, irritated*) Oh no! For goodness' sake, enough of this. I feel a right idiot. You've been making a fool of me for a whole hour. First it was my wife, then your husband. Poor bastard, if he'd to put up with all this stopping and starting...

WOMAN: Not at all, it was quite different with him. He yielded right away.

MAN: (*Surprised*) What do you mean 'yielded right away'?

WOMAN: Just what I say. In his case, it was me who invited him up to my place, so it was up to me to make him succumb. (*Pompously*) If we separate the pleasure of conquest from love, what's left? Regrettably my husband has always been lamentably spineless and he gave in at once; (*Pause*) so I despise him. But with you, I have a feeling it will be different. You are so resolute once you make up your mind. Go on, be resolute.

MAN: Yes, I am being resolute. I resolve that we go through there right now.

The two are about to go out, in each other's arms, when the telephone rings. They stop in embarrassment, not knowing what to do.

MAN: Who could that be?

WOMAN: Your wife?

MAN: No, no... My wife... Why should she be phoning? Who would she be ringing? Certainly not me. She believes I'm at my mother's. Anyway it doesn't sound like a long distance call. It must be one of those heavy breathers or someone who's got the wrong number. (*Taking her in his arms again*) Let's go through, it'll stop in a minute.

But the ringing continues regardless.

WOMAN: Please, make it stop, it's driving me mad.

MAN: (*Moves towards the phone, picks up the receiver and shuts it in the drawer of the telephone table*) There you are. It won't bother us now. I've knocked it off the hook.

WOMAN: (*In despair*) Oh my God! What have you done? Now they're bound to know that you're at home. Who else could have removed the receiver?

MAN: (*Realising, with dismay, that she is right*) What a fool! You're right. And they might even have suspected that I'm not on my own. They'll think I'm trying to hide something terrible.

WOMAN: Thank you very much. Why don't you come right out and tell me that you only want me for one thing?

(*Bursting into tears*) Just as I was letting myself be convinced... serves me right.

MAN: (*Doing his utmost to appear in command of himself*) My dear, don't misunderstand me. Don't let's lose control for goodness' sake... let's stay calm... after all, why should they imagine for one moment that it was me who picked up the receiver? It could have been anyone, it could have been...

He does not know how to go on.

WOMAN: (*Ironically*) Certainly, someone just passing by.

MAN: (*Awkwardly, with no conviction*) Why not?

WOMAN: (*In the same tone*) Someone passing through by the merest chance... a burglar for example.

MAN: Yes, could be... (*Realising the absurdity*) What do you mean 'a burglar'? If they thought that, they'd call the police.

WOMAN: Right, and who knows, maybe they've done that already. (*Terrified*) Oh God! they'll find us here together, they'll arrest us. (*In a near scream*) The police! I want to go home.

So saying, she rushes towards the door, followed by the MAN who tries to hold her back. At the same time the terrified BURGLAR comes out of his hiding place.

MAN: No, don't go away. Calm down.

BURGLAR: The police, that's all I bloody need. Where the hell do I go now?

MAN: (*From outside the living room*) Wait. Act your age.

WOMAN: I'm frightened. Let's get out; there's no time to lose.

MAN: All right. Let's go, but I suppose you'll want your fur coat.

WOMAN: Oh yes, my fur coat. I'm completely mixed up. What a mess.

The BURGLAR in the meantime has been undecided

whether to escape through the window or wait until the two have gone out, but hearing them return he darts back to his hiding place. As he climbs back into the body of the grandfather clock, he strikes his head against the pendulum with a deep, resonant 'Dong'.

BURGLAR: They're coming back! Nothing else for it. Move over, pendulum, be a pal. Ouch my head!

WOMAN: (*Frightened*) What's that?

MAN: (*Smiling*) Nothing my dear. Just the grandfather clock. It struck one.

WOMAN: I'm sorry, I'm a bundle of nerves.

The MAN has the fur coat in his hand and is about to help the WOMAN put it on. The WOMAN notices that the receiver is still off the hook.

WOMAN: You're not so calm and collected yourself. Look, we were going to leave the phone off the hook.

She replaces the receiver. No sooner has she said these words than the phone begins to ring again. The two stare at each other, once more overcome by terror. The MAN almost hypnotised by the sound, grabs the phone and very slowly raises it to his ear.

MAN: (*With a strained voice*) Hello.

As before the figure of the BURGLAR'S WIFE appears and at the same time her intensely irritated voice is heard.

BURGLAR'S WIFE: About time too, I've been trying to get through for a full hour. Are you going to tell me why you cut me off?

MAN: I'm sorry, who's speaking please?

His lover puts her ear close to the receiver so that she too can hear.

BURGLAR'S WIFE: Oh that's lovely, now you don't even recognise your own wife's voice.

WOMAN: (*Nearly fainting*) Your wife! I knew it! Oh my God!

BURGLAR'S WIFE: Who's that with you? How could you! I distinctly heard a woman's voice. Who is it?

MAN: (*Turning to his lover*) Calm down my dear. There must be some mistake. I have no idea who's on the phone. I've never heard this voice before.

BURGLAR'S WIFE: But I have. There's no point in you trying to wriggle out. You brute, you swine, I've found you out at last! Now I understand why you didn't want me to come to that house. But you'll need to come here sometime and I'll be waiting...

The BURGLAR *looks out of his hiding place to follow the conversation, and hearing his* WIFE'*s voice he cannot help being gravely concerned.*

MAN: (*Speaking into telephone*) Look, there's been some mistake. You've got the wrong number. This is the Frazosi house.

BURGLAR'S WIFE: I know that fine. Frazosi, 47 Via Cenini, Flat number 3. Now stop playing the fool and don't try disguising your voice any more. You don't do it very well. You swine... after telling me you didn't want to be disturbed at your work!

MAN: Who said he was working?

BURGLAR'S WIFE: Some work right enough! Mucking about with other women! Traitor, phoney, cheat, liar! They always said that a liar is a thief... I mean a thief is a liar.

MAN: What do you mean? Thief, phoney, who do you think you're talking to?

BURGLAR'S WIFE: To my husband. Who else?

MAN: If your husband is a phoney thief, that's your business, but I am not your husband, but the husband of my wife, who's not here, thank God, otherwise...

WOMAN: We'd all be done for!

BURGLAR'S WIFE: First of all, my husband is not a phoney thief. He's a real thief...

MAN: Congratulations, Madam.

BURGLAR'S WIFE: And if you are not my husband, what are you doing in that house?

MAN: My dear lady, this is my own house.

BURGLAR'S WIFE: Oh excellent. You're in your own house, with a woman who is not your wife... alone, at this time of night, after spreading the word that you were out of town.

WOMAN: We've been found out!

BURGLAR'S WIFE: So, just like my husband, you too are a traitor, a cheat, a liar and therefore a thief.

MAN: I don't give a damn for your husband. But I would be very grateful if you would tell me who said I would be out of town.

BURGLAR'S WIFE: My husband. He always tells me where he is going. He's been keeping you under observation for ten days.

MAN: What?

BURGLAR'S WIFE: Yes, he was waiting for the right moment.

MAN: He was waiting for what? Why on earth did your husband want to know...

WOMAN: (*Covering the receiver with her hand*) But don't you see? Your wife has had you followed by that woman's husband, who must be a private detective.

MAN: Ah. Now I understand. So your husband offers this splendid service.

BURGLAR'S WIFE: Well, he's only doing his job.

MAN: A marvellous job too, if you think it's respectable to do everything you can to make a wife leave her husband.

BURGLAR'S WIFE: My husband make a wife leave her own husband? Watch what you're saying!

MAN: Stop acting the goat. And don't let on that you know

nothing about it. (*Changing tone*) My wife... playing a dirty
trick like that on me. (*Pompously*) There's no doubt that in
this world mutual trust is dead and buried, fool that I was
to have deceived myself. 'There are certain things my wife
would never stoop to,' I said to myself. 'She is a real lady,
of the kind they do not make any more, even if she is a bit
on the simple side.' It was me that was simple.

BURGLAR'S WIFE: What are you getting at? Are you
implying that your wife and my husband...

MAN: What do you mean 'implying'? I couldn't be more
certain. For God's sake, quit the clowning.

BURGLAR'S WIFE: All right, all right, where is my husband
now?

MAN: How should I know, if you don't know yourself?

BURGLAR'S WIFE: I only know that less than one hour ago
he was there in your house.

MAN: Here, in this house?

BURGLAR'S WIFE: Certainly, I phoned him myself. In fact
I thought he was still there.

WOMAN: He must have got the keys from your wife.

MAN: Precisely, so that he could come and go at all hours of
the day and night. I bet he's already down at the Villa
Ponente.

BURGLAR'S WIFE: Villa Ponente. And why should my
husband be down there?

MAN: (*Ironically*) Oh come on. Didn't he tell you? I thought
he never hid anything from you about what he was doing
and where he was going. Anyway, just to keep you happy,
here's the address. Villa Ponente, 34 Via Aristide
Zamboni, telephone number 7845... My wife's there...
though she won't be my wife much longer.

*With these words, he puts down the phone in a temper. The
other* WOMAN *bursts into bitter tears. The figure of the*
BURGLAR'S WIFE *vanishes.*

WOMAN: What a scandal! I'll be disgraced. When my husband finds out, it'll be a terrible blow for him, poor thing. When I think of all the sacrifices I've made to keep him in the dark... to hide even the tiniest details from him... so as not to upset him... even this most recent affair... and now, caught in the act...

MAN: And do you not think it's worse for me? I had just made up my mind to retire from the town council, but now, after this scandal, they'll put me up for mayor.

WOMAN: Well, what can we do? We can either run away or give ourselves up.

MAN: There's no need to go over the score, give ourselves up! To whom, may I ask? And what for? What are we supposed to have done after all? It's not as though they caught us red-handed. No, we were just having a chat... we were talking about children...

WOMAN: That's true enough. I was just telling you how much I liked children.

MAN: Exactly. But perhaps it would be better not to mention that. People can be very evil-minded. They would accuse us of premeditation. What an outrage, I'd shoot myself.

WOMAN: What a good idea! Perhaps that's the best way out, the only real solution.

MAN: What? The only solution! Are you mad? I can just see the headlines! 'Local Councillor, after presiding at over fifty civil weddings shoots himself for adultery.' They'd laugh their heads off at the town hall!

WOMAN: I am glad you find it all so funny... sometimes I wonder about you... you've no sense of responsibility.

MAN: Why should I blame myself? We're in a trap and there's nothing for it but to wait an hour or two until my wife arrives from Villa Ponente. (*Thinking it over*) An hour or two? Why not make full use of it? At least they'll have something to sentence us for. (*He goes towards the* WOMAN *who is still seated on the sofa*) Let's go in there now.

WOMAN: Don't be so vulgar, please.

She pushes the MAN, *who ends up in the same position as previously, full length on the settee with his head over the back which has again given way.*

MAN: (*Cursing, striking his open hand against the settee*) And I bought the bloody thing myself!

WOMAN: Is it asking too much for you to show even the tiniest bit of concern... of understanding for me? Don't you understand that I am in despair?

MAN: You always exaggerate! 'In despair.' Would you be kind enough to tell me what you want of me. (*With a theatrical pose*) Do you want me to shoot myself? All right then, I'll shoot myself. I keep a little pistol handy for emergencies. (*The* MAN *takes a pistol from a drawer and aims it at his forehead*) Maybe now you'll be happy.

WOMAN: Nooooo! What are you doing? Stop it. Give me that.

She takes the gun from his hand while the MAN, *who has obviously made the gesture only to frighten her, laughs quietly.*

MAN: (*Ironic but satisfied*) What? Now you don't want me to shoot myself?

WOMAN: My dear, you'll have to take off the safety catch and put a bullet in the gun. Like that. (*She snaps the loaded gun together and hands it back to him*) There you are. Now you can shoot yourself.

MAN: (*With a strangely squeaky voice*) Ha... Ha... Now I can...

WOMAN: (*Raising the gun until it is level with his face*) Come on, hurry up. You don't want to be still alive when your wife gets here now do you...

The MAN, *petrified, puts the gun against his forehead and just at that moment the grandfather clock strikes twelve-thirty. At the first sounds, the* MAN *starts back and stares at the gun in terror.*

WOMAN: What a funny clock, first it strikes one, and then it strikes midnight... seems to be going slow... I mean going backwards.

MAN: It certainly is strange... that never happened before... perhaps it's a sign from heaven. The hand of destiny that comes to arrest the suicide's hand... to remind him that time, that life can be ended but that no traveller returns from that undiscovered bourne. Oh my grateful thanks to you, blessed heavenly hand! My darling grandfather clock you have saved my life!

With these words, he goes up to the clock, embraces it warmly as if it were a person in flesh and blood. The clock goes on striking and seems to spring to life.

BURGLAR'S VOICE: (*Obviously unable to hold back cries of pain caused by the pendulum striking his head*) Ouch... Oh... damnation... stop.

MAN: (*Leaping backwards and going over to embrace the WOMAN who is now rigid with fear*) Destiny!!

BURGLAR: (*Comes out massaging his head*) Oooh, the pain! ...that was sore! Good evening. If you don't mind, could you let me have some soda water? I'm coming up in huge lumps all over.

WOMAN: (*Scandalised*) Lumps! A bit vulgar for Destiny!

MAN: Who in the name of God are you? What are you doing in my house? Answer, or else I'll give you a sight more than lumps.

WOMAN: Please, don't you start being rude as well. After all, what harm can it do to give him a drop of soda water?

BURGLAR: Come on, just a teensy weensy glass of soda water, after all...

MAN: (*Very decisively, pointing the gun at him*) Don't make me lose my patience. Who are you? Who are you?

BURGLAR: (*Terrified*) There's no need to be pointing that at me. I'll tell you right away sir... I am the husband... you see, that woman who phoned a while ago, she's my wife...

and I'm her husband.

MAN: Ah... You're the husband... good.

BURGLAR: Yes. We got married in church.

MAN: I'm pleased to hear it. So you'll have the good fortune to be buried in consecrated ground.

BURGLAR: Buried! No, No, No. You can't get rid of me like that. (*Turning to the* WOMAN) You've no right. Madam, you're a witness that I am unarmed. You'd better watch out. Anyone who shoots me will catch it, and no mistake. Paragraph 127 of the Criminal Justice Act. You can, at the most, fire in the air if I attempt to escape. But since I'm not escaping, you can't. I warn you that the charge would be first degree murder.

WOMAN: You people are always well up on the law... of course the law is always on your side. But suppose we just decided to shoot you in the back, as they do with spies. (*Turning to the* MAN) That's what to do. Shoot him in the back. (*To the* BURGLAR) Kindly turn round.

BURGLAR: I'm awfully sorry, but I really don't like war games. Why don't we just call the police?

MAN: Ah! He's smart, this one. Call the police! The police uncover the adultery, we're sent packing and he carries off the reward.

BURGLAR: A reward! Me? From whom?

MAN: From my wife.

BURGLAR: You're out of your mind. I've no idea who your wife is.

WOMAN: What a hypocrite. You don't know her! Shoot him at once, please, he's getting on my nerves.

MAN: Just a moment. How long were you in there?

Pointing to the clock.

BURGLAR: From precisely 13 minutes to twelve. I went in just as you arrived. Why?

MAN: So if he was inside the clock, he can't have phoned yet.

If we get a move on, we might still be safe.

WOMAN: Yes, safe, with him there ready to blow the whistle on us.

BURGLAR: (*Without understanding what they are talking about, willing to do anything to remove the danger*) No! Me blow a whistle! I don't know how to blow a whistle. I never learned, strike me down dead if I tell a lie. (*He blows into the barrel of the gun, which is only a few inches from his mouth, as if it were a whistle*) You see?

MAN: Besides, if we killed him, it would be a bit too obvious.

WOMAN: Suppose we just gave him a really serious wound.

MAN: What good would that do?

BURGLAR: I couldn't agree more. What good would it do?

WOMAN: I know what good it would do. If you could get him on one particular nerve. (*She touches him at the back of the neck*) For example in the neck, this one which passes right behind here, between the atlas and the epistropheus. He would lose his memory completely.

MAN: Are you sure?

WOMAN: Positive. In any case, he'd be completely paralysed, he wouldn't be able to speak and from our point of view that would be just as good.

BURGLAR: (*Who already feels paralysed*) But not for me it wouldn't. Is there not some other way, a little less risky? Come on lady, think up another idea. You've got brains.

WOMAN: (*Flattered*) Yes, there might be another solution: get him drunk. No one would believe the evidence of a drunk.

MAN: That's true. I've always thought you were marvellous.

BURGLAR: (*With a sigh of relief*) Absolutely marvellous. I knew it as soon as I saw you (*Rubbing his hands*) Well, what have you got to drink? If it's all the same with you, I'd rather have red wine. White wine gives me indigestion. Ever since I was a boy...

MAN: No, not wine, it takes too long. It's far better with gin or whisky. Three good glasses should do the trick.

BURGLAR: Well... whisky doesn't really agree with me. It smells of oil.

WOMAN: (*Who in the meantime has filled a glass to the brim*) There's no oily smell with this one. It's genuine Scotch whisky.

MAN: What's it like?

BURGLAR: (*Savouring it like a real connoisseur*) Very good indeed! Quite excellent.

MAN: (*Drinking in turn*) It damn well ought to be. It cost me a packet.

BURGLAR: (*Pretentiously*) Could I have another soupçon?

MAN: (*To the* BURGLAR *who holds out his glass to have it filled up again*) Take it easy. If you swallow the lot, what are we supposed to have?

WOMAN: Where are your manners? Anyway, it's him who is supposed to be getting drunk isn't it?

BURGLAR: Yes, it's me. (*Becoming bolder*) But if you want, why don't you get sozzled as well? Ha, Ha, Ha, wait till my wife hears about this. She'll never believe it. (*The thought of his wife wipes the smile from his face*) Talking of my wife, what did you tell her to drive her into such a temper? You've landed me right in it. You two go and phone her right away and explain your little ploy to her.

MAN: Ploy? What ploy?

BURGLAR: You know. That you're getting me drunk to stop me talking... about whatever it is that's bothering you.

WOMAN: Do you hear that? He wants a witness, the villain. You were right all along. Better to shoot him at once, and get it over with.

MAN: Yes, much better. (*He goes to get the gun which he has left in the drinks cupboard, but the* BURGLAR *gets there first, seizes the gun and aims it at the* MAN) Now none of this nonsense! That's my gun! Give it back to me this minute.

BURGLAR: It's all change now. First you keep me locked up in that tomb getting knocked about by the pendulum, then you set my wife against me, then you want to paralyse me with my epistropheus. Time to stop fooling about. I came here to burgle, not to play the clown.

MAN: To burgle!

BURGLAR: Indeed. I'm a burglar. The real thing.

WOMAN: (*Amused*) A burglar. Now it all comes out. I've never heard such nonsense. Where's your black mask, your striped jersey, your felt shoes?

MAN: Exactly. Where are they?

BURGLAR: Black mask! Felt shoes! This isn't a cartoon in one of your colour supps. Anyway what do you know about burglars and robbers?

WOMAN: (*Pompously*) For your instruction, I know everything there is to know about robbers, thieves, swindlers, burglars etc. I was on a TV quiz show. My subject was 'Celebrated Crimes and Thefts'.

MAN: Oh now I see where all your knowledge about the use and care of guns comes from. (*To the* BURGLAR) I'm sorry... bad luck... choose another profession. This just won't do at all.

BURGLAR: Listen you, have you ever heard of the Martello gang?

WOMAN: (*In the tone of someone repeating by heart*) The Martello Gang, leading members Mangia, Serafini, and Angelo Tornati nicknamed Stanca.

BURGLAR: Angelo Tornati nicknamed Stanga, with a g. It's a dialect word meaning long.

WOMAN: Long... don't be absurd... he's just a little fellow.

MAN: (*Just to say something*) You mean 'smallish'.

BURGLAR: Why, do I seem smallish to you?

MAN: What have you got to do with it?

BURGLAR: What have I got to do with it? Allow me to introduce myself. I am Angelo Tornati, nicknamed Stanga. And if you don't believe it, here are my release papers from St Stephen's Prison. (*He pulls out some documents*) I did three years.

WOMAN: (*A smile spreading over her face after glancing at the papers*) Wonderful! It really is him. Stanca, sorry Stanga. Marvellous. May I? (*She embraces him, kisses him on the cheek*) A robber, a real robber... I've never met a real robber before... let me have a look at you.

MAN: (*Jealous*) What are you up to now? This scoundrel comes to burgle my house... and you kiss him... it's disgusting.

WOMAN: Watch your language! 'It's disgusting.' What do you know about it? Have you ever kissed a robber?

MAN: No.

WOMAN: Well then. You try, and then tell me if it's quite as disgusting as you say.

At that moment the doorbell rings.

WOMAN: Who can that be?

BURGLAR: I bet it's my wife again. (*Lifting the phone*) Perhaps now you'll be good enough to explain to her. Hello Maria. You've landed me in a right fix with your telephone calls. I've told you time and again that when I'm at work you must leave me in peace. You must not disturb me, even if the house goes on fire. I want you to stay at home and not bother about anything.

MAN: It's not the phone... it's the doorbell.

BURGLAR: (*Looking at the phone with annoyance*) So that's why she let me talk.

He hangs up.

MAN: (*Opens the window and looks out*) Who is it?

WOMAN'S VOICE: Who do you think? It's me, Anna.

WOMAN: (*Turning pale*) Oh God... this time it really is his wife.

MAN: (*Trying to sound perfectly natural*) Ah it's you, dear. I wasn't expecting you. What's happened?

ANNA: That's what I wanted to ask you. I had some mad female on the phone shouting insults.

BURGLAR: A mad female! That's my wife. I might have known.

ANNA: Why don't you open the door? What's keeping you?

MAN: Just coming... (*Moving away from the window*) Now we're for it. What do we tell her?

BURGLAR: Bye, Bye, don't call me. I'll leave by the window.

MAN: (*Grabbing him by the collar*) Oh no you don't. Very convenient. It's thanks to you and your wife that we're all in this mess, so it's up to you to get us out.

BURGLAR: Me! What do you want me to do?

MAN: (*Turning to the* WOMAN) Just a minute, if you two could pass yourselves off as man and wife... we'd be OK.

WOMAN: What! Me married to him! We haven't even been introduced.

MAN: Don't worry, love follows after. Anyway, it's always better to be taken for the wife of a phoney husband than the lover of a real husband. (*Preparing to go and meet his* WIFE) Right then, everybody ready. (*Picking up the gun*) I'll take this now, thank you. Remember, no fooling about, otherwise... (*Clicks the gun shut*) I don't want to have to use this.

WOMAN: Oh my God, how dreadful. (*Looking the* BURGLAR *over from head to toe*) If you're going to be my husband, stand up, let me see you. Couldn't you have put on something neater? It's always the same, when we're visiting other people, you always make me so embarrassed... You know that when a man looks untidy, it's always the wife's fault.

BURGLAR: I know, I know but... I didn't exactly expect

things to turn out like this. I've got a nice checked suit at home. I'll pop over and put it on, if you like.

WOMAN: No you won't. (*Looking at his bulging pockets*) Your pockets are stuffed with things.

BURGLAR: (*Straightening up like a tailor's dummy*) It's the latest style didn't you know?

ANNA: (*Voice heard coming from outside*) So what's all this? Who's here with you?

MAN: That's what I was trying to tell you. There's been a misunderstanding but now it's all cleared up.

ANNA: Misunderstanding? You can say that again. You were supposed to be at your mother's, but instead I find you here.

MAN: (*Entering, followed by* WIFE) I'm trying to explain. Here we are, this is my friend Doctor Angelo Tornato.

BURGLAR: (*Drily*) Tornati.

MAN: (*With a weak smile*) Sorry. And this is his wife.

BURGLAR: It was your husband who made us get married. Love follows after, so he told us.

MAN: (*Covering up*) In my official capacity, at the registry.

WOMAN: Please forgive this intrusion, I realise it's a bit late, not very convenient for you, but we had to turn to your husband, because... it so happened... well you see...

ANNA: (*Drily*) Never mind that. Was it you who telephoned me?

MAN: (*Intervening quickly*) Yes. It was her. But you must understand, the poor thing was so distraught.

WOMAN: Do forgive me, but I was nearly driven crazy by jealousy, I don't know why, but I had the idea that my husband was having an affair with you. But now that I see you, I don't know how I could have thought such a thing.

ANNA: Why, do I look as though I'm past it? Or do you want to come right out and say that I'm some kind of monster.

WOMAN: No, no I didn't mean that at all. You look very elegant. I meant, knowing the vulgar tastes of my husband as I do...

BURGLAR: Me! Vulgar tastes!

ANNA: I am sorry that you feel vulgar, my dear, since your husband married you, but that doesn't mean that you have to consider me low enough to end up with a man like your aforementioned spouse.

BURGLAR: That's quite enough, first vulgar, now low and aforementioned.

MAN: (*Evidently attempting to defuse the situation*) No need to overdo it, dear. He is not much to look at but he might be all right for some tastes!

ANNA: What a husband I have! Instead of being outraged when they cast aspersions on his own wife, he says that I might get to like my supposed lover. The man's mad!

WOMAN: No, your husband didn't mean that. He just meant that when a woman is in love, she always thinks that other women might like her husband no matter how vulgar his tastes are.

ANNA: That's lovely that is. You mean that because I'm fond of my husband, you must be fond of him as well, is that it? Seeing you are here, why don't you take him as your lover?

WOMAN: No thank you.

ANNA: (*Turning to* BURGLAR) And what do you say to all this?

BURGLAR: To be quite honest, I'd sooner have her as a lover than as a wife... always assuming your husband had nothing against it... it's all up to him. It was him who married us.

ANNA: (*Bursting out laughing, in obvious good humour*) Very good, very witty. Now I see why your wife is afraid of other women. Witty men are the most dangerous. Especially if they have vulgar tastes.

BURGLAR: (*To the* WOMAN) She called me vulgar again!

WOMAN: (*Affectionately, putting her arm around him*) Ah yes, he really is dangerous. You've no idea.

MAN: (*Annoyed*) You're overdoing it a bit. (*Correcting himself*) All men are dangerous, to some extent.

ANNA: Certainly not you, my love! (*Looking at the* BURGLAR *and the* WOMAN *who are holding hands tenderly*) Aren't they lovely. They look like two newly-weds on honeymoon. You were made for each other... weren't they dear?

MAN: (*Getting riled*) Yes, but now... it's time to be saying goodnight... it's getting late.

ANNA: Where are your manners? Take no notice, just stay as long as you please. Why don't we all have a little drink?

BURGLAR: Why not? The same whisky as before for me.

He grabs the bottle but the WOMAN *signals 'no' to him.*

WOMAN: (*Whispering*) Put that down! (*In a strained voice, to* ANNA) You're very kind, but we've already taken advantage of your courtesy... (*The* BURGLAR *puts the bottle in his pocket*) It really is late, and I wouldn't want my husband to come and (*Realising what she has said*) ...I mean, him to get home too late... we live quite a way off, right at the other end of the town, and he must get up early tomorrow morning, isn't that right dear?

BURGLAR: Eh?

ANNA: Well, why not stay the night? We've got a spare room. Go on, dear, you make them.

MAN: (*His mind elsewhere*) Yes, why not sleep here tonight. (*Realising what he has said*) What am I saying? Perhaps they prefer...

BURGLAR: Oh, we'd be quite happy.

ANNA: Good, you see. They'd rather stay here. I can't tell you how pleased I am.

WOMAN: (*Making a last effort*) But really... we've got nothing with us, and my husband can't sleep without his pyjamas.

ANNA: If that's all. (*To her* HUSBAND) You can give him your pyjamas, the ones you haven't worn yet, can't you?

MAN: (*In despair*) Yes!

ANNA: (*To the* WOMAN) Would you like to come with me and I'll show you the room. You'll be perfectly comfortable, I'm sure. (*To the* BURGLAR) I'll have to steal her from you for a moment.

The two WOMEN *go out. The two* MEN, *left alone, stare at each other, the one with embarrassment, the other with hatred. The first to speak is the owner of the house.*

MAN: Did you really have to go on like that? You're nothing but a half-witted Casanova... but if you think you're going to sleep with my... my... my pyjamas... you can get that idea out of your head right away.

BURGLAR: Whose idea was it in the first place? Who had the great idea of making me pretend to be the husband of your lady-friend? And then you go all of a twitter... A man who's never had a day's luck in his life comes here to earn his living... not only do you stop him going off with as much as a broken alarm clock, but you make him take part in your cavortings! No, no, I'm very sorry, but now you phone up my wife... No, a better idea, let's get your wife in here and we'll tell her everything... then I'll call the police. I'd sooner be interrogated by a police sergeant than by my wife.

MAN: Listen to that! An officer and a gentleman! I do believe he's offended. We disturbed him at his back-breaking work. You came here to burgle. All right, get on with it. Burgle away. (*He opens the silverware drawer*) There are some gold teaspoons there, help yourself.

BURGLAR: (*Takes out his bag, opens it but then thinks better of it*) No thank you, but stealing things in this way is not my style. Another time perhaps.

MAN: (*Who is beginning to get jumpy. He makes as though to take the gun from his pocket*) I have ways of making you. With this!

BURGLAR: If you really insist. (*He handles a spoon very delicately*) Yes, quite a pleasing little piece, this spoon.

He sticks it into his jacket pocket.

MAN: (*Taking out his gun menacingly*) I told you to steal... so do it thoroughly. I don't want you to go around telling people there's nothing much to steal in my house... or complaining that we exploit burglars.

BURGLAR: I never said that.

MAN: You're just the type to say it. Come on, take these as well.

He opens a drawer and hands him a bundle of silver spoons.

BURGLAR: I really don't want to abuse your kindness, your hospitality.

MAN: No need for scruples. Just get on with the job. I've got a gun, remember.

At that very moment, the BURGLAR'S WIFE *comes in, and seeing the* MAN *pointing a gun at her husband, lets out a piercing scream and throws herself between the two, clinging to her husband.*

BURGLAR: Maria! How did you get here?

BURGLAR'S WIFE: The door was open.

BURGLAR: And I had to clamber three flights up a roan pipe to get here.

BURGLAR'S WIFE: Forgive me, it was all my fault, I know... I only understood too late... but now you'd better give everything back... even if they give you a few months, it's quite near the festive season and it's not too bad doing a stretch at this time of the year... they even give you Christmas cake and tangerines... please give yourself up.

MAN: Not his wife, not her as well! What am I going to tell my wife when she finds out that he has two wives?

BURGLAR'S WIFE: Who has two wives?

BURGLAR: (*His voice high-pitched from terror*) I've nothing to do with this, remember. It was him that told me to take her as my wife in case his wife found out that she wasn't my wife... just a wife...

BURGLAR'S WIFE: Give me that gun. I'll teach him a lesson. (*Snatches the gun from the* MAN's *hands and points it at her husband*) Ah ha! you wicked traitor, liar, villain... fool that I was to believe that you were getting along fine with your wife when you've had another wife all the time... and she's not even his wife... I'll kill you. (*Tries to remove the safety catch*) How does this thing work?

MAN: I'll show you. Oh God what am I doing? Never mind (*Snatches the gun*) For God's sake don't make such a din. If the other two wives hear us, I'm done for and no mistake, but so's your husband. Listen to me one minute. I am not going to explain all the whys and wherefores, it would take too long, but if you want to save your husband, stay calm. (*Footsteps are heard, coming nearer*) Damn... here they are... what in God's name can we say now!

ANNA: (*Entering*) What a lovely woman you married, Signor Tornati... she's waiting for you... I've brought you down these pyjamas myself because if I were waiting for my husband... (*She stops, surprised at seeing the new guest whom the* BURGLAR *and her husband are trying to hide from her view*) ...I have... Sorry dear... Who is this lady?

MAN: (*As if unaware of her existence*) Who?

BURGLAR'S WIFE: I'm a wife... Maria Tornati.

ANNA: What? Another wife?

MAN: (*Trying to redeem the situation*) Yes, I was just going to tell you... this lady claims to be...

BURGLAR'S WIFE: Claims to be! I am the wife.

MAN: Exactly, I am the wife... she is the wife. (*Staring hard at her, as if trying to hypnotise her*) The first wife of my friend Tornato.

BURGLAR: (*Correcting*) Ti.

MAN: (*Uncertain*) To – ti.

BURGLAR: Ti... ti... ti... Tornati.

MAN: The first wife from whom he is now divorced.

The BURGLAR'S WIFE *tries to interrupt, but her husband nudges her with his elbow.*

ANNA: Are you foreigners?

BURGLAR: Eh... no, we are...

ANNA: Then how were you able to get divorced?

BURGLAR: (*Asking the* MAN *for help*) Eh? Able?

MAN: (*Turning to* BURGLAR'S WIFE) Able?

ANNA: Ah... I understand... your friend works in the cinema.

MAN: Yes, yes, yes, he works in the cinema. He's a film producer.

ANNA: A producer! And what kind of films does he make? (*Noticing the bag he has in his hand*) What's that in your hand? (*Opens the bag*) My best silver! What are you doing?

BURGLAR: A spot of burgling.

MAN: Noooo... he was telling me about the subject of a new film of his... where there is a scene involving a theft... and he was showing me...

ANNA: Oh how interesting. So you're a specialist.

BURGLAR: Yes, father and son...

ANNA: Your wife too?

BURGLAR'S WIFE: No... not me. My husband won't let me, he always leaves me at home.

ANNA: No, I meant... this business of the divorce... if they are divorced, how come his wife is still his wife... he seems to have two.

MAN: Precisely... He got divorced... then remarried... but then the State, over-riding Church Law, didn't recognise the divorce, even though it had earlier recognised, in civil law, the second marriage... so that the poor thing now finds himself at one and the same time a bigamist, an adulterer, a public sinner and a devout Catholic.

BURGLAR'S WIFE: What! (*To her husband*) You never said a word to me.

BURGLAR: I didn't know. (*To the houseowner*) What do you mean, a devout bigamist?

The MAN *pushes him away from the women.*

ANNA: (*To the* BURGLAR'S WIFE) Just as well for you. There are some things it's better not to know. Even when you do know them, you still don't understand. Poor thing! Who knows where it'll all end. Maybe they'll put him on trial and send him to jail like a petty thief.

MAN: Maybe. Just like someone who makes off with the cutlery (*Pointedly*) and all because he has a wife.

ANNA: What?

MAN: I mean two wives.

ANNA: (*To the* BURGLAR) Which reminds me, your other wife, shouldn't we let her know that she's here. (*Pointing to the* BURGLAR'S WIFE) What bad luck for her. I don't see what else we can do. Even if you all agreed, it's really just a one-and-a-half sized bed. You wouldn't be very comfortable.

MAN: Never mind... we'll fix something up.

BURGLAR'S WIFE: You'd better... you're not getting off that lightly.

BURGLAR: (*Would like to take the bag, but is obliged to leave it so as to push his* WIFE *towards the door on the left*) Yes, yes... but let's get out now. Damn! I'll have to leave the takings.

MAN: (*To* BURGLAR'S WIFE) Don't go yet. Come in here and meet your husband's wife... I mean... this way.

BURGLAR: I'm coming too.

ANNA: (*Watches the three go out and shakes her head with compassion*) Poor woman! (*Then, seeing the bottles scattered on the table*) What a mess. They've certainly been drinking.

She pours herself a drink. In the meantime a man appears at the door and calls quietly to her.

ANTONIO: Anna... are you alone?

ANNA: Oh my God! Antonio, are you out of your mind? Go away... at once... my husband's at home.

ANTONIO: What on earth's up? You were just not making any sense on the phone. What's all this about my wife phoning you?

ANNA: Nothing, nothing at all. It's all been a mistake, thank God! I had a phone call from a woman who insulted me because of her husband.

ANTONIO: And you thought it was my wife?

ANNA: Exactly, I don't know your wife, much less her voice but I got such a fright. Anyway, you can't stay here. Away you go. I'll see you tomorrow.

ANTONIO: Ah, you want me out of the way now. No, no, I'm not having that. What do you take me for? A telephone call, some funny misunderstanding, your husband coming home when he's supposed to be at his mother's... no, no, there's more to all this. You know what I think? I think it was all set up to cancel our date so that you could meet someone else here. Who it was I don't know, but certainly not your husband.

ANNA: You're mad. How can you think such a thing?

ANTONIO: Stop lying. What about these glasses. It's quite clear... you were preparing yourself, spiritually. Where is... what's his name? Speak, it'd be better for you. (*Seizing her by the shoulders*) Who is he?

At that moment the BURGLAR *appears with the pyjamas still under his arm. He's come back for the bag. But at the sight of this scene and of the new guest, he drops the bag in fright, at which* ANTONIO *turns round.*

BURGLAR: Don't let me disturb you. I'm just picking up my bag.

ANTONIO: Ah, here he is... with his pyjamas neatly rolled

up… the young gentleman's ready and willing.

BURGLAR: (*To* ANTONIO *who has grabbed his arm*) Just lay off, the lady gave me these herself. You can have them if you like. There's no need to get all worked up over a pair of pyjamas.

ANTONIO: I know she gave them to you, don't I just! And now I'll make you both pay. (*With these words, he locks the door and puts the key in his pocket*) No one's leaving until you explain.

ANNA: Antonio… I beg you… you're making a terrible mistake… this man's a friend of my husband's and he's here as our guest with his wives…

From the other rooms, the shouts of the two WOMEN, *evidently quarrelling, can be heard.*

VOICES OF THE TWO WOMEN: No, no I'm not the village idiot, you know… don't give me all that stuff, you little whore. (*Other voice*) Who are you calling a whore? Just mind your language.

ANTONIO: (*Releasing his grip*) So they really are your wives? How many have you got?

The BURGLAR *makes a gesture of his hands as though to say 'quite enough'.*

ANNA: Please, please, please, Mr Tornati… don't breathe a word of this to my husband.

BURGLAR: No, no, not a word.

ANTONIO: That's very good of you. I'm sorry about this misunderstanding.

BURGLAR: What's one more misunderstanding among friends? What a night this has been!

ANNA: You must fly now. Where have you put the key?

ANTONIO: In my coat. (*He searches in his pocket*) Oh damn! It's slipped down into the lining. There's a hole in the pocket. Ooooh, what next? Don't just stand there. Give me a hand.

He takes off his coat to make the search easier. All three take part in the operation to locate the key, which seems to have a life of its own and keeps eluding them.

ANNA: Got it! No, you knocked it out of my hand.

BURGLAR: Stop. Here it is. Oh no, where's it got to now?

ANTONIO: Take it easy. You're ripping the lining apart. Hell, it's gone into the sleeves now.

The voices from the adjoining room draw closer.

ANNA: Here, they're coming. Now what do we do?

BURGLAR: Come over here. I was in here for a couple of hours. (*Opens the grandfather clock*) You can make yourself quite comfortable. (*Pushing him in*) Just watch out when it starts striking… You can get a right nasty one… and no smoking!

The two women come in, followed by the MAN… *They are somewhat distraught.*

BURGLAR'S WIFE: (*To her* HUSBAND) Since these two are not going to tell me anything, let's go home and you can explain everything.

BURGLAR: Go home? What's the rush? We're all having such a wonderful time. What lovely people! Look, they've even given me a pair of pyjamas. Anyway, I don't know how on earth we're going to get out. There's no key.

BURGLAR'S WIFE: (*Shaking the door*) It shouldn't be very hard for you to pick the lock. That's your job isn't it.

The BURGLAR *takes an enormous bunch of keys out of his pocket.*

BURGLAR: Would one of these do?

ANNA: (*To her husband*) What a lot of keys! What's he got all them for?

MAN: I told you, he's a film producer, and you show me a film producer that doesn't have at least five or six offices, two or three villas, and a couple of pied-à-terres.

At that very moment, the grandfather clock begins to strike. First a blow, then a shout of pain and the unfortunate inhabitant of the clock comes out cursing.

ANTONIO: Ouch, that was sore... my poor head... ooooh.

BURGLAR: I told you so! I told you you'd get it in the skull, and there's not even any soda water in this house.

WOMAN: (*Panic-stricken*) It's my husband. (*Trying to appear nonchalant*) Hello dear.

ANTONIO: Julia! What are you doing here?

ANNA: What. You know Mr Tornati's wife?

ANTONIO: Whose wife? You must be joking, Julia's my wife.

MAN: (*Turning to his wife*) No, no, dear, don't worry. There's been a misunderstanding.

BURGLAR: Another one! What a lot of misunderstandings this evening.

WOMAN: You'll have to explain to me what you were doing in that clock. (*To* BURGLAR) Was he in there when you were there?

BURGLAR: (*After a moment's perplexity*) Well it's hard to say. It's very dark inside.

MAN: It's all clear now, totally clear, just give me a minute and I'll clear up the misunderstanding. Well then...

BURGLAR: Well... O help! There's no misunderstanding. It's like this. Now...

Before he has time to go on, the others, afraid that he will uncover their individual affairs, interrupt hurriedly.

ANNA: Of course there's been a misunderstanding... obviously there has.

ANTONIO: Yes I understood that at once. In fact I'm astonished that our friend here hasn't gathered that yet. It's all one big misunderstanding.

WOMAN: It's so clear that even a child could understand it.

MAN: So there's really no need of explanations. You can't explain misunderstandings, otherwise it would hardly be a misunderstanding, would it?

BURGLAR: (*To his* WIFE) Come on, let's get out.

BURGLAR'S WIFE: Just a minute. Don't pull me like that.

BURGLAR: Let's go before they notice.

As they pass the switch, the BURGLAR *puts out the light.*

ANNA: Who's put out the light?

WOMAN: What's going on?

ANTONIO: Stop them! Where are those two off to?

WOMAN: He's so crazy he might even go off and give himself up... this minute.

MAN: Quick, stop them, don't let them get away.

WOMAN: They've gone out through the garden... run.

MAN: It's impossible. You two go out that way. You come with me.

They all go out. Silence. From the window appears the light of a torch. The light comes right into the room and stops on the bag filled with the BURGLAR's *takings. At that point the others return.*

SECOND BURGLAR: Nice place here, the cutlery already parcelled up. Very thoughtful of them. (*Pause*) Somebody's coming.

MAN: He's come back in through the window, the scoundrel. He actually came back to get the silverware.

ANNA: Grab him.

WOMAN: Quick... hold him... don't let him get away.

MAN: Switch on the light.

When the light comes on, a SECOND BURGLAR, *surrounded by his four pursuers, is seen.*

ANNA: That's not the great Tornati. It's another one!

SECOND BURGLAR: Ah no, no. This is a bit much. You're

starting to lay traps, leaving the window open, the loot all tied up and ready... and then just as I'm about to move, Bang! It's a fair cop Guv! No, that's just not playing the game. I'm going to see my union about this, so I'll bid you all good night.

EVERYONE: Noooooo!

MAN: No, for goodness' sake, listen, there's been a misunderstanding.

SECOND BURGLAR: A what?

EVERYONE: Misunderstanding.

MAN: Now, with your permission, we'll explain everything.

EVERYONE: It's like this...

The following lines are to be spoken simultaneously, so that there will be a great din without a single word being understood.

WOMAN: Earlier this evening I was with my husband. I got a phone call and came here at once...

ANNA: I was at Villa Ponente. The phone rang and at the other end I heard a woman's voice insulting me...

MAN: I was at my mother's. We were just sitting down to eat when all of a sudden I remembered I'd left the office keys at home...

ANTONIO: I was at the cinema earlier on. The usual stuff, sex and violence, when...

The SECOND BURGLAR, *assaulted by the clamour of voices and meaningless words, moves back until he bumps into the sofa. He sits, then falls full length at the mercy of the four unfaithful liars who talk and talk and talk.*

Blackout

One Was Nude and One Wore Tails
A One-Act Farce

translated by Ed Emery

Characters

FIRST ROAD SWEEPER
SECOND ROAD SWEEPER
WOMAN
NAKED MAN
PATROLMAN
MAN IN EVENING DRESS

We find ourselves in a street on the outskirts of town. A couple of lamp posts, a withered hedge, a dilapidated park bench, a newsvendor's kiosk (which is closed) and a trestle with a sign indicating 'Road Works'.

Enter several ROAD SWEEPERS, *pushing their carts. They sing in unison:*

> The wise man sleeps on a bed of wool,
> The lazy man sleeps on a bed of feathers.
> The rheumatic sleeps on wood,
> And the rogue on a pretty girl's breast.
> At night we clean the streets,
> The long avenues, dirtied during the day.
> Dead leaves, deformed by the frost,
> Or by the doings of a dirty dog;
> We pick up litter and rags,
> And dog ends walked on and flattened,
> Before, by the sad vagaries of fate,
> They all end up blocking the drains.
> Sometimes we find a thousand-lire note.
> Hell, but it's one of the old ones... not worth a thing,
> So we stick it on the bonfire.
> But then we are seized with remorse,
> And we give it to a blind beggar.

Exit the ROAD SWEEPERS. *Only two of them remain on stage. They talk quietly for a while. Then one of them raises his voice:*

FIRST SWEEPER: Listen, you know what I say? I say that it's best to speak the truth, and have done with it. At least, that's the way I see it...

SECOND SWEEPER: Ah, yes, the truth, you say... And what is the truth? You will tell me that the true is the opposite of the false... Correct. So, now tell me: what is false and what is true? Is that which is true true, or is that which is false true? Thus, if the true and the false are one and the same... (*The* FIRST SWEEPER *moves away, irritated*) ...Hey, wait, why are you running off in such a hurry?

FIRST SWEEPER: Because I want to be on my own... that's why.

SECOND SWEEPER: I say... You wouldn't happen to be angry with me, would you?

FIRST SWEEPER: Who said anything about angry...? The fact is, I am sick of hanging around here giving myself a headache with your speeches every night. You rave on with your mad theories, and then it starts me thinking. I've already told you that thinking gives me a pain right here.

He points to his forehead.

SECOND SWEEPER: That's because you're not trained for it... The brain is a muscle, and when it is not subjected to regular strenuous exercise...

FIRST SWEEPER: Oh yes, brilliant! You know what? I bet, if I start exercising my brain muscle strenuously, afterwards, I guarantee I'll get brain strain... Wonderful!

SECOND SWEEPER: (*Amused*) Brain strain! Ha, ha! I like that!

FIRST SWEEPER: That's right. And what's more, I don't understand why you, with your well-trained muscle, and with all your education, still carry on working as a roadsweeper.

SECOND SWEEPER: Because for me, being a roadsweeper is not a job, but a mission...

FIRST SWEEPER: Here we go again, more crazy notions!

SECOND SWEEPER: Not at all. Sensible, if anything. To start with: what is the most important thing in life? Answer me that!

FIRST SWEEPER: Well, I should say it's that a person should have good health and happiness...

SECOND SWEEPER: ...That way he can reach true happiness?

· **FIRST SWEEPER:** Yes, and then if he doesn't give a damn for anything or anyone... that's even better.

SECOND SWEEPER: There you go! Well done. I have to admit that I was mistaken about you. You're not really as stupid as you look. That's exactly correct: in order to be truly happy, one must raise oneself above life's wretched vicissitudes, forget one's own ambitions, suppress one's feelings and passions...

FIRST SWEEPER: Not give a damn! Exactly! But that's easier said than done...

SECOND SWEEPER: Ah, indeed, it is not easy... But the means do exist.

FIRST SWEEPER: Like what?

SECOND SWEEPER: Have you never heard of yoga?

FIRST SWEEPER: Eh? What's yoga?

SECOND SWEEPER: I have to admit that I was *not* wrong about you... You really are as stupid as you look. Yoga is an exercise, a psycho-physical discipline, which enables those who practice it to achieve the most absolute sublimation, and thereby reach a state of beatitude, in other words, happiness.

FIRST SWEEPER: Alright... But what's this yoga got to do with being a roadsweeper?

SECOND SWEEPER: It's got a lot to do with it... Basically, it's the same principle. What can be more suitable than a roadsweeper's life, in order to suppress within us that baggage of arrogance, pride and ambition which prevents us from stripping ourselves of pointless vanities, and going forward, naked but happy, to attain the bliss and ecstasy of the platonic world of ideas?

FIRST SWEEPER: Naked? There, I knew it. Now I'm starting to get a headache! What do you mean, naked?

SECOND SWEEPER: Naked! Naked outside, but clothed within, with our spirit clothed...

FIRST SWEEPER: Our spirit clothed! Hey, I like that! I'll have to remember that... But what does it mean?

SECOND SWEEPER: I'll explain it in a couple of words... You, for example: do you see yourself as someone?

FIRST SWEEPER: What a question! I'm a roadsweeper... What do you expect me to see myself as...?

SECOND SWEEPER: Precisely. You don't see yourself as anyone. You see yourself as nobody, in short, a nothingness... But is not nothingness perhaps the beginning of everything, in other words, the absolute? And the absolute, as Plato says, is God, and therefore you are God...

FIRST SWEEPER: Me?

SECOND SWEEPER: Yes, you!

FIRST SWEEPER: Oh come on... You're just saying that because you like me... But look, when you get to know me better... Ha...! They've been telling you stories about me, and you fell for it.

SECOND SWEEPER: Lucky you, to understand so little! Look... A person could dress you up as absolutely anything: a king, a clown, a soldier, a priest... Stark naked, or in evening dress, you will always be yourself, a roadsweeper. In fact, not even a roadsweeper – a nobody, because you are nobody, and therefore everything...

FIRST SWEEPER: And since everything is God, as Plato says, I am God...

SECOND SWEEPER: Well done! I see that it's sinking in at last!

FIRST SWEEPER: Yes, yes, it's not so hard really... But tell me, does the Pope know that I am God?

SECOND SWEEPER: The Pope?

Enter a WOMAN, *running. She looks very worried.*

WOMAN: Hell... This time I'm really done for... Oh, excuse me... Maybe you can help me...

SECOND SWEEPER: Happy to oblige... In what regard might we be of assistance?

WOMAN: They nabbed me... Just as I was negotiating with a client...

FIRST SWEEPER: *Who* nabbed you?

WOMAN: The Vice Squad. There they are. They're coming! Oh, for pity's sake, help me... Do something!

FIRST SWEEPER: Let's hide her in the bin! There's plenty of room, as long as she squeezes up a bit.

SECOND SWEEPER: Don't be stupid... Such a good-looking woman... In among all that rubbish...?!

WOMAN: Thanks for the compliment... But unfortunately the fact that I am good-looking, as you say, isn't going to help me a lot... The Vice Squad don't mess around. They lock you away as soon as look at you. Last time, a gentleman saved me by passing me off as his fiancée, but this time...

SECOND SWEEPER: Oh yes, I can just see it! Just imagine if we said that you were our fiancée... that *would* make people laugh... Roadsweepers, as everyone knows, are incapable of love...

FIRST SWEEPER: Yes, one fiancée between two... It wouldn't be right... On the other hand, though...

SECOND SWEEPER: Oh yes, how stupid of me... I didn't even think of that...

FIRST SWEEPER: Yes, we could take it in turns... Me first! I thought of it first...!

SECOND SWEEPER: Behave yourself, and take this. (*He*

removes his roadsweeper's cape) The caterpillar is transformed into a butterfly; it throws off its old skin and flies. (*He tosses his cap and cape into the bin, and then pulls a top-hat from his toolbox*) Let us go, my love. Tonight I shall be your protector...

WOMAN: Oh, thank you, you're very kind... And you look like a real gentleman... I really don't know how I can repay you.

SECOND SWEEPER: Don't worry, I'm sure we shall find a way. (*Theatrically*) Cling to me, treasure; Love will save us...

FIRST SWEEPER: Just a moment, before you two start clinging to each other, what am I supposed to do with this bin of yours? I can hardly go round with two bins at the same time, can I! Supposing I run into a supervisor...?

SECOND SWEEPER: You're right... What can we do?

FIRST SWEEPER: Well, maybe there is a way: I'll hide my bin behind that little wall, and I'll take yours to the depot, and I'll tell the supervisor that you felt ill, and that you had to go off... I won't say who with, though...

SECOND SWEEPER: Well done... You're divine!

FIRST SWEEPER: Yes, I know, you've already explained that. You don't have to go telling everyone, though... These are delicate matters, you know! Let's go.

WOMAN: Thank you too... It's been a real miracle running into you.

FIRST SWEEPER: There, you see...? A miracle now! If word of this gets out... Come on, hurry up. Go.

WOMAN: Yes, yes, we're going. Goodbye... and thank you again.

The two of them exit, arm in arm. The FIRST SWEEPER follows, wheeling the SECOND SWEEPER's bin.

A few seconds of blackout, to indicate the passage of time.

FIRST SWEEPER: (*Re-entering*) Hey, let's not start playing

tricks… Who's shifted my bin? (*The bin, which was on-stage prior to the blackout, has now been shifted behind a hedge*) Ah, here it is… Just as well… That gave me a fright… (*He starts picking up litter*) That would have been a fine thing… A fellow worries about another fellow's bin, and in the meantime his own one gets stolen… If I find the rat who shifted it…

He opens the bin lid, and throws in the rubbish that he's collected.

NAKED MAN: (*Annoyed, popping up out of the bin*) Good God! Mind where you're throwing that rubbish… I suppose you think that's funny.

FIRST SWEEPER: (*Not believing his eyes*) Oh, excuse me…

NAKED MAN: (*Dusting down the top hat which he's wearing*) Excuse me be damned! If you think that's funny… I can assure you that your jokes are in extremely bad taste…

FIRST SWEEPER: Hey, now look, you, you're a bit mad…

NAKED MAN: Ah, so I'm mad now, am I? That's lovely – now you start insulting me into the bargain. And what's to stop you starting to hit me too? Come on, feel free! However, I must warn you that you are about to hit a… naked man.

FIRST SWEEPER: A naked man? Let me see this naked man.

NAKED MAN: Please, go ahead… (*He stands up, to show the top half of his body, which is indeed naked*) That'll do. After all, we hardly know each other! And anyway… don't you think you're going a bit far? Alright, I can imagine that, with your job, accustomed as you are to living among all kinds of filth… I'm sure that the sight of another's nudity is hardly going to embarrass you… But fortunately, in my case, modesty prevents…

FIRST SWEEPER: (*Losing his temper*) Right, that's quite enough, eh? Either you pack that up, or I'll make you pack it up…! I'll take my bin, with you in it, and I'll tip the whole lot into the first ditch I find…

NAKED MAN: (*Soothingly*) There's no need to get all worked up like that. Come on, calm down...

FIRST SWEEPER: No, my friend... It is *you* who should calm down... and cut the fooling about... Because I am quite capable of calling a policeman, and *then* you'll be sorry!

NAKED MAN: No, please... I humbly beg your pardon... on my knees... don't turn me in to the police... Because that would be the same as leading me to suicide... Please, don't call the...

FIRST SWEEPER: Alright, I won't call the police... But listen, just so that I know: how on earth did you end up in my bin, and naked into the bargain?

NAKED MAN: I ended up in here precisely because I am naked... I don't have to tell you that if I had been clothed, I wouldn't have come anywhere near your bin.

FIRST SWEEPER: Are you sure you didn't take off your clothes just to see how it felt being naked in a bin, eh?

NAKED MAN: No... I got undressed for quite another reason... the most sublime of reasons... for love... But unfortunately, just as we were getting down to it, HE had to turn up... the husband... just like some third-rate farce.

FIRST SWEEPER: Ha, ha! Just like in the cartoons...

NAKED MAN: Precisely. And in order to avoid reacting in the traditional way, which would have sent me scurrying under the classic bed, or into the even more classic wardrobe, I took my hat, (*He points to the black top-hat he is wearing*) I gritted my teeth, and went out onto the balcony just as I was...

FIRST SWEEPER: Stark naked, but with a top-hat on your head and your teeth gritted. Forgive my laughing, but things like this make me laugh.

NAKED MAN: Go ahead, go ahead. I wish I could do the same, but, as you can imagine, it is difficult to laugh when one is naked and up to one's neck submerged in filth.

FIRST SWEEPER: Yes, yes, it's hard, I know, but all the

same, it makes me laugh… Ha, ha.
Anyway, how did it go, how did it go…? Wait a moment…
It was really good… Ah, yes, that's it: (*He declaims,
imitating his philosopher friend*) The important thing is to
be naked, but clothed… that is, naked outside, but clothed
inside… And since you are inside, obviously, you are
clothed…

NAKED MAN: I don't understand.

FIRST SWEEPER: It's philosophy… It would take too long
to explain… I'm sorry, but I'm going to have to continue
my round… So I must ask you to get out of my bin, because
otherwise there won't be any room for the rubbish.

NAKED MAN: Oh no, please, you wouldn't want to leave me
out in the street like this, would you? I mean, it wouldn't
be decent! Come on!

FIRST SWEEPER: What do you mean, it wouldn't be
decent? So, in your opinion, what am I supposed to do.
Supposing I run into a supervisor, what am I supposed to
do? He'd probably end up reporting me for unauthorised
hire of a vehicle for illicit purposes, or something!

NAKED MAN: If you could just be so kind … and so
understanding… as to take me home…

FIRST SWEEPER: Home? I mean…! What do you take me
for, a taxi?

NAKED MAN: It's not really so very far… And, look, as a
token of my appreciation, take this… I'll give you my
watch. (*He removes it from his wrist*) The only thing that
I'm still wearing, apart from my hat. Take it… it's a
valuable watch… 18-carat solid gold.

He hands him the watch.

FIRST SWEEPER: (*Taking it, embarrassed*) And you are
giving me this valuable, 18-carat, solid gold watch, just for
taking you home?

NAKED MAN: Indeed… and I regret having nothing else
with which I can demonstrate…

FIRST SWEEPER: Alright, it doesn't matter. Settle down. Where are we going?

NAKED MAN: Via Donini... number 27...

FIRST SWEEPER: 27 via Donini...? And that's supposed to be not very far? That's two miles on foot, you know! You can keep your watch, because I don't want trouble... Supposing I run into a supervisor, what am I going to tell him?

NAKED MAN: There you go again with your supervisor...! Can't you think of anything other than your supervisors? What kind of sons-of-toil mentality is this...? It really is true what they say: once a road-sweeper, always a road-sweeper.

FIRST SWEEPER: Now then, go easy... Who says that, anyway?

NAKED MAN: I say it... And I also say: that people like you make me ashamed of being human... because I can accept anything – cowardice, poverty, ignorance – but not nothingness...

FIRST SWEEPER: Ah yes, nothingness... But, in case you didn't realise it, nothing is everything, and everything is God. And you can say what you like... but hands off my divinity. (*At that moment, a* NIGHT PATROLMAN *appears from the back of the stage. The* NAKED MAN *sees him, and immediately disappears into his bin. But the* SWEEPER, *who has his back to the* PATROLMAN, *continues talking*) Because I become an animal, and I don't care who you are...

NAKED MAN: (*Hissing at him*) Stop it, shut up! Look out...!

FIRST SWEEPER: Stop it? You're telling me to stop it? (*He thumps his fist on the bin-lid, which closes again*) You're the one who should stop it... Dirty old man... First you go flirting with other people's wives, then you get yourself caught, and then you come and start making fun of people... But I'll sort you out. (*He gives the bin a kick*) And thank your lucky stars you've got no clothes on – because otherwise… (*He bangs his fist on the lid*) …that ugly head of yours… Damn you… (*The* PATROLMAN *behind him can't restrain a laugh*) Yes, yes, go ahead, laugh! Ha, ha! But I'll have the last laugh… Enjoy yourself, carry on with your little jokes… When I tip you into the canal, ha, ha, I'd like to see how you get on in the water… Ha, ha! Help, help… And down you'll go… glug, glug… Like a submarine.

At this point, the SWEEPER *becomes aware of the* PATROLMAN's *presence* Glug… Glug… *He stops for a moment, perplexed, but then continues unperturbed, miming the sinking of a submarine. He sings.*

The submarine goes Glug, Glug, Glug
The little fishy too goes Glug, Glug, Glug
And the submarine goes Glug, Glug, Glug.
All together now, Glug… Glug… Glug…

All this is accompanied by a kind of tap dance, which ends with the SWEEPER *kicking the bin.*

PATROLMAN: Um… Ah… Are you not feeling well?

FIRST SWEEPER: No, no… You see, I was just… well, just passing the time… Glug… Glug…

PATROLMAN: So just to pass the time, you start kicking this poor bin? But what's it done to you?

FIRST SWEEPER: It's… well… it's made me angry… It's made me… Every now and then, who knows why, bang… it stops… and there's no way to get it moving. Look… You see… it's making fun of me… the wretch! (*He gives it another kick*) But believe me, one of these days… (*He gives the bin a push*) There you go, you see? (*The bin has moved*) Now it's moving… It's got frightened… because you're here… I tell you… dustcarts are like children… If you don't treat them roughly every once in a while, if you don't shout at them, they end up doing just what they want. They show you no respect, they… (*He starts talking to the bin*) Come on, get a move on… and don't pull any more stunts… because, if you do, I'll call the Park Keeper again... and Park Keepers are not to be trifled with! Come on, come on, you shout at it too...

PATROLMAN: (*Embarrassed*) Ah, yes, if it's all the same with you, I... I... Well, I'd better be going... See you...

He gets on his bicycle, and exits rapidly.

FIRST SWEEPER: Yes, yes, see you... (*He mops the sweat from his brow, and from inside his hat*) Phew! What a terrible five minutes...

NAKED MAN: (*Cautiously sticking his head out*) Has he gone?

FIRST SWEEPER: Yes, yes... You almost landed me right in it, there... Look, I'm all sweating...

NAKED MAN: Well I don't have to tell you what it was like for me... If he had hung about for just one minute longer, I would have died of suffocation...

FIRST SWEEPER: Would that it was true, dear boy!

NAKED MAN: (*Leaning out of the bin like a preacher out of his pulpit*) Oh, don't be like that... I've realised it now, you know. You... There's no point in you pretending to be a hard, heartless person, because you're really very kind... Thank you., thank you for what you've done for me... I assure you that I shall reward your sacrifice, once you get me home.

FIRST SWEEPER: Home? Ah, here we go again... You must be mad if you think that I'm taking you home...

NAKED MAN: Well, look, tell me, how much wages do you make in a month?

FIRST SWEEPER: Me? Well... It depends... For example, this month... Wait, I've got my wage packet... I picked it up today... Here we are... Twenty-two thousand and fifty... exactly. Why, what's it to you?

NAKED MAN: Right. Consider it doubled... And I'll throw in my watch too, for good measure.

FIRST SWEEPER: What...? You're going to give me your

18-carat gold watch, plus twenty-two thousand and fifty lire... just for taking you home?!

NAKED MAN: Certainly... As soon as we reach 27 via Donini... you wait downstairs for me a moment, while I go up... Oh, no... no... I can't...

FIRST SWEEPER: What do you mean, 'I can't'? First you say you can and then you say you can't. Make your bloody mind up!

NAKED MAN: But... what did you think I meant? I was just saying that I can't go home in the condition I'm in now.

FIRST SWEEPER: But why? Who do you think is going to see you at this hour?

NAKED MAN: My wife... Since I haven't got my keys, I imagine that she will come and open the door... and when she sees me naked and without my evening dress, what am I going to tell her?

FIRST SWEEPER: Without your evening dress?

NAKED MAN: Yes. Before this misfortune, I was wearing evening dress... I'd told my wife that I had to attend an embassy *vernissage*.

FIRST SWEEPER: An embassy *vernissage*, in evening dress? Just a moment, this evening dress, is it a jacket with long, long tails?

NAKED MAN: Yes, why?

FIRST SWEEPER: Because in that case, there's one coming towards us on a bicycle...

NAKED MAN: An evening dress on a bicycle!?

FIRST SWEEPER: Yes, look... (*He points off-stage, behind the* NAKED MAN) It must be one of those fellows who go round at night selling flowers.

NAKED MAN: So it is...! A real evening dress...!

FIRST SWEEPER: Relax, I'll see to this... Hey, Evening Dress... Stop, a minute...

MAN IN EVENING DRESS: Are you referring to me?

FIRST SWEEPER: Yes... Listen... Are you looking for business?

MAN IN EVENING DRESS: You're not going to start telling me that roadsweepers buy flowers too, these days?

FIRST SWEEPER: No, I want to buy your evening dress... and immediately, too. Tell me how much you want. Let's have a look what it's made of... (*He lights a match, and holds it up to the tails of the tailcoat*) Hum... cheap wool. Pretty tatty!

MAN IN EVENING DRESS: Wretch, mind what you're doing with that match! And get your dirty hands off... I've just had it dry-cleaned, if you don't mind.

FIRST SWEEPER: You'll see... after all it's not exactly solid gold... I just wanted to pass a bit of business your way... But seeing that you're playing hard to get, you can keep your evening dress... Anyway, people who wear evening dress always strike me as a bit lacking in taste...

MAN IN EVENING DRESS: So, if it's so lacking in taste, why do you want to buy it?

FIRST SWEEPER: Because I'm depraved... psychologically depraved... And I only like things which disgust me...

MAN IN EVENING DRESS: Like being a roadsweeper... for example.

FIRST SWEEPER: Correct. You've hit the nail on the head. So, do you want to do this bit of business? In exchange I shall give you this valuable 18-carat gold watch. And in addition I shall give you 15,000 lire, in cash. Come on, it's a deal... Take it or leave it.

MAN IN EVENING DRESS: Leave it, be blowed... Even if I wanted to, how am I going to...? I can hardly go home naked!

FIRST SWEEPER: That's true, and then what are you going to tell your wife?!

MAN IN EVENING DRESS: What wife...! I'm not married, you know...

FIRST SWEEPER: Well then?

MAN IN EVENING DRESS: Well, just think a moment... Can you imagine me, nude, on my bicycle?

FIRST SWEEPER: Ha, ha, that's even better than that other fellow, nude on the balcony... Ha, ha...

MAN IN EVENING DRESS: Balcony? What's balconies got to do with it?!

FIRST SWEEPER: Nothing, nothing... I forget! But now I think of it, there would be a way... Once you were naked, you could put yourself in my bin...

MAN IN EVENING DRESS: What, what? Me, naked, in your bin?

FIRST SWEEPER: Yes... And it's not all that bad in there... it's been tested... You settle down in there, nice and comfortable, and I take you home... Door to door service... Everything included... It's a deal: either take it or leave it.

MAN IN EVENING DRESS: But you must have some kind of screw loose... I mean, me, nude, in the bin...?! While we're at it, why don't we have it so that I've got a dummy in my mouth and a baby's bonnet on my head, and we can play at nanny taking baby for a walk in the pram?

FIRST SWEEPER: Oh, why do you have to make things so difficult...? If you really want to know, there's one fellow already in there. (*He points to the bin*) He's been in there for a couple of hours, and *he* hasn't been complaining all along, like you...

MAN IN EVENING DRESS: What, what? There's a man in your bin?

FIRST SWEEPER: (*Offended, giving him a mean look*) Certainly... what did you think was in there?

MAN IN EVENING DRESS: A living man?

FIRST SWEEPER: Obviously living. You wouldn't expect a corpse, would you? I'm not an undertaker, you know... Alive, and nude.

MAN IN EVENING DRESS: Impossible... Let me see!

He makes as if to go over to the bin.

FIRST SWEEPER: Hey, gently... Stand over there... You're not at home now... Don't you think you should knock first? You might find that he's not in the mood for guests today... And wait over there, because he's not a great one for trusting people. (*Knocking*) May I? Am I disturbing you? Excuse me, Ambassador... (*Turning to* EVENING DRESS)) He's from the Embassy!'(*Turning back to the* NAKED MAN) If you don't mind, I wanted to introduce you...

NAKED MAN: (*Lifting the bin lid*) Eh...? Ah, it's you... (*Noticing* EVENING DRESS, *who stares at him in amazement*) But what on earth do you think you're doing? Don't you understand that in my present state... I mean, are you really trying to ruin me? Introducing me to a complete stranger, in my present condition...?

FIRST SWEEPER: Yes, yes, a stranger, but he's got an evening dress... And if we don't find some way of settling an agreement, then, I regret to say, there's no chance of your getting home...

NAKED MAN: Alright... We shall tolerate this further humiliation... A pleasure... my friend.

He extends his hand, condescendingly.

MAN IN EVENING DRESS: A pleasure... But I don't understand... What on earth has happened to you?

FIRST SWEEPER: Nothing, nothing... it's a long story... Anyway, now you can guess why I wanted to buy your evening dress...

MAN IN EVENING DRESS: Ah, it's for him... Well, I'm sorry, there's no way that I'm going to strip naked and dive into that bin, in his place.

NAKED MAN: Well, maybe there could be a solution. You strip, you give me your suit, and you put on the sweeper's clothes...

FIRST SWEEPER: (*Swiftly calculating the odds*) And I end up naked. Wonderful!

NAKED MAN: But you can go in the bin…

FIRST SWEEPER: Even better… You both go off home, and I hang around here, waiting for somebody to cart me off to the police station…

MAN IN EVENING DRESS: There must be some other way… (*Pointing to the* SWEEPER) How about you put on my evening dress… and I dress up… as a roadsweeper…

FIRST SWEEPER: (*More swift calculations*) And he's still left, stark naked… Wonderful, wonderful…

NAKED MAN: Yes, it is wonderful, because once we've got the evening dress, everything's resolved. (*Turning to the* SWEEPER) You'll take me back to your house… You must have another suit at home…!

FIRST SWEEPER: I've got an ordinary suit.

NAKED MAN: Very good. So we'll do a swap…

MAN IN EVENING DRESS: Alright, so if we're going to go through with this, let's get on with it. But you'll have to agree to buy my flowers too…

FIRST SWEEPER: Why? What are we supposed to do with flowers…?

MAN IN EVENING DRESS: And what am I supposed to do with them, once I've sold my evening dress, and dressed up as a roadsweeper? Who am I going to sell these flowers to, after that? I can hardly go into night clubs dressed as a roadsweeper…

FIRST SWEEPER: And how much do you want for these cabbages…?

MAN IN EVENING DRESS: Let's see… (*A swift calculation*) There are 25 of them… five times five is twenty-five… seven thousand and fifty, plus 15,000 in cash for the evening dress, that makes 22,050. Not one lira less, though…

FIRST SWEEPER: Take it or leave it?

MAN IN EVENING DRESS: Yes...

FIRST SWEEPER: I'll leave it... (*He throws him the flowers.* EVENING DRESS *catches them*)

NAKED MAN: Take it!

Having caught the flowers, he gives them back to the SWEEPER.

FIRST SWEEPER: I don't want to end up without a lira...

NAKED MAN: I'll reimburse you the money. (*He grabs the wallet from the* ROADSWEEPER'*s hands, and hands it over to* EVENING DRESS)

FIRST SWEEPER: Hey, you could at least leave me my wallet...

MAN IN EVENING DRESS: And what are you going to do with an empty wallet...? Come on, let's get a move on with this strip-tease before you change your mind...

He makes as if to get undressed.

FIRST SWEEPER: Slow down... You're surely not going to strip off just like that in the middle of a public highway... Supposing somebody comes by... Three naked men in one go... it's a bit much...

MAN IN EVENING DRESS: There I make you right... Let's go behind there...

FIRST SWEEPER: Allow me...

NAKED MAN: Go ahead, go ahead... But be quick...

The two of them disappear behind the news kiosk. Enter from stage left, the NIGHT PATROLMAN *whom we already know, on his bicycle. He sees the bin centre-stage, and stops. The* NAKED MAN *only just disappears in time.*

NAKED MAN: Action stations...! Dive...!

PATROLMAN: How irresponsible... He just dumps his bin here, and wanders off... It must be that lunatic from before! (*Looking around*) Where's he got to? (*He bends* *over to look at the number plate on the bin*) Ah, there's his number... 30... I bet he's had another row with his bin! (*He tries to lift the lid, but can't*) Ooof...! It must be jammed...

Enter the WOMAN. *She tiptoes up to him and kicks him up the backside.*

WOMAN: Hands up!

PATROLMAN: (*Reaching instinctively for the gun in his holster*) Who's that... Ah... it's you...

WOMAN: Ha, ha... That frightened you, eh!

PATROLMAN: I can do without jokes like that... More to the point, you wouldn't happen to have seen the owner of this junk-heap anywhere around?

WOMAN: Why do you ask me...? I don't hang out with road sweepers, you know...

PATROLMAN: True, except once a month... On payday...

WOMAN: So, what's that supposed to mean? I'm not ashamed of it... Anyway, when all's said and done, they part with their wallets better than a lot of others I can think of... I tell you, sometimes these road sweepers can surprise you... This evening, for example, I picked up one...

PATROLMAN: ...with your usual story about the Vice Squad being after you? Watch out, because one of these days somebody's going to tumble you, if you'll excuse the expression...

WOMAN: I will watch out... Anyway, as I was saying, I picked up one of them, and if it hadn't been for the fact that I knew he was a roadsweeper, I would have felt really bashful... You should have heard how he spoke, he was like a real professor!

PATROLMAN: Oh yes, I know, a professor of roadsweeping!

WOMAN: Yes, yes, that's right, make fun of me...!

PATROLMAN: Me, make fun of you? The very idea...! Anyway, would you do me a favour: I've got to go over here to make a phone call, to get them to come and pick up this bin... Make sure that nobody runs off with it.

WOMAN: OK, but get a move on. I've got things to do.

PATROLMAN: I'll be back in a couple of minutes.

No sooner has the PATROLMAN *left the stage, when from behind the news kiosk emerges the* ROAD SWEEPER, *in evening dress.*

FLOWERSELLER: (*Previously the* MAN IN EVENING DRESS. *From off-stage*) Ha, ha... God you're goodlooking... You look like the Chief Undertaker!

FIRST SWEEPER: Well, you're a pretty fine sight, yourself... a right sight... With that overcoat hanging down to your feet. (*Noticing the* WOMAN) Good evening... miss... (*He tries to hide his face with the bunch of flowers that he's holding. He has recognised her, and does not want to be recognised in turn*) A warm night, eh?

WOMAN: (*Flattered that such a distinguished gentleman should strike up conversation with her*) Oh, yes... the heat is unbearable... I had to come out... because I felt I was suffocating... And you? I heard you joking with your friend... You must be a great joker, you...

FIRST SWEEPER: Yes, I find very great pleasure in jokes...

WOMAN: But, you know, now that I see you better... I feel as if I've seen you somewhere before!

FIRST SWEEPER: No, no, it's not me... the one you mean... He's someone else... I... I am... an ambassador...

He begins walking like a circus horse, with long, sweeping strides.

WOMAN: Good heavens...! An ambassador...! I've never seen one from close up.

FIRST SWEEPER: (*His horse-like gait has now carried him across the stage. Now he casually leaps the Road Works trestle, as if it was a fence at a horse show*) You know, we ambassadors don't tend to let ourselves be seen from close up. We have this terrible shyness...

WOMAN: That's where I've seen you... on television... Or in the newsreels...

FIRST SWEEPER: Well, yes... maybe... Sometimes I do go to the cinema...

WOMAN: But then, if you are an ambassador... I suppose you must be a count too...?

FIRST SWEEPER: Count? No, we are not a count...

He positions himself between the WOMAN *and the bin.*

WOMAN: Don't try to deny it... I understood immediately that you were a count... You have such a refined way about you...

At this point, the lid of the bin lifts, and the NAKED MAN *pokes his head out. He signals to the* SWEEPER *to get a move-on.*

FIRST SWEEPER: That must be because of the long tails (*He preens himself*) which we ambassadors carry behind us.

WOMAN: No, I wouldn't even have thought of that... I would have noticed at once, even if you had been dressed, let's say... as a roadsweeper.

FIRST SWEEPER: As a roadsweeper? (*The* NAKED MAN *grabs a tail of his dinner jacket, and tugs at it*) Well, excuse me, duty calls... I have to go.

WOMAN: What a shame...

FIRST SWEEPER: Yes, unfortunately... You see, I have to take these flowers.

So saying, he sticks his bunch of flowers in the bin, arranging them as if they were in a vase.

WOMAN: I envy the lucky woman who's going to get them...

FIRST SWEEPER: If you would like one... here... (*He offers her a rose*) It's been a pleasure...

WOMAN: (*She offers her hand to be kissed. The* SWEEPER *has a moment of embarassment, but then pulls himself together, and kisses her hand*) How kind... The pleasure is all mine. Oh, thank you.

The SWEEPER, *slightly embarassed, bows, and then exits, with his horse-like gait, pushing his bin before him.*

FIRST SWEEPER: Goodbye.

WOMAN: (*She sighs ecstatically, but then notices his curious exit, and is a bit bewildered*) But... what... why...? Your excellency... ha, ha... How eccentric... (*He takes the bin, and off he goes, as if it was a Lambretta*) Ha, ha!

Enter the PATROLMAN.

PATROLMAN: What are you laughing at...? And what about the bin? Did he come to take it?

WOMAN: Who?

PATROLMAN: The roadsweeper.

WOMAN: But that was no roadsweeper, that was a count...

PATROLMAN: A count...? A count took away the sweeper's bin?

WOMAN: Certainly...

PATROLMAN: What, what? A count with a bin? But why didn't you say something?

WOMAN: I did... I told him that he was a lovely fellow... and he gave me a flower, and kissed my hand... just like he'd do with a lady. What gentlemen these counts are!!

PATROLMAN: He kissed your hand, and carried off the bin? But what's he going to do with it?

WOMAN: Well, just for a joke... you know, one of these things that gentlemen do...

PATROLMAN: Ah, just to amuse himself, I suppose... I'll teach him to play pranks with Council property... He went over that way, did he?

WOMAN: Yes... But surely, you're not going to start rowing with a count...? And over a dustbin, at that...? Wait for me...

But the PATROLMAN *is already on his bicycle, and exits.*

The WOMAN *also exits, running. From the other side of the stage, enter the* ROAD SWEEPER *in evening dress, pushing his barrow.*

FIRST SWEEPER: (*Addressing the* NAKED MAN *whose head is sticking out from among the flowers stuck in the bin*) And what are you complaining about now? There you are, in the middle of my flowers, looking like something out of Botticelli's Primavera, and you're still whinging: 'Hurry up, hurry up.' How do you expect me to go any faster than this...? And, what's more, when one is in evening dress, one must walk in a refined manner... One cannot start running like those who are not in evening dress, you know!

NAKED MAN: But was it really necessary for you to waste all that time playing Don Giovanni with that girl... If you really want to know, I'm sick to death of being stuck in here like a sardine in a can!

FIRST SWEEPER: Well, you can imagine how sick *I* am, having to be your servant for the last three hours...

PATROLMAN: (*From off-stage*) Hey... Sir... Stop!

NAKED MAN: What's happening now?

FIRST SWEEPER: Action stations! Dive!

NAKED MAN: Dive!

He disappears.

FIRST SWEEPER: (*He arranges his flowers around the head of his unfortunate passenger, and sings softly as he awaits the* PATROLMAN):

Look at all the pretty little flowers,
Pretty flowers that bloom in Spring...

PATROLMAN: Excuse my stopping you... but why have you walked off with that bin?

FIRST SWEEPER: What bin? (*Looking at the barrow as if seeing it for the first time*) Oh yes, it's a bin!! I hadn't even noticed... I had bought these flowers, you see, and not knowing where to put them, I put them in here... I mistook it for a flower vase...

PATROLMAN: A flower vase? On wheels?

FIRST SWEEPER: Yes, you know, one of those modern vases… A mobile vase…

PATROLMAN: So, you're in the mood for silly jokes, eh?

FIRST SWEEPER: Yes, to tell the truth, I'm very much in the mood… You know, I am quite a joker… And you?

PATROLMAN: Well, I… But wait a moment… You know what, your face is very familiar.

Enter the WOMAN, *panting after her long run.*

WOMAN: Whew… what a run…! Good evening.

She thrusts her hand under the SWEEPER's *nose, in order for him to kiss it.*

PATROLMAN: I'm sure I've seen you before… somewhere…

WOMAN: Of course you have… You must have seen him at the pictures, or on television… I told you, he's a count, and an ambassador…

PATROLMAN: An ambassador?

WOMAN: Yes… and now you've gone and made a fool of yourself… You should have listened to me… Look – now you've offended him.

FIRST SWEEPER: Oh, don't worry about offending me… sticks and stones may break my bones…

WOMAN: How kind you are… Thank the count…

PATROLMAN: Thank you… You must understand, sir, if it was up to me… you'd be welcome to take all the barrows you want… (*The flowers sticking out of the bin start waving in an agitated manner. Evidently the stowaway wants his driver to get a move on*) But this is Council property, and without proper authorisation, I regret…

FIRST SWEEPER: I understand… You're only doing your duty… But I have no intention of stealing it… I only want to borrow it.

WOMAN: Yes, that's right... borrow it... Otherwise, how's he supposed to get all those flowers home...? You surely don't expect a count like him to carry them in his arms?

PATROLMAN: He can carry them how he likes, but without a proper authorisation, I am not authorised... (*Now the flowers begin to look too unnatural as they wave around; the* SWEEPER *gives them a slap, pretending to brush off flies*) And what's more, haven't you thought of the poor road sweeper. If you take his bin away, he's going to lose his job.

FIRST SWEEPER: Precisely... that's precisely the reason... that I'm not taking it away... my bin...

PATROLMAN: Oh, that's rich, that is! Here you are – you, Lord Muck, amusing yourself by getting road sweepers the sack. And as we all know, there are still people around who vote for the monarchy!

FIRST SWEEPER: Hey, no, let's not start getting into politics... Because in that case, I shall just have to tell you the truth: here there is no count, and no ambassador... because, if you really want to know, I am a road sweeper!

PATROLMAN: Yes, and I am an elephant.

FIRST SWEEPER: (*Observing him with incredulity*) An elephant? With a gun? Don't think you can fool me, because I'm an expert on elephants...

PATROLMAN: Fool you? I would never dream of it! Seriously, though, rest assured, I realised immediately that you were a road sweeper...

WOMAN: What do you mean?

PATROLMAN: Obviously, he's a road sweeper in evening dress... it's their new uniform, isn't it. Everybody knows that the Council has ordered a new style for municipal employees: we're going to have road sweepers in dinner jackets, dog-catchers in morning dress, and sewermen in party frocks... what's odd about that?

FIRST SWEEPER: Alright then, since you want to start being comical about it... I'll show you my card... (*He searches in*

his jacket) Hell... it was in the wallet that that
money-grubber took off me...

PATROLMAN: But I told you, there's no point in trying to
convince me. I'm already convinced... But now you're also
going to have to convince the Inspector, who is a man
absolutely devoid of imagination... and if he does not get
his hands on something... or rather, his handcuffs...

FIRST SWEEPER: Ha, ha... that was good... His
handcuffs... I was only joking, though!

WOMAN: Yes, that's right, leave him alone... He was
joking...

PATROLMAN: Alright then, will you pick up your flowers,
and leave me the bin? (*He turns to the* WOMAN, *turning
his back on the* SWEEPER, *who leans against the barrow*)
And from now on, mind your own business...

NAKED MAN: (*Popping out of the bin*) No I won't!

He dives back in immediately.

PATROLMAN: (*Thinking that the words came from the*
SWEEPER) No? Alright, then... I must warn you that
anything you say will be taken down and may be used...

WOMAN: Leave him be... Don't go getting yourself into
trouble.

The PATROLMAN *turns his back again.*

NAKED MAN: (*As above*) Go ahead, arrest me... But in the
end, you're going to regret it!

PATROLMAN: (*Aggressively*) So, do you think you frighten
me? I would advise you to stop fooling about... Because
otherwise, you could end up in trouble...

The WOMAN *tugs at his jacket. The* PATROLMAN *is
distracted.*

NAKED MAN: (*Taking advantage of the situation, he slaps the
hands of the* PATROLMAN, *who is holding the*
SWEEPER *by the collar*) And get your dirty hands off, you
lout...

He hides again.

PATROLMAN: Who are you calling a lout? (*He responds by slapping the innocent* SWEEPER *about the face*) I warned you...

FIRST SWEEPER: Hey, ouch... gently... That hurts, eh?!

WOMAN: Have you gone mad? Now he's going to sue you for assault... and quite rightly, too...

PATROLMAN: (*Again turning his back on the barrow*) Oh yes, he's in the right, because he's a gentleman... In this world of idiots, the rich can amuse themselves, making a fool of you, insulting you, kicking you in the face...

NAKED MAN: (*Throwing an apple at his head*) And throwing rotten apples at your head...

PATROLMAN: (*Turning round, furious, and again grabbing the* SWEEPER *by the scruff of the neck*) Wretch...! So you really do want me to give you a good hiding?

FIRST SWEEPER: No, no... I don't...

He receives another backhander across the face, and a punch in the stomach... The WOMAN, *terrified, covers her face with her hands.*

WOMAN: He's killing him... Oh God... Stop it... Help... He's killed the ambassador...

NAKED MAN: (*From his hiding place among the flowers, he watches the punch-up with glee*) Ha, ha... Nice one... a left hook...

At that precise moment, the SWEEPER *ducks, and the* NAKED MAN *gets a punch in the face. The* PATROLMAN's *momentum carries him pirouetting around the stage. When he finally stops, the* NAKED MAN *has disappeared, unconscious, into his bin, after dropping some of the flowers. The* SWEEPER *swiftly puts the lid down.*

FIRST SWEEPER: (*Seeing the* PATROLMAN *returning to the attack*) Pax. Pax. I'm not playing any more!

PATROLMAN: Ah, so you've finally come to your senses...

FIRST SWEEPER: Yes, yes, I have... You can keep the barrow, with everything that's in it.

WOMAN: Did he hurt you much? (*Turning to the* PATROLMAN) You've done a fine job there, Officer. I hope you're proud of yourself...

PATROLMAN: Yes, fairly much: if nothing else, I've taught him that you don't mess about with other people's bins... (*He picks up the bunch of flowers from the ground*) And now, will you please take your flowers...

FIRST SWEEPER: No, no, you take them... It's a present... for the winner. That's the custom...

PATROLMAN: Thank you... With pleasure. (*Without looking inside, he tosses the bunch of flowers into the bin*)

FIRST SWEEPER: The pleasure is all mine... Happy Easter...

The PATROLMAN *gets on his bicycle, and exits, pulling the bin behind him.*

WOMAN: Why did you wish him a Happy Easter?

FIRST SWEEPER: Because at Easter you open your Easter egg, and in your Easter egg, you always find a surprise...

He laughs.

WOMAN: Stop laughing like that... Because, otherwise, I'm going to start crying...

FIRST SWEEPER: Why, is my laugh that bad?

WOMAN: No, it's just that when I see other people laughing, and I can't laugh because I don't understand what it is that's making them laugh, I get so angry that I want to cry...

FIRST SWEEPER: But why?

WOMAN: Because I always end up thinking I'm stupid... you know... always the last person to catch on...

FIRST SWEEPER: And instead you should be happy,

because, as they say: the last shall be first, the penultimate shall be second, and the third from last the third, and so on...

WOMAN: What a pleasure it is listening to you talk. It must be good to feel that you're somebody...

FIRST SWEEPER: To tell you the truth, I don't really see myself as anybody at all... a nobody in fact... in short, a nothingness. But since nothingness is... (*He sits down on the bench, dismayed*) There, now I've forgotten what nothing is... But never mind... Anyway, just to give you an example... If I dress up as a priest, or as a jester, or as a general, or in evening dress, it's as if I was naked. In other words, a roadsweeper... You see?

WOMAN: Noooo...! You see, I really am the last to catch on.

FIRST SWEEPER: No, now that I think about it, *I'm* the last one to catch on... Because if you two (*Referring to the* WOMAN *and the* PATROLMAN *who has just left*) have not understood that I was naked, in other words, a roadsweeper, then it means that when I'm wearing evening dress, then I am someone... And so I'm no longer God... Do you follow?

WOMAN: Not really... After all, you're still a count and an ambassador...

FIRST SWEEPER: Look, I *told* you, I have never been either a count or an ambassador... And now I'm not even a roadsweeper... I've lost my money and my job, all in one go... At least they could have let me stay God... And now what am I going to tell the Pope?! He'll be very upset...

WOMAN: (*Touching his forehead, worried*) Have you still got a headache?

FIRST SWEEPER: No, no, now I feel quite alright... You won't believe this, but as far as I'm concerned, the fact of not any longer being everything makes absolutely no difference to me... Because I may no longer be everything, but at least I feel that I am someone... and the best part of it is, that others also think that I am someone... and so I am happy...

WOMAN: And I'm happy too...

FIRST SWEEPER: How strange life is. You go banging your head against a brick wall, you go to incredible lengths to find happiness, and then, all of a sudden, all you need do is change your suit, and, zap...! You've got it... And all because I met a naked ambassador...

WOMAN: What naked ambassador?

PATROLMAN'S VOICE: (*From off-stage*) Stop him, stop him...

FIRST SWEEPER: That one...

He points to the back of the stage, where we see the NAKED MAN, *in his barrow, crossing the stage at speed, pushing himself along with the broom, as if poling a punt.*

Blackout